SEX LIVES OF THE
GREAT COMPOSERS

SEX LIVES OF THE GREAT COMPOSERS

NIGEL CAWTHORNE

First published in Great Britain in 1998
This edition published 2004 by

Prion
an imprint of the
Carlton Publishing Group
20 Mortimer Street
London W1T 3JW

A catalogue record for this book is available from the British Library

ISBN 1 85375 542 7

Printed in Great Britain
by Mackays

CONTENTS

INTRODUCTION

I admit it. I was a philistine. I never really listened to classical music until I started writing this book. I had always written in complete silence during the day. In the evenings, I might have the TV on. But television is only moving wallpaper. Talk radio is too distracting, while TV only requires a tenth of your concentration to follow.

Now, though, I listen to classical music while I work. Why the transformation? Now that I have studied the lives and loves of the great masters, I understand where they are coming from. Music is sex, bottled. Most of the great composers admitted as much. They sublimated their sex to make music, or indulged themselves in it to find inspiration.

During the nineteenth century particularly, the composers were seized by the Romantic ideal. They fell in love with unattainable women, then had it off with any prostitute or peasant girl who happened to be passing. Syphilis was the inevitable result. Then a fatal disease – in its day far more pernicious than AIDS – it did not stop them fulfilling their erotic dreams. Many of them gave their lives for their art.

When we listen to their music today, we are voyeurs in the fantasy world of the great composers. They speak directly to our emotions. And our emotions are the stuff of our sexuality – and of our very life itself.

SEX LIVES OF THE GREAT COMPOSERS

The composers really *lived*, despite their medical and spiritual condition. They glimpsed the true nature of existence and expressed it. They were committed to the task. Nothing would stand in their way of their sexual destiny. They were driven by the force that drives life itself – the desire to unite with one another, flesh to flesh, and occasionally, if you get unlucky, to create new life itself.

Just as pop stars today inspire erotic thoughts in their female fans, so the greatest composers had their groupies. Who could fail to fall for a composer who, at his desk, at the piano or on the rostrum could drive the audience to a frenzy? Few on either side resisted.

It should be remembered that modern romantic love was invented by musicians for the expressed purpose of getting their leg over. Love was devised by the troubadours of thirteenth century France as a way to seduce the mistresses of the lords set above them.

But it was the artists and composers of the nineteenth century who drove it to its climax. Music propelled talented and driven men from the lower orders into the company of upper-class women with all their décolletage. They met in glamorous concert halls or in the drawing rooms for a private piano lesson, thigh to thigh on the piano stool, one on one. But then, at night, the composer would have to return.

Most of the great composers presented here, as in life, are men. Psychologists say that men produce great music – and, for that matter, great writing, great art, great science and great thought – as a way of showing off to women. And the more they show it off the better. The great music, of whatever variety, that fills our CD collections is the result.

So writing this book has brought me into contact with music. And I am beginning to enjoy it. For those readers who already enjoy music, this book will give them a unique insight into the composers they love and the source of their inspiration. For those who do not enjoy music, this is another amusing study of mankind's most basic urge. It is comforting to note once again, as in all the books in my *Sex Lives...* series, that we are all the same. First, everyone is doing it with someone – even if it is only themselves or their god. Secondly, everyone, no matter how rich and famous, falls in love with the wrong person – the wronger the better. In the love stakes, passion is always ahead of the field and reason was scratched.

Everyone cheats and lies about sex. That is why polls on sexual attitudes and activities come up with such palpably ridiculous results. The pollsters cannot get anyone to tell the truth. Remember, if your sexual partner is not actually doing it with someone else, they are thinking about it. So are you. Some have the good grace to be discreet about it.

And everybody writes adolescent poetry and embarrassing letters, the more the better. So, if we compare our own sex lives to those of the great composers, we can take comfort from the fact that our sex lives are not quite such the disaster areas we thought. It is just that the great composer's disaster areas have a better soundtrack.

Nigel Cawthorne

1

THE ORGANMEISTER

Johann Sebastian Bach is often called 'the father of modern music'. That is debatable, but he was certainly the father of twenty legitimate children.

The Bachs were a marrying clan; and they were prolific. The family dominated music in northern Germany in the seventeenth and eighteenth centuries. They were organists almost to a man. Only nine of the eighty-six Bachs shown on the family tree in *Grove's Dictionary of Music* did not join the family profession.

The Bachs married young and often. Johann's father Sebastian married twice, taking his second wife only seven months after the death of the first. He had a twin brother, and they were so alike, it was said, that even their wives could not tell them apart. I wonder how they put that to the test. But young Johann Sebastian Bach was different. He waited until he reached the ripe old age of twenty-two before tying the knot.

It was not that he did not like women. At the church in Arnstadt, where he was organist, he was reprimanded for 'having allowed a strange woman to show herself and make music in the choir'. Women did not sing in German churches in those days. There was also talk of the 'strange maiden' accompanying him in the organ loft. Bach's excuse was that this 'music making' was a private matter, just as long as it did not take place during Sunday services.

But this censure of his private life led Bach to try and find another post. He visited the celebrated organist Dietrich Buxtehude at Lübek and well overstayed his leave. This may have had something to do with the fact that Buxtehude had a 30-year-old spinster daughter, Anna. Buxtehude was old and there was talk of Bach taking over his post. But when Bach discovered that getting married to Buxtehude's daughter was part of the deal, he scuttled back to Arnstadt where he married his twenty-two-year-old cousin Maria Barbara Bach.

Handel, of *Water Music* fame, was the next up for Buxtehude's daughter, who by that time was thirty-four. The eighteen-year-old Handel also made a dash for it. In the end he never married, and only had one other near miss. The beautiful, gifted, seventeen-year-old singer Vittoria Tesi, who sang in his first Italian opera *Rodrigo*, became so infatuated with him that she followed him from Florence to Venice. His biographers say that Handel, then twenty-four, turned her down out of prudence because he was a penniless composer at the time and could not afford a wife. In fact, he turned her down out of discretion. Vittoria was the favourite mistress of the Grand Duke of Tuscany. Later, she married a common labourer to escape the unwanted attentions of a nobleman. After one of her would-be lover's impassioned appeals, she went out into the street and gave the first man she met 50 ducats to marry her. Her new husband could not believe his luck, but on the wedding night he was informed that the marriage was in name only.

Anna Buxtehude eventually got her man. An organist called Schieferdecker took up her father's offer, married the ageing Anna and took over Buxtehude's post, which was then the most distinguished and best paid in Europe.

Bach's new wife, Maria Barbara Bach, was the daughter of Johann's Uncle Michael, the organist at Gehren. Such close, practically incestuous, liaisons were common among the Bachs. It kept the music-making genes in the family.

The romance with Maria Barbara sprang from the young composer's stout defence of her honour. They were in the market place together when a group of six students led by the bassoonist Johann Heinrich Geyersbach approached. There was an exchange of insults. Bach said Geyersbach made the bassoon bleat like a nanny-goat. Geyersbach threatened Bach with a stick. Renowned for his fiery temper, Bach drew his sword. Maria Barbara was deeply impressed.

According to the parish register at Dornheim where they were married, Maria Barbara was a 'virtuous maiden'. But she was not a maiden for long. Bach got a job as organist in Mühlhausen and they set about producing a large family.

Within a year, they moved to Weimar where Bach fell under the influence of Italian composers and their evocation of a land of cheap wine, perpetual sunshine and well-disposed maidens. This obviously inspired him. Maria Barbara gave birth to a family of seven, including a pair of twins, but only four lived to grow up. Three of them, Wilhelm Friedmann, Carl Philipp Emanuel and Johann Gottfried Bernhard, became composers.

In 1720, while Bach was away for nearly a year with the court in Carlsbad, Maria Barbara became ill and died. Fortunately, Maria Barbara's sister lived with the family and took over many of her duties. Bach was still a vigorous thirty-six-year-old and eighteen months later, he married a second time, this time to a woman sixteen years his junior. Her name was Anna Magdalena Wülken and she was the twenty-one-year-old court singer at Cöthen where Bach was then musical director. He wrote love poetry for her, calling her 'sweetest maiden bride'. And he had her portrait painted, which was rare outside the nobility.

As well as looking after the four children he already had, Anna Magdalena bore him thirteen more. The last, his daughter Regina, was born in 1742, when Bach was fifty-seven. Three years later Bach died. Anna Magdalena lived for another ten years, in penury.

Bach left no will and members of the family made off with his manuscripts. The sons went to other towns, where they scored some notable successes. Anna Magdalena and her three daughters were left to fend for themselves, ultimately depending on charity.

SEX LIVES OF THE GREAT COMPOSERS

Anna Bach died in 1760, in an almshouse. The only mourner was her daughter Regina, though some public school children followed the coffin to the grave as was the custom at a pauper's funeral. Regina lived until 1801 by 'public subscription' to which Beethoven contributed.

It was a sad postscript to a blissful married life, which was a rare thing indeed among the great composers – and Bach had two of them.

2

A MAN FOR ALL SEASONS

Antonio Vivaldi was a Catholic priest, but that did not mean he was not a lover too – not in eighteenth-century Venice. This was the city of Casanova. Its bordellos were famous throughout Europe and the city boasted more than 11,000 working prostitutes. Men from all over Europe came to Venice for their sport. And music of every description throbbed out across the waters of the Lido as the gondolas sped their passengers on their amorous quests.

Nor were the religious immune. The nuns of the S. Lorenzo were notorious for their casual behaviour. They dressed in white and wore such sheer fabric across their neck and breasts 'that 'twas next to nothing at all,' one visitor wrote. Later, the habits grew even more daring, and by 1738 they were cut so low that they uncovered 'no more and no less than the Roman costumes of our actresses'.

Vivaldi was known as the Red Priest, *Il Prete Rosso,* because of his bright red hair. But shortly after being ordained, he decided that he no longer wanted to continue the religious life and went to teach music at the Pietà, an orphanage for girls whose occupants were principally the unwanted daughters of courtesans. The orphanage was also run by nuns 'who knew no other father but love'.

They may not have known their fathers but their mothers had not abandoned them completely. On Sundays and holidays, the Pietà was the place to visit as ''tis the rendezvous of all the coquettes of Venice and such as are fond of intrigues have both their hearts and hands full' there. Music was played on these occasions and the performance of Vivaldi's young girls was soon famous across the city.

As Vivaldi's reputation grew, gossip began to circulate about his relationship with Signorina Anna Girò, the daughter of a French wigmaker who had a considerable musical career in her own right. He met her in Mantua. Although not an orphan, she became his pupil at the Pietà. Under his guidance she became an opera singer and was known as *L'Annina del Prete Rosso*-the Red Priest's Little Anna.

She made her first appearance in an opera by Vivaldi in 1726, though by all accounts she did not have a very good voice. Even so, her striking looks and her stage presence caused a sensation. Both the Spanish and the Neapolitan ambassadors mentioned her in dispatches and she was denounced to the Holy Inquisition.

Although she was not beautiful, she was certainly attractive. She had 'a delicate figure, beautiful eyes, lovely hair and a charming mouth'. She had a long association with Vivaldi, and one musicologist even says they were married. For fourteen years they travelled together throughout Europe. They were always accompanied by Anna's sister Paolini, who acted as Vivaldi's nurse and was probably his mistress as well.

The three of them lived together in a *ménage à trois* in Venice. This led Cardinal Tomaso Ruffo to ban one of Vivaldi's operas in Ferrara, which was then part of the Papal States. The production was already well advanced and could probably have gone ahead had Vivaldi dropped Anna from the cast. But he refused to put on an opera without his star. Cancellation cost Vivaldi a great deal of money and he complained bitterly of the stain Cardinal Ruffo's slur had put on the character of La Girò and her sister. These two poor women, he said, had been accepted wherever he had travelled. Out of loyalty to his mistress, he left Italy for good. In Graz, he put on his opera *Catone in Utica,* with Anna singing the lead.

A MAN FOR ALL SEASONS

In 1741, Vivaldi died in poverty in Vienna. Cut off from Italy, his fame was already on the wane. Seven years later, Anna married a nobleman, and how she affected his life is not known. She had certainly put a spring in Vivaldi's step. The sensual sweep of the *Four Seasons* is hardly the work of a celibate priest.

3

AMOROUS AMADEUS

'To my mind,' Mozart said, 'a bachelor lives only half a life.' Not that, as a bachelor, he was starved of female attention. 'If I had to marry every girl I flirt with, I would have at least two hundred wives,' he once wrote.

As a child prodigy, Johann Wolfgang Amadeus Chrysostom Sigismund Mozart was the darling of the ladies. As precocious in flirtation as he was in music, he was caressed and pampered by the beauties of the Viennese court. He would jump onto the Empress's lap, throw his arms around her and smother her with kisses. He lost his head over poor Marie-Antoinette, who was a young Austrian princess when he was at court. One day, when she picked him up after a nasty fall on slippery floor, he said: 'When I am a man I will marry you.' But it was she who lost her head during the French Revolution.

However, Marie-Antoinette was just one among many. The young Mozart was a Wolfgang in sheep's clothing. He was promiscuous with his affections and promised to marry most of the great ladies of his day. His sister Maria Anna 'Nannerl' was his confidante and partner in *l'amour*. She would be dispatched as his go-between with ladies of the court.

He was not yet in his teens when he sent a note to Nannerl, saying: 'I beg you not to forget your promise to make a certain visit. Pray present my regards in that quarter in the most impressive and tender manner – most tender. And oh! I beg you to give my compliments to Roxalana ... Make all sorts of pretty speeches to Mlle Mizerl. She must not doubt my love. I have her constantly before my eyes in her fascinating *negligée*. I have seen many pretty girls here, but not one whose beauty can be compared to her.'

He was very advanced for his age. But in Venice, his sexual precociousness got the better of him. Seven young girls tried to hold him down and beat his bare backside with a hairbrush. It was an incident he frequently harked back to during his adult life.

The women of the court were high above him in social status, so the young Mozart also approached young women who were more within his reach. He became infatuated with the court doctor's daughter, Thérèse von Barisani. But she was quickly replaced in his affections by Rosa Cannabich, the daughter of the music director Christian Cannabich. The affect she had on him was like 'a magnet', he said. His needle was always pointing north.

He needed little encouragement to give private lessons to the pretty young daughters of the aristocracy, even if they were less than gifted in the music department. One of them, Josepha Auerhammer, fell in love with him and there were rumours that they were to be married. Mozart tried to quash the rumours, assuring his father: 'She is as fat as a farm-wench, perspires so that you feel inclined to vomit, and goes about so scantily clad that really you can read as plain print: "Pray, do look here." 'His repudiation of her is so vehement that it is hard to believe that there was nothing to it.

In Munich, he conceived a violent fancy for a Mademoiselle Keiserin, an opera singer. She was the daughter of a cook and amenable. Mozart was just sixteen and wrote later that he was 'a little ashamed of his easy enthusiasm'. But not so ashamed that he did not immediately launch into an 'affair' with the daughter of a baker in his native Salzburg.

When he exhibited some reluctance to go on tour with his mother, Mozart explained in a letter to his father that the baker's daughter was 'the cause of my reluctance to leave home, and finding it to difficult to go', and implored his father to be discreet.

'I hope that this thing is not known all over Salzburg by now,' the love-struck young Mozart wrote. 'I beg you, dear papa, most urgently to keep it quiet.

But the thing was known and, in adolescent embarrassment, the baker's daughter withdrew to a convent. Mozart was heart-broken, of course. But while he had been away on tour he met his 'little girl cousin' in Augsburg. Her name was Maria Anna Thekla, but Wolfie called her *Bäsle*. She was two-and-half years younger than him, a noted beauty and seems to have been much more experienced in the intricacies of love.

'Like me, she's a bit naughty,' he said. But he was not the only one. 'She knocks around with priests rather too much,' he wrote jealously and he began to call her *Pfaffschnitzl* – or, euphemistically, 'Parsons' Pleasure'. But still she found ways to titillate him.

'Yesterday, my dear little *Bäsle* dressed up in the French manner just to please me,' he wrote, 'and it made her five per cent more beautiful.'

Mozart's father grew worried that he was spending too much time playing with Maria and not enough playing his music. The two were separated. They wrote a series of obscene letters to each other. In them, Mozart signed himself *dein alter junger Sauschwanz* – 'your old young pig's prick' – and promised to be 'faithful until the grave, as long as I live'.

Marie indeed proved to be a *Pfaffschnitzl*. In 1784, she gave birth to an illegitimate child. The father was Canon Berbier of Augsburg Cathedral. He who had something of a reputation. A visitor to the city that year said that the canon collected 'the maidenheads of the free-and-easy citizens by the dozen'. Through his influence in the Catholic church, the Canon got *Bäsle's* child legitimised.

Little is known of her fate after that, though she kept the young Mozart's letters, in bundles tied with ribbon. They fell into the hands of Sigmund Freud, who had a good time picking over them. In later life, Maria lived in Bayreuth and died there in 1841 at the age of eighty-three.

When Mozart's father heard about Maria's unplanned offspring, he was furious. Pretty young *Bäsle* had come close to ruining his son, he chided. Mozart protested his innocence.

'The voice of nature speaks as loud in me as in others, louder perhaps than in many a big strong lout of a fellow,' he wrote. 'But I simply cannot live as most young men do these days. I have too great a love of my neighbour and too high a feeling of honour to seduce an innocent girl. And I have too much horror and disgust, too much dread and fear of diseases and too much care for my health to fool about with whores.'

But then Maria was hardly an 'innocent girl'. So was Wolfgang still a virgin?

'I can swear I have never had relations of that sort with any woman,' he told his father. 'If such a thing had occurred I would not have concealed it from you. After all, to err is natural enough in a man. To err once would be mere weakness, although if I had erred once in this way, I would not have stopped short at one slip.'

How well he knew himself. And he begged his father to allow him to marry. He already had someone in mind.

In Mannheim, Mozart had met the music-copyist Fridolin Weber, uncle of the composer. He had one son and five daughters. Mozart immediately fell for the sixteen-year-old, raven-haired Aloysia. He raved over her 'lovely pure voice'. She seems to have put her heart and soul into the dramatic interpretation of some of his love duets.

He wrote to his father asking permission to take Aloysia to Italy, where he intended to build her a career as an opera singer. But his father insisted that Mozart go on to Paris instead, with his mother and without his precious Aloysia. He asked his son whether he wanted to become 'a commonplace artist who the world will forget, or a celebrated composer whose name posterity would read in books'. Mozart had a choice to make. Either he could be 'infatuated with a pretty face and, one day, breathe your last on a straw sack with your wife and children in

12

a state of starvation, or, after a well-spent Christian life, die in honour and independence, with your family well provided for'. Some choice.

But Mozart would not be shaken. He proposed taking his darling Aloysia to Salzburg, 'to make the acquaintance of dear papa'. He praised Aloysia's musical ability as well as her voice. But dear papa insisted that his son make a favourable match to 'get great people on your side'.

When a friend married for money, Mozart wrote: 'I hope I'll never marry this way. I wish to make my wife happy, but not to become rich by her means. The nobility must not marry from love or inclination, but from interest, and all kinds of other considerations. But we poor, humble people are privileged to be able to choose a wife who loves us, and whom we love. Because we are not noble, nor high-born, nor rich, we can and do this. We have no need of a wealthy wife, for our wealth, being in our heads, dies with us. And this wealth, no man can deprive us of, unless he cuts them off. In which case we need nothing more.'

But father held the purse-strings and Mozart did what he was told and dropped Aloysia. Hurt and rejected, she married the painter Joseph Lange. Mozart was fiercely jealous.

'As far as the Lange woman is concerned, I was a fool,' he wrote bitterly, 'but who isn't when in love? I did love her though, and still can't feel indifferent to her. It's lucky for me that her husband is a jealous fool and doesn't allow her out anywhere, so I seldom get the opportunity of seeing her.'

Behind her back, Mozart was describing Madame Lange as a 'false, malicious person and a coquette'. And he set about seducing her older sister, Josepha, who he was soon denouncing as a 'lazy, gross perfidious women, and as cunning as a fox'. Perhaps he thought it would be a case of third time lucky when he turned to his 'dear Constanze', the third of the Weber sisters. But he did not do so with any great enthusiasm.

'She is not ugly, but at the same time far from beautiful,' he wrote to his father. 'Her whole beauty consists in two little black eyes and a pretty figure. She has no wit, but she has enough common sense to enable her to fulfil her duties as a wife and mother.'

Not only was she not beautiful, she had no sense of humour and dressed badly. But Mozart's mother had died in Paris, so the matter of marriage had become more pressing. 'I have never been able to look after my own clothes, or do my washing,' he wrote, 'and I cannot think of anything more necessary to me than a wife.' Two can live as cheaply as one. Constanze even did her own hair, Mozart told his father. This was no mean feat in those days.

Mozart outraged his father by moving in with the Webers, and soon he found himself forced into marriage. Constanze's father had died and her guardian – and probably her mother's lover – Johann von Thorwardt, the finance director of the Vienna National Theatre, drew up a marriage contract. Mozart was compelled to sign.

'Certain busybodies and nosey-parkers have spread certain stories about me,' he explained to his father. A rival, the composer Peter von Winter, had spread the story that Constanze was a slut and Mozart's mistress. 'What could I do?' Mozart said. 'I was obliged to sign the contract or renounce the girl. Who that sincerely and truly loves can forsake his beloved?'

The contract stipulated that Mozart would either marry Constanze within three years, or pay her 300 florins a year thereafter. But signing the contract, he said, was 'the easiest thing in the world', although he could ill afford the alternative of 300 florins a year. 'I knew it would never come to that, as I'd never leave her,' he wrote. Constanze herself was no party to this cynical entrapment. When her guardian left the house, Constanze – 'the angelic girl' – got hold of the contract and tore it up. 'I don't need a written contract from you,' she said. 'I believe every word you say.'

But the course of this true love never ran smooth. The lovers had frequent tiffs. Constanze's mother threatened to call the police more than once. Mozart said that his courtship 'degenerated into a race between the priest and the policeman'. The priest won and on 4 August 1782, only a day after Mozart's father gave his grudging consent, the couple married in St Stephen's, Vienna. The bride was nineteen; Mozart twenty-six.

'When the ceremony was over, both my wife and I shed tears,' Mozart wrote. 'All present – even the priest – were touched on seeing the emotions of our hearts ...'

'I was willing to stake my very life,' he wrote to his father, 'that you will rejoice still more in my happiness when you really know her; if, indeed, in your estimation, as in mine, a high-principled, honest, virtuous, and pleasing wife ought to make a man happy.'

But Constanze was not constant. Within weeks of their honeymoon, Mozart had to chide her for playing a game of forfeits which ended with 'the size of your leg being measured by a gentleman'. No girl with becoming modesty would have permitted such a thing,' Mozart said. Constanze excused herself by saying that the Baroness Waldstädten had also permitted the gentleman to get his tape measure around her calf. 'That is quite another thing,' railed Mozart. 'The Baroness is a passé elderly woman, who cannot possibly inspire passion.'

Mozart often wrote of his 'strong appetite' though he was a small eater. He and Constanze produced six children in rapid succession, though only two sons survived infancy. As his fame grew he toured a lot. His letters home to her reveal his great passion for his 'little pussy'. When he received a letter from her, he would kiss it over and over again, he said. And there were kisses in his letters too. In one, he enclosed 1,095,060,437,082 of them.

And there was hot sex talk. On one occasion in 1789, he wrote to tell her that he would soon be on his way home to her.

'The first thing I shall do is take you by the arse-feathers,' he promised, 'and give you a sound spanking on your dear little kissable arse. You can count on that.'

When he was on tour, he would take her portrait with him in a slip-case. He said he would slide it in and out faster and faster, crying 'higher, higher, higher', before saying 'good night little mouse sleep well'.

The frustration of being away from her was often unbearable.

'On the night of the 4th – the 4th – I intend to sleep with my darling little wife', he wrote to her from Berlin. 'Arrange your dear sweet nest very daintily, for my little fellow deserves it indeed, he has really behaved himself very well indeed and is longing to possess your sweetest [the word here has been scratched out by Constanze's second husband]. Picture the little rascal in your mind's eye. Even as I write he is trying to creep up on the table. I gave him a good whack on the nose, but the rogue only – . Now the rascal is burning hot and I'm almost incapable of keeping him under control. Come to me by the first coach.'

But Mozart suspected that Constanze was being unfaithful to him while he was away. He begged her to consider 'your honour and mine' and to 'keep up appearances'.

She would frequently go off to Baden to take the cure with his composition pupil; Franz Xavier Süssmayr. Mozart pleaded with her not to 'make yourself quite so cheap'. One of the couple's surviving sons was probably not Mozart's. Even if he had been conceived as soon as Mozart returned from Germany on 10 November 1790, he would still have had to have been seventeen days premature. The child was named, coincidentally, Franz Xavier. Mozart plainly accepted the situation. That is how things were in Vienna in the eighteenth century. Five years before his marriage, Mozart said quite blithely that he would be a cuckold.

And what is sauce for the goose is sauce for the gander. Despite Mozart's constant assurances in his letters to Constanze that he was faithful, there were plenty of rumours about his behaviour on tour. Even in Vienna it was said that: 'To keep him from intercourse of the hazardous kind, his wife patiently took part in everything with him.'

One early biographer wrote: 'Mozart was attached to Constanze, but that did not prevent him from conceiving a fancy for other women, and his fancies had such a hold over him that he could not resist them.'

Another said: 'He was a husband, brought up two children … and had many intrigues with lively actresses and other women.' While another version portrays Constanze as 'a worthy wife, who tried to deter him from his many follies and debaucheries.'

As for his other loves, there are several candidates. His name was linked with 'Madame B.' – Henriette Baranius, a soprano at the Berlin opera. He had a long association with the singer Josepha Duschek, who had married her music teacher, who was twenty-three years her senior. When Mozart toured Europe, their paths would often cross. With Constanze safely at home, they met in Dresden, Prague, Potsdam, Leipzig and Berlin. During these trips, Mozart wrote home constantly, reassuring Constanze of his enduring love – though he teased her by telling her that he had been to parties, but that all the women there were ugly.

According to musicologist Alfred Einstein, the 'only woman of whom Constanze would really have had a right to be jealous' was the English soprano Nancy Storace. Mozart was plainly partial to sopranos and he created the role of Susanna in *The Marriage of Figaro* for Nancy.

During his last year of life in Vienna, Mozart was the centre of scandalous gossip. He was a friend of the notoriously promiscuous theatre manager Emanuel Schikaneder, who was said to have introduced the great composer to the 'seductions of the Viennese demimonde'. During the production of *The Magic Flute,* Mozart was rumoured to be having affairs with several members of the cast, notably Barbara Gerl and Anna Gottlieb. Gerl, it was said, was a 'pretty and attractive woman who had completely entangled Mozart in her coils'. When Mozart died, Gottlieb lost her voice and left the opera. In later years, she broadly confirmed that she had had a romantic liaison with Mozart.

Meanwhile there were rumours that he was having an affair with one of his pupils, Magdalena Hofdemel, the wife of his friend and creditor; Franz Hofdemel. Constanze was away at Baden at the time. Magdalena even had a child, conceived around the time that Constanze gave birth to Franz Xavier.

When Mozart died of rheumatic fever and typhoid in

Vienna, 5 December 1791, Constanze threw herself on the bed, hoping to catch the disease and die with him. By the time of the funeral she was prostrate with grief and too ill to visit the cemetery. Consequently, the pauper's grave where Mozart was buried 'three corpses deep' remains unidentified to this day.

On the day of his burial, Franz Hofdemel tried to murder Magdalena, who was pregnant once more. In a fit of jealousy, he slashed her face and neck with a razor. Magdalena survived the attack but Hofdemel committed suicide. The scandal sheets drew the obvious conclusion. Magdalena fled to her father's home in Brünn, where she gave birth to a son who she named Johann Franz Hofdemel. Johann was the name Mozart was christened with and it came first before the Wolfgang.

Constanze was just twenty-eight when her husband died. She had wanted to marry Süssmayr, but refused to give him the score of the *Requiem* that Mozart had wanted him to complete. In a huff, he left her. Although her temper quickly cooled, he never saw her again. She remained a widow for eighteen years, before marrying her lodger, the Danish diplomat Nicholas von Nissen. Nissen became Mozart's biographer and wrote: 'As a man he may have had many weaknesses ... He was high-spirited and pleasure-seeking, even in his youth.'

As Mozart's reputation grew, he was credited with intrigues with every pupil he had taught and every singer for whom he had written a song. As Joseph Henikistein, a Viennese banker whose sister had taken lessons from Mozart, remarked: 'Mozart would not take pains in giving lessons to any ladies except those he was in love with.' Constanze dismissed all this talk but admitted in later life that her first husband had indulged himself with what she called 'servant girlies'.

4

IN SEARCH OF THE
IMMORTAL BELOVED

The immortal Beethoven was the Byron of the world of music. His lifelong friend Dr. Franz Gerhard Wegeler said: 'Beethoven was always in love and occasionally made a conquest that would have been difficult if not impossible for any Adonis.' Yet he remained single throughout his life.

He was attracted to unattainable women who were far above his station. One of these was his 'Immortal Beloved', the unnamed woman to whom he wrote three passionate love letters that were found in a secret drawer in his desk after his death. 'Unfortunately, I have no wife,' he once said. 'I have found only women who I shall never possess.'

Like many other romantics, Beethoven loved to love those he could not have. To possess such an elevated love object carnally was to defile her. Even with ordinary women, he was shy. When the younger members of the orchestra played a trick on him and got a comely waitress to come on to him, he boxed the poor girl's ears.

He relieved the pains of love furtively with prostitutes, while leaving his great loves unsullied. This gave him a double romantic thrill. He could both enjoy the act and then torment himself with guilt and remorse at his human weakness.

One evening he was seen in one of Vienna's red light districts and was asked what he was doing there. 'Blame it on my dick,' he said simply. But in private he was not that blasé. In his diary, after a visit to a brothal he wrote: 'From today on, I will never go to that house, with feeling shame at craving such a thing from a woman.' He noted that: 'Sensual gratification without spiritual union is bestial. Afterwards one feels no trace of noble feelings, save remorse.'

The violinist Ignaz Schappanzigh reported that 'once, after a merry party, I took Beethoven to a girl, and then had to avoid Beethoven for weeks'. Otherwise he would have had to take the blame for Beethoven's casual indulgence.

This kind of sex had its dangers, of course. Beethoven kept a copy of *How to Guard Against and Cure Sexual Diseases* on his bookshelves, alongside works on how to treat diseases of the ear. This came in handy, as he caught the clap at least once.

But he did not have to go with whores. Beethoven is probably the only composer whose likeness most people would recognize. Both his portrait and his bust show a romantically handsome figure. He is the Heathcliffe of the classical repertoire, windblown, square-jawed and ruggedly handsome. However, his biographers often say that he was physically unattractive. Small – just 5 feet 5 inches tall – stocky, slovenly and surly. His face was pockmarked and unshaven; his nose stubby; his fingers short and hairy; his complexion, as they said at the time, was 'ruddy and coarse'. His appearance was 'demonic'. His wild and crazy behaviour was almost certainly designed to scare off female admirers. One book even compares him to a demented Robinson Crusoe, fetched up in the middle of post-Enlightenment Europe.

As a young man though, Beethoven was a real dude. When he was the court organist in Bonn, he wore a sea-green dress coat, green knee-breeches with buckles, white silk stockings, a white, flowered waistcoat trimmed with gold lace and a white frilly cravat. He had his hair fashionably frizzed and tied in a pony tail, carried his hat not on his head but under his arm in the style of the time. He also sported a sword, though there is no record of him using it.

At twenty-six, he was seen wearing thigh boots, a ring with

a seal and a pair of stylish lorgnettes. It was only in later years, with his increasing deafness, that he let himself go. Even when he was profoundly deaf, friends said that he used to 'stare amorously at a handsome peasant girl and watch her working in the garden', only to be mocked by her for his attentions.

Throughout his life, Beethoven longed to be married. 'Love and love alone, can give me a happy life,' he said. And marriage would keep him away from prostitutes: 'Please God, let me find a woman who can keep me on the path of virtue, one that I may rightly call my own.' It was not as if he lacked opportunity. While in Vienna as a youth, Dr Wegeler recalled; 'Beethoven was always in love.' With those women in his range, he could have had the pick of the bunch. The problem was, Beethoven was fickle.

'Beethoven had a great liking for female society,' wrote one pupil, Ferdinand Ries, 'especially young and beautiful girls. Out of doors, when he saw a charming face, he would turn around, raise his lorgnettes and gaze eagerly at the girl. He would smile and nod if he found I was watching him. And he was always falling in love, but generally his passion did not last long. When I teased him about his conquest of a very beautiful woman, he said that she had been his most enduring love – lasting a full seven months.'

One evening, Ries came for his lesson to find Beethoven occupied with a young lady. Ries was employed to play for them, with his back to the action. After a time, there was a sudden commotion. Beethoven had done something to offend the lady. She stormed out. Once his passions had cooled, Beethoven wanted to go after her. Ries was surprised to discover that Beethoven did not know what her name was or where she lived.

Ries and Beethoven went out to try and follow her. They glimpsed her in the moonlight, but then she disappeared. They searched fruitlessly for another hour and a half. This drove Beethoven half crazy. He told Ries: 'I must find out who she is and you must help.' Ries came across her later and discovered that she was the mistress of a foreign prince.

Still looking for a wife, Beethoven wrote to his friend Baron Ignaz Gleichenstein asking him to help. 'If you find a pretty one,' Beethoven wrote, 'one who may perhaps lend a sigh to my harmonies, do the courting for me.' And Beethoven knew exactly what he was looking for. 'She must be beautiful. I cannot love anything that is not beautiful. If I could, I should fall in love with myself.'

Beethoven was fastidious when it came to physical beauty. He mocked both the violinist Ignaz Schuppanzigh and the publisher Carlo Boldrini for being fat, calling them both Falstaff. In a restaurant or tavern, if an ugly person sat opposite him, he would move. Beautiful women were constantly inspiring him to write great music, he complained. This meant that he was not commissioned and was writing for free, solely in the hope of some amorous reward.

By the time Beethoven found his 'Immortal Beloved', he had been seriously in love a good few times. The first time was in his home town Bonn with Eleonore von Breuning. She was the daughter of the widowed Frau von Breuning who looked after him when his own mother died and he was seventeen. The pretty young Eleonore soon became his willing pupil. He called her 'Lorchen' and wrote tender love letters to her. In return, she knitted him a waistcoat and a scarf which 'brought tears to his eyes'. He kept a silhouette of her to his death.

At the time, though, his love was not so constant. When Jeanette von Honrath came to visit Eleonore from Cologne, Beethoven was quickly captivated by her blue eyes. She was 'a beautiful, vivacious blonde, of good education and amiable disposition, who enjoyed music,' he wrote. When she sang, Beethoven showed himself to be her slave on the keyboard. She would tease him about it and blow on his hair.

'Poor lad,' wrote Wegeler, 'exposed for the first time to the fire of these innocently feminine coquetries, he turned hot and cold, and the light breath that played through his hair infused a new life into his whole being.'

But it was not to be. Jeanette was high born and married an Austrian recruiting officer in Cologne who went on to become a field marshal. So Beethoven fell hopelessly in love with another aristocratic beauty, his pupil Fräulein von Westerholt. But then, according to Wegeler, 'there was never a time that Beethoven was not in love, and that in the highest degree.' Sadly, Fräulein von Westerholt was the daughter of the chief equerry to the Elector of Münster, and married a count.

Beethoven was also infatuated with Babette Koch, the daughter of Widow Koch who ran the Zehrgarten Café in Bonn where Beethoven took his meals. He wrote to her twice after he moved to Vienna. But even setting his cap at one of his own rank did not help. Babette went on to become the governess in the house of Count von Belderbusch, who she eventually married.

Beethoven proposed to the singer Magdalena Willmann. She turned him down 'because he as very ugly and half crazy'. He also pursued the famous singer Christine Gerhardi. But again she was far above him socially. She married Dr Joseph von Frank in 1798 and moved away from Vienna. Then there was the 'beautiful and cultivated' Julie von Vering, who encouraged him, but then took off with one of the von Breunings, whom she married in 1808.

According to Beethoven's pupil Karl Czerny, he was 'seriously in love' with another pupil, Anna Louise Babette, who he called 'Barbara'. He dedicated his Piano Sonata Opus 7 to her. Early on, it was known as the 'In-Love Sonata'. But Anna Louise was a countess and married a prince. Beethoven continued to dedicate pieces, including his famous C major Piano Concerto, to her in her married name. She died in 1813 while still very young.

Beethoven then fell in love with Giulietta, Countess Guiciardi, and dedicated his 'Moonlight Sonata' to her. He was thirty; she was sixteen. She was another of his pupils, a pert-looking girl who was exceedingly pretty. Her wild looks and her brown ringlets captivated him and optimism got the better of him.

'I am now leading a slightly more pleasant life, for I am mixing more with my fellow creatures,' he wrote. 'This change was brought about by a dear fascinating girl, who loves me and whom I love. After two years I am again enjoying a few blissful moments. For the first time I feel that marriage might bring me happiness. Unfortunately, she is not of my class and at the moment I could not marry. I still have to bustle about a good deal.'

Suffering repeated bouts of illness, he said he felt her love making him stronger every day. She visited him regularly and her brother Franz 'adored' Beethoven. But class was not something that could be overlooked. Beethoven soon found he had a rival in love, the aristocratic young composer Count Wenzel Robert Gallenberg. Giulietta married her count in 1803 and moved to Italy. Then, suddenly, she returned to Beethoven.

'She sought me out, crying, but I scorned her,' he told his secretary Anton Schindler. But later, he mellowed and slipped into a triangular relationship. 'She loved me very much,' he told Schindler, 'far more than she ever loved her husband. Meanwhile, he was more of a lover to her than I was. Heaven forgive her. She did not know what she was doing.'

When Giulietta told him that her husband had fallen on hard times, Beethoven sought out a rich man to sponsor him. Explaining the act of generosity, Beethoven said of Giulietta's husband: 'He was always my enemy; it is for that reason I was as good to him as possible.' But Giulietta's place in his affections was soon taken by her cousin Josephine Brunswick.

In 1799, Josephine had been compelled to marry Count Deym, a man thirty years her senior, who died in January 1804. Josephine gave birth four weeks later, then had a nervous breakdown. Beethoven was brought in to give her piano lessons. It was therapy for both of them.

'It's just a little dangerous,' her sister Thérèse wrote. 'May she be on her guard ... her heart must have the strength to say no.' But it did not. According to Thérèse's diaries, Josephine vacillated rapidly between periods of chastity and promiscuity. She gave herself 'freely without concern', but then went into paroxysms of guilt afterwards. This was a torment for all concerned.

The cause of the problem was that Josephine, a healthy young woman, had sworn an oath of chastity after her husband's death.

'That I cannot satisfy this sensuous love, does this cause you anger?' she asked Beethoven. 'I would have to break holy vows were I to listen to your desires.'

Beethoven reassured her. 'Oh beloved J.,' he wrote. 'It is no desire for the other sex that draws me to you, it is your whole self with all your individual qualities.' Men have always told women these sweet little lies. 'You have conquered me,' he wrote. She responded: 'I love you inexpressibly.' But her vacillation drove Beethoven into fits of jealousy. He watched her every turn, imagining that when she was not giving herself to him she must be giving herself to someone else.

'Do not doubt me,' she wrote. 'I cannot express how deeply wounding it is to be equated with low creatures.' But there was some foundation to Beethoven's suspicions. Josephine suddenly fled from Vienna on the arm of Count Wolkenstein. Again Beethoven had lost a lover to the aristocracy. He may have drawn some small crumb of consolation from the fact that Josephine's second marriage was not a happy one. She and Wolkenstein rowed – to the point where the police were called.

'The morality of the Countess does not appear to enjoy a good reputation,' read a police report of 1815. 'It is stated that she cannot be absolved from having given grounds for conjugal quarrels.'

Meanwhile, Beethoven had moved on to Josephine's sister Thérèse, the Countess Brunswick, who was another of his students. Five years his junior, she presumably knew what she was letting herself in for. Both Thérèse and Josephine could have been the 'Immortal Beloved', but both died with their lips sealed.

There was another Thérèse in the picture, a Thérèse von Malfatti, the beautiful niece of Beethoven's doctor. They had an amorous interlude and he dedicated some piano pieces to her. But soon Beethoven complained of the 'volatile Thérèse who takes life so lightly'. Well, she was nineteen, while he was forty.

Nevertheless, he drew up marriage plans with her in 1810. Then the volatile Thérèse took life so lightly that she spurned him. When she had married someone else, Beethoven wrote: 'Farewell, my dearest Thérèse. I wish you all the good and charm that life can offer. Think of me kindly, and forget my follies.'

By that time, Beethoven had been taken up by the prominent intellectual Bettina Brentano, who called his forehead 'heavenly'. She had already captivated Goethe. Beethoven wrote passionate love letters to her, though slightly less passionate than those to his 'Immortal Beloved'. But when he discovered his 'dearest, fairest sweetheart' had a sweetheart of her own he was crushed. Courageously, he wrote wishing her every happiness and, without tears, bade her farewell. Then, after she was married, he began wooing her all over again.

In 1812, Beethoven was working on his 8th Symphony in Töplitz, but that did not 'prevent him making love with much ardour'. The object of his affections was Amalie Sebald, who he called 'a nut brown maid of Berlin'. She was a singer and the composer Weber was also 'a devoted admirer of her virtues, her intellect and her beauty'.

She visited Beethoven frequently for an hour or so, though she occasionally complained that he was 'a tyrant'. But when he decided to leave Töplitz, Amalie was so upset that she would not even say goodbye. Beethoven soon realised his mistake.

'Everyday I am angry at myself,' he wrote to a friend at Töplitz. 'It is a frightful thing to make the acquaintance of such a sweet creature, and to lose her immediately. Nothing is worse than to have to confess one's own foolishness like this.' And he urged a friend to give Amalie 'an ardent kiss – if there is nobody there to see'. Amalie, not surprisingly, married someone else.

After Amalie, Beethoven declared that marriage – which he had once hoped would be the joy of his life – was now an impossibility and that, although he had never proposed to her, he could never get her out of his mind.

Once famous, Beethoven began attracting groupies. One

was Fräulein Roeckel. But she dropped him in favour of J.N. Hummel, who was once thought to be the equal of Beethoven himself.

Beethoven was impressed when Marie Bigot, sixteen years his junior, played his '*Appassionata*' at first sight. But when he invited her out for a walk, her husband grew jealous. Beethoven protested at his distrust, but Monsieur Bigot stood firm. Marie lovingly preserved Beethoven's autographed copy of the '*Appassionata*', which her husband bequeathed to the Paris Conservatoire after her death.

The pianist Elise Müller sent him love letters and presents, even though she was married. Fanny Giannatesio del Rio, the passionate Spanish-Italian daughter of the principal of the school where Beethoven placed his wayward nephew Karl, also makes the A list. Ludwig Nohl published Fanny's diary after her death. In 1816 and 1817, she claimed she was in love with Beethoven, 'a violet blooming at his feet in utter disregard'. She said he loved her in return and that she would have made him a good wife, but she could not declare herself.

Women admirers wrote to Beethoven asking for locks of his hair. Once, as a joke, Beethoven's friend the violinist Karl Holz sent a lady a tuft he had cut from the beard of a billy goat instead. The lady cherished it until she found out the truth. She angrily confronted Beethoven, who immediately lopped off a great handful of hair and gave it to her.

Although, in general, Beethoven preferred very young women, he occasionally entertained ladies of a certain age. Schindler noted that the Princess Lichnowsky was a 'second mother' to him. While Nanette Streicher who, as a girl, had captivated Mozart with her playing, gave him household advice.

Beethoven was always on the look out for a casual conquest. When he remarked on the charms of a plump young waitress, a dinner companion promised to procure her for him. He openly admired the 'magnificent arse' of the young wife of one of his friends, the conductor, Counsellor Peters, who offered to share his wife with him. When Peters went off on a trip to Italy, he suggested that Beethoven sleep with his wife 'because it is cold'. Frau Peters had a reputation for promiscuity, of which Peters knew and approved. 'When I am away my place is taken by amenable friends,' he said. It was better than her sleeping with a stranger, I suppose.

Whether another friend, the singer Franz Janitschek, made a similar suggestion is not known. But Beethoven received a note from Janitschek's wife saying: 'Why don't you come and visit me? My husband is away.' Janitschek and his wife were estranged soon after. And, in between, there were prostitutes. In his correspondence, Beethoven referred to them as fortresses. 'Keep away from rotten fortresses: for an attack from them is more deadly than one from well-preserved ones.'

His friend Baron Nikolaus Zmeskall procured prostitutes for him. Beethoven liked the girls to come around at half past three or four o'clock in the afternoon, so that he would have his evenings free. This continued until the end of his life. Well into his fifties, Beethoven warned Ferdinand Ries to take good care of his wife. 'You think I am old,' he said. 'But I am a very youthful old man.'

During the rehearsals for the debut of his 9th Symphony, Beethoven flirted with the singers, nineteen-year-old Henriette Sontag and twenty-year-old Karoline Unger. When they kissed him on the cheek, he said he would prefer they kissed him on the mouth. Beethoven grew jealous when he heard that Unger was going out with a young man. She tried to reassure him by telling him that she cared for him more than any twenty-three-year-old beau.

By this time, he was profoundly deaf and friends communicated with him via a Conversation Book. Karl Holz regaled Beethoven with the juicy tale of how Unger had lost her virginity to the thirty-year-old flutist Louis Drouet. Unger, Sontag, Holz and Drouet had all been out to dinner together after a concert in Baden. Afterwards they had gone for a walk in a nearby beauty spot. The couples became separated. After over an hour, Unger and Drouet returned looking flushed and embarrassed, and Unger had a huge bloodstain on her white dress.

Beethoven died in 1827. It was then that his secret letters

were found and the search for his 'Immortal Beloved' was on. The three letters to her were dated Monday, 6 July, Monday evening, 6 July and 7 July. No year is given, which makes it harder to work out who they were to.

As Beethoven's music scaled new heights of passion, so did his love letters. His 'Immortal Beloved' letters are obviously to someone who is married or otherwise unattainable, who he addresses as 'My Angel, My All, My Very Self', He wrote them when he was on his way to see her, but had been delayed by weather and the state of the roads. He rails against the fact that she is not entirely his, and he not entirely hers. But, on the other hand, this may be a good thing.

'Can love endure except through sacrifices?' he enquires. However much she loves him, he says he loves her more. 'Is not our love a truly heavenly edifice, firm as heaven's vault?'

The third letter begins: 'While still in bed, my thoughts press into thee, my Immortal Beloved.' Most men feel this way when they wake in the morning. He insists that he is faithful to her as 'never can another possess my heart'. 'Your love has made me the happiest and, at the same time, the unhappiest of men.' He signs off: 'Ever thine, ever mine, ever each other's.'

So who, then, was this 'Immortal Beloved'. Giulietta Guiciardi is an obvious candidate. She had a long relationship with Beethoven. They were still in contact eighteen years after she was married. Although she was a leader of Italian society, she was unhappy with her husband and, who knows, might have longed to be free one day.

The 'Immortal Beloved' was not Fanny del Rio. She was heartbroken when she overheard a conversation between her father and Beethoven. Her father, as fathers do, asked Beethoven if there was anyone else. He replied that he had met someone five years previously. 'To be united with her, I would have considered the greatest happiness of my life. But it was unthinkable, impossible, a fantasy,' he said. 'I have not been able to get those words out of my mind, they were so painful to me,' Fanny wrote.

If the woman Beethoven talked of to Fanny's father was his

'Immortal Beloved', several other women are in the frame. Many come to the conclusion that the 'Immortal Beloved' was Countess Thérèse Brunswick. He dedicated his sonata in F sharp minor to her and she seems to have been the model for Leonora, the heroine of *Fidelio*.

Miriam Tenger, who befriended Thérèse Brunswick in later life, claims that Thérèse was secretly engaged to her piano teacher-Beethoven . She said that Beethoven always included a sprig of *immortelle* in his love letters to Thérèse.

On one occasion Beethoven left after Thérèse's music lesson and absentmindedly forgot his coat and scarf. Thérèse rushed out into the cold after him. Her mother was scandalised that a well brought up young lady should run after a lowly piano teacher.

Plainly marriage was out of the question. Thérèse could not defy her parents and was afraid of Beethoven's temper. But Beethoven grew impatient and when he broke it off, he returned her love letters in a bundle. Tucked under the ribbons was a note: *L'Immortelle à son Immortelle – Luigi.*

When Thérèse died, thirty years after Beethoven, it is said that she was laid to rest with her head cushioned on the sprigs of *immortelle* saved from his letters, her last connection to the man she had loved.

Whether Thérèse Brunswick was the 'Immortal Beloved' or not we shall probably never know. In some ways, Beethoven's life was a lifelong search for an immortal beloved. But, meanwhile, he made do.

One of those he made do with was Johanna Reiss, the daughter of a prosperous Viennese upholsterer, who was already four months pregnant when she married Beethoven's younger brother Kaspar. The child, Karl, was nine when his father died. Beethoven immediately took over as the child's guardian. One theory to explain this is that Beethoven was the real father of Karl, and Kaspar, who was already terminally ill, married Johanna to save his brother from scandal. Beethoven accused Johanna of being a whore and forbade the child to see his mother. He and Karl lived together in a somewhat disorderly house with a couple of loose-living chambermaids. One, Karl reported, 'sat up in bed with her breasts exposed and looked at me in a brazen way'. Johanna never returned the insults Beethoven hurled at her.

He had sexual fantasies about her, imagining her turning up naked to the Artists' Ball and offering herself to him for 20 guilders. After Kaspar died, Johanna gave birth to an illegitimate daughter, who she called Ludovica – the feminine form of Ludwig. It was not a name that ever caught on. Johanna could also have been the mysterious, heavily veiled woman who visited Beethoven on his deathbed. Perhaps, she was truly his 'Immortal Beloved' if he had but known it.

Late in life, Johanna and Beethoven had been reconciled after Karl tried to kill himself by shooting himself in the head. But by that time, Beethoven had realized that marriage was not for him.

Marriages are seldom happy, he said, and they 'should not be such an indissoluble, liberty-crushing bond'. He said he was glad that none of the women he had loved so passionately had become his wife, though he thought at the time that they would have been 'the highest joy on earth to possess'. One of them, the brokenhearted Fanny del Rio, confided wistfully to her diary: 'I think I know a girl who, beloved by him, would not have made his life unhappy.' But then, women always think that.

5

FRANZ JOSEF 'SALAMI' HAYDN

Haydn is regarded as the Father of the Symphony and during his lifetime he was affectionately known as 'Papa Haydn'. But his wife, he frequently complained, was 'barren' – by this he meant that she did not like sex. It is likely, though, that he did father a child by one of his long-term mistresses.

Haydn was one of those men who was chaste in his youth and whose interest in sex grew with the passing years. At the age of twenty-seven, he was accompanying a pretty young countess when her neckerchief became undone. The poor boy became quite hot and flustered. But, however much this turned him on, as a young penniless composer he could not possibly aspire to bedding a countess, especially as he was physically unprepossessing.

'He was undersized and painfully thin,' wrote one contemporary. 'His legs were so short that they hardly reached the ground. His nose was long, and beaked, and disfigured, with nostrils of different shapes. His lower jaw jutted out like a bull-dog's and his face was pitted with small-pox.' He was so dark skinned that people called him 'nigger' and he always wore a wig although they were long out of fashion.

When he first moved to Vienna, he was lucky enough to find lodgings with a barber named Keller. To pay his keep, he gave one of the young ladies of the house harpsichord lessons and, in the way of young men, fell hopelessly in love with her. But the beautiful Thérèse did not reciprocate his feelings. She was so turned off by the prospect that she took the veil. Haydn was so infatuated, however, that he wrote the music which was played when she took her nun's vows. Brokenhearted, he consoled himself with her older, plainer sister Maria, which was something he would live to regret.

They married in St Stephen's in Vienna – the same church where Mozart was married – in 1760. Haydn was twenty-eight; Maria thirty-one. At that age, Herr Keller must have been grateful to get her off his hands. Friends called her 'not pretty nor yet ugly'. Hardly passionate about his new wife, Haydn believed that he might grow to 'like' her if she behaved in a reasonable way. Of course, she did not.

Like her pretty younger sister, Maria had a religious bent, which may have explained the dearth of sex. She filled the house with priests who ate and drank at Haydn's expense. Haydn was earning just £20 a year as music director to Count Morzin. Worse still, she used his scores as curling papers and underlays for her pastry.

When his genius became widely known, he complained that his wife did not care whether he was a cobbler or an artist, just as long as he brought in the money. When he was away in London, she wrote asking him to send cash so that she could buy a house she had seen. She liked it, she said, because it was 'a cosy size for a widow'.

'My wife,' Haydn wrote, 'is an infernal beast. She is ill most of the time and always in the same miserable temper. But I do not let it distress me any longer. There will sometime be an end to this distress. Sometime.' In such a situation, there is only one consolation.

'My wife is incapable of bearing children,' he told a friend. 'Therefore I was less indifferent to the charms of other women.'

After seven years of marriage, Haydn went with Prince Eszterházy to Bratislava, where he met a young woman called Catherine Csech. She was lady-in-waiting to Princess Grassalkovics. When the time came to return to Vienna, Haydn could not tear himself away. He delayed his departure by three days with excuses about the weather.

Although their time together was painfully short, Catherine Csech must have made a powerful impression on him. He never saw her again, but when he died, forty-three years later, he left her 1,000 guilders in his will – a vast sum in those days.

Haydn had good reason to entertain himself with a lady-in-waiting. By this time, his wife had taken a lover, the artist Ludwig Guttenbrunn who had been commissioned to paint Haydn's portrait. So perhaps she was not so averse to sex after all – only sex with him. When they finally split years later, one of the few things Frau Haydn held on to was Guttenbrunn's portrait of her husband.

Dalliances with young women while away from home were all well and good, but Haydn needed a more permanent solution. He hired the ailing violinist Antonio Polzelli and his young wife, the soprano Luigia. She was slim, chestnut-haired and olive-skinned, and Haydn, who was then forty-seven, took the nineteen-year-old as his mistress. Her husband, it seems, went along with this. He was considerably older than his wife and the arrangement clearly suited him. Indeed, when he was fired, Haydn intervened with the palace authorities and got him reinstated.

Luigia was not a singer of the first rank and Haydn constantly scaled down his arias for her. But Haydn was blind to her shortcomings. In his letters to her, he wrote 'if only four eyes would close' – those of his wife and Polzelli – they would get married.

She bore him a son, Alois Anton Nicolaus, and, when her husband died, Haydn signed a document promising to marry her if he ever became free. But, by the time his wife died, he had tired of her and she subsequently married someone else. Nevertheless, he left her an annuity of 150 guilders in his will – small beer compared with his bequest to Catherine Csech.

The Polzelli affair did its job though. At first Frau Haydn's suspicions were aroused. She became jealous and watched her husband like a hawk. Eventually he could bear the situation no longer and offered her generous alimony payments in return for a separation. She accepted and he paid up without fail. But Haydn's wife never achieved the widowhood she so ardently longed for. She died in 1800, nine years before him. He then moved into her cosy widow-sized house. 'And now,' he wrote in 1806, 'it is I who am living in it – as a widow.'

After separating from his wife, Haydn set about the ladies with a will. In 1791, on a trip to England, he fell in love with a Mistress Shaw who, he wrote in his notebooks, was 'the most beautiful woman I ever saw'. For years, he treasured a piece of ribbon she was wearing when they first met.

Then there was Mrs Hodges who was, again, 'the most beautiful woman I ever saw'. He always set his cap at beautiful women.

He was quite taken with the singer Mrs Elizabeth Billington and was quickly embroiled in scandal. Her letters had fallen into the hands of an unscrupulous publisher, who offered to return them for ten guineas. She refused, took him to court and lost. She then offered him £500 for their return. But the publisher knew a hot property when he had one and published them. They contained accounts of her amours, written to her own mother. By three o'clock on the day of publication the book was sold out. She was also said to have illegitimate children and that her own father had a hand in certain affairs.

'Such stories are common in London,' Haydn wrote to Luigia Polzelli, who may have grown suspicious of his friendship with Mrs Billington. 'The husband provides opportunities for his wife so that he can profit from it, relieving his "brothers-in-law" of up to £1,000.'

The reason Haydn did not marry Luigia when his wife died was that he was already in love with someone else. When a friend asked him about a bundle of love letters he carried around with him, Haydn replied: 'They are from an English widow who loved me. I should in all likelihood have married if I had been single.'

But the widow was no widow at all. Her name was Rebecca Schroeter and she was the former wife of Johann Schroeter, brother of Corona Schroeter, an amoretto of Goethe. The German musician was music master to Queen Charlotte, wife of George III, a position he had taken over from Bach's son. Like other music masters Schroeter also gave music lessons to the daughters of the nobility. But Schroeter crossed the line. He secretly married one of his aristocratic pupils, the fair Rebecca. A law suit ensued and Schroeter agreed to an annulment in return for a £500 pension. But apparently this left Rebecca Schroeter with an unquenchable craving for music teachers.

'Mrs Schroeter presents her compliments to Mr Haydn,' the thirty-five-year-old 'widow' wrote in June 1791, 'and will be very happy to see him whenever it is convenient to him to give her a lesson.' Having been trained by the queen's music master in her youth, it is difficult to see what the fifty-nine-year-old composer could have taught her. But she must have been a willing student, as the lessons continued with increasing regularity.

By 7 March 1792, she wrote telling him that she wanted lessons 'both in the morning and the evening'. Later she wrote to tell him that that she would provide food as they would be making music until all hours. 'I hope to see you my dear love on Tuesday as usual to dinner,' she wrote, 'and all night with me?'

But Rebecca Schroeter was not his only pupil. Women fans sent poems to him. They wore badges and headbands with the name 'Haydn' embroidered on them. The matrons of Old England behaved like a bunch of teenage girls over the latest boys' band. When Rebecca went to one of his concerts, she thanked him a thousand times for the entertainment. 'Where your sweet compositions and your excellent performance combine, it cannot fail to be the most charming concert,' she wrote. 'But apart from that, the pleasure of seeing you must ever give me infinite satisfaction.' This woman was thirty-five, not fifteen.

Haydn certainly enjoyed his fair share of groupies. When criticised for this, he said simply: 'It's part of the business.' But it is possible that Haydn found it all a little too much. At times, he seems to have feigned a headache. When he set off back to Vienna, Rebecca Schroeter told him that she would always consider her acquaintanceship with him the chief blessing in her life.

Haydn returned to England in 1794, but no more letters from his English widow have been found. However, when he left London for the last time, he left behind him the scores of his last six symphonies 'in the hands of a lady'. Could that lady have been the widow Schroeter?

6

SCHUBERT'S UNFINISHED

Schubert did not finish his famous symphony because he died of the pox at the tragically early age of thirty-one. He was much the same in love, never seeming to finish what he had started. Although he teased his friends on their affairs, he never seemed to steer his own through to a satisfactory conclusion. The result was binge sex with ladies of the night who gave him the disease that finished him off before he could finish off his *Unfinished Symphony*.

In September 1814, the Congress of Vienna was called to tackle the European situation after Napoleon's defeat and exile to Elba. Into the city trooped two emperors, two empresses, four kings, some 250 members of reigning families, all with their entourages, plus generals, diplomats, technical experts, bankers, cartographers, journalists, cooks, barbers, valets, ladies' maids, coachmen, equerries, interpreters, spies – not forgetting wives, mistresses and prostitutes – some 10,000 people in all. You would have thought there would have been plenty of scope there for an amorous young composer. But with the pick of Europe within his grasp, Schubert fell in love with a young lady with the unappealing name of Thérèse Grob. She was the young daughter of a widowed friend of the family and sang the soprano part in his mass in F when it was performed in the church in Liechtenthal. She was no great beauty, being small, plump and with a pock-marked face. And he was in no financial position to marry.

'I loved her very deeply and she loved me,' he wrote. 'She wasn't pretty but she was good. She had kindness of the heart. For three years, I hoped to marry her but I could find no position that would keep us both provided for.' He was seventeen; she a year younger. He wrote her many poignant love songs during their affair, which lingered on until into the 1820s when she married a wealthy baker.

'When she married someone else, I was deeply hurt,' Schubert wrote. 'I am still in love with her, and since then no other woman has pleased me as much. But she wasn't for me.'

Schubert went for long walks in the country and tried to forget her. Friends begged him to put away this 'ridiculous infatuation'. One remarked: 'From the time he lost the girl he loved, Schubert showed much antipathy toward other girls.'

Anna Wilder, a lady's maid turned singer, tried to comfort him and acted as 'a sort of nurse to Schubert, sang his songs in public, and gave him advice,' it was said. But she aspired to higher things in life and married a rich jeweller. Then Marie Pachler, who had been an intimate of Beethoven, brought some relief, but only temporarily.

'For many years I sang my solitary song,' he wrote. 'If I sang of love, it turned to pain. If I would sing of pain, it turned to love. Thus I was torn between joy and sorrow.' Much like the human condition then, or the symptoms of a well-known disease.

Schubert was definitely not a ladies' man. He was awkward and shy around the opposite sex and not attractive. He was stooped and round-shouldered, with plump arms and stubby little hands. His moon-shaped face was puffy. His forehead was low, his lips thick, his eyebrows were bushy and his nose short and upturned. Apparently, he had nice eyes but they were hidden by glasses which he wore even in bed.

'Schubert was a cold fish towards the other sex and not exactly a gallant man,' said a friend. 'He paid no attention to his clothes or his teeth. He smelled of tobacco and was not turned out to be a suitor.'

So what was this man doing falling in love with a countess?

In the winter of 1818, Count Eszterhàzy was visiting Vienna and hired Schubert as piano teacher for his two daughters, Marie and Caroline. At the end of the season, Eszterhàzy was so taken with Schubert's musical output that he invited him to accompany the family to their summer-house at the foot of the Styrian Hills in Hungary. There, in the servants' hall, Schubert began to open up a bit.

'The cook is rather jolly,' he wrote to a friend. 'The ladies' maid is thirty. The housemaid is very pretty, often quite social. The nurse is a good soul and the butler is my bitter rival.'

But Schubert's intentions remained firmly above stairs. 'The count is rather rough,' he wrote. 'The countess is haughty, yet with a kind heart. And the young countesses are nice girls.' Marie was fourteen, but it was the younger one, eleven-year-old Caroline, that attracted the twenty-one-year-old Schubert's attention. She was certainly aware of his feelings towards her.

'Why do you not dedicate any of your compositions to me?' she once asked.

'What would be the use,' he replied. 'All that I do is dedicated to you.' In fact, only one of his works, the 'Fantasia' in F minor, is dedicated to her and it was not published until after his death. It is a piano duet.

Although marriage was out of the question, there was no rupture in the relationship until Schubert's death in 1828. Then Caroline waited another sixteen years before she settled down to a comfortable marriage with an army major.

However, Schubert's failures in heterosexual love have given rise to certain inferences. His spacious Viennese home was bedecked with Turkish upholstery, Arabian carpets and Persian pipes. Schubert was an opium smoker, as well as a heavy drinker. He was also a friend of Liszt, who seemed to play a dominant role in his affairs. And there has been speculation that they had a gay affair.

The biographer Maynard Solomon claims to have found the coded references used by the Viennese homosexual subculture in Schubert's writings. Once when he is 'out of sorts' it is said he 'needs "young peacocks", like Benvenuto Cellini'. Solomon says that 'young peacocks' are the beautiful boys, often transvestites, that Cellini was reputed to have chased. Others have pointed out that in early 19th century Vienna, eating peacocks was thought to be a cure for syphilis.

There is little doubt, however, that Schubert did surround himself with young male admirers, all of whom had been educated in single-sex schools and colleges. He wrote erotic letters to male friends. But his closest companion, Franz von Schoder, was a well-known womaniser.

Despite Schubert's legendary shyness, he had social relationships with Josefine von Koller, Sophie Müller and Josefine 'Pepi' Pöckelhofer, who he met in Zseliz in 1818. In fact, Pepi Pöckelhofer's account of their encounter is positively suggestive. While others speculate that he was in love with the singer Emilie Neuman.

Schubert's death certificate records that he died of *Nervenfieber* – nervous fever. But from the medication he had been prescribed before his death, it is certain that Schubert had syphilis, among other things. The doctor who treated him had written two books on the subject.

There was a flourishing trade in female prostitution in Vienna at the time. Schoder was one of their best customers and Schubert's friends blamed the 'seducer' Schoder for leading the composer into 'the slough of moral degradation' and leaving him 'bathed in slime'. Close friends all said that syphilis played a part in his death.

'Schubert loved girls and wine,' said Wilhelm von Chézy in his *Memoirs* of Vienna. 'With his liking for the pleasures of life, he strayed on to those wrong paths that generally admit no return, at least no healthy one.'

Schubert appears to have contracted syphilis around 1822, which should have ruled out all further sexual contact. This would have made his young countess, who he continued to visit, even more unattainable. But it certainly did not stop him indulging his *passions mauvaises* that were said to 'enslave' him. He was a man of powerful sensuality and strong passions.

Chézy said: 'His work proclaims a genius of divine creation, unimpaired by the passions of an eagerly burning sensuality.'

Once he had the disease, Schubert rejected the marriage bed in favour of buying sexual favours in brothels and other meeting places for prostitutes where syphilis was endemic. When drunk, it was said, he resorted to 'hypersexual activity', seeking out sordid sexual satisfaction in seedy inns. Once the disease had caught hold, he might as well indulge himself with prostitutes who would, more than likely, have the pox already.

Towards the end, Schubert was tormented with recurring headaches, loss of appetite, violent mood swings, hallucinations, bouts of being bedridden and general malaise, which were brought on by the mercury he was taking to treat his syphilis as much as the disease itself. But he did not give up the heavy drinking and chain-smoking which further weakened his constitution. All the while he maintained his double life, hiding his secret vices. Despite his squalid end, or perhaps because of it, Schubert's songs, more than any other's, have inspired generations of happy, and unhappy, lovers unafflicted by sexually transmitted diseases. Schubert himself ran through the whole gamut of syphilis – its primary, secondary and final, fatal, tertiary stages. It was one thing in life that he did really finish. And it finished him.

7

SCHUMANN AND HER TWO MEN

As well as being a great composer in her own right, Clara Schumann bedded two other great composers; her husband Robert Schumann and Schumann's young disciple Johannes Brahms. It was a musical ménage de tra-la-la. Clara was a child prodigy. Her father, Friedrich Wieck, was a noted piano teacher whose dedication to encouraging Clara's youthful talent bordered on the sadistic. When Clara was five, her mother and father divorced and from then on he watched Clara's every move. He coached her and dressed her and even wrote her diary for her. When she travelled, he shared her bedroom and he kept her well away from the company of boys.

At the age of eight she performed a Mozart concerto at the salon of Frau Agnes Carus, the wife of a famous doctor. The eighteen-year-old Robert Schumann was also there and he became infatuated with Frau Carus, who was eight years his senior. He used to play Schubert's piano duets with her which, like Schubert, he found an arousing experience.

'Only one kiss from her and I would be ready to die,' he confided to his diary. There are other entries spelling out his adolescent arousal: 'She at the window – terrible sweaty night'; 'Excited night and beautiful, magnificent dreams of her, of her'.

Already Schumann was no stranger to love, in July 1827, when he was seventeen, he wrote to a schoolmate: 'Now only do I feel that purest, highest love which is not forever sipping the intoxicating cup of enjoyment, but finds happiness in tender contemplation and reverence. Oh, friend. Were I but a smile, how I would flit about her eyes. Were I but joy, how gently would I throb in all her pulses. Yea, might I be a tear, I would weep with her; and then, if she smiled again, how gladly would I die on her eyelash, and gladly, gladly be no more.'

In the same letter he says he has given two girls the push. One was Liddy – 'a narrow-minded soul, albeit the perfection of female beauty which, if petrified, every critic would pronounce superb'. 'I think I loved her,' he goes on. 'But I knew only the outward form in which the rose-tinted fancy of youth often embodies its inner most longings.' The other was Nanni – 'a most glorious girl'. But the love he felt for her had now turned into 'just a quietly burning sacred flame of pure divine friendship and reverence'.

He complained a few weeks later of his bitter disappointment at not seeing her when he visited Dresden and in his mind 'went over and over again all the hours I dreamed away so joyfully in her embraces and in her love'. Nanni is his Madonna, before whom he must worship. Although, according to his diaries, he had been torn between the two girls, he also took an interest in a girl called Mili who had large breasts that bounced up and down as she danced.

A few months later he declared that he was in love with Clara von Kurrer in Augsburg. Even though she was practically engaged, his ardour knew no dampening. When he returned to Leipzig as a university student, the image of Clara 'sweeps before my eyes in my waking and sleeping moments'.

On 19 August 1928, he noted that he had dreamt not only of Clara, but of Agnes Carus as well. A piano duet can easily turn into a 'duet for two hearts, or a quartet for four legs,' he muses. At the same time, he was also having an affair with Frau Miersch, the wife of a delicatessen owner. Proudly, the nineteen-year-old Schumann records stealing hot kisses and embracing her loins under the nose of her husband.

Schumann also fancied himself as a writer and his stories at the time often featured bare-breasted women wafting through cemeteries. And some of his poetry was openly homosexual:

And how wildly one youth loves the other youth,
And how he embraces him, and how they weep together,
That's how you are right now; once you were my feminine
  beloved.
And from the blossoms of your love
Arises friendship softly.

After a trip to a tavern in March 1829 with his friend Johann Renz, he mentions 'pederasty' in his diary. He went back the next evening and passed a 'voluptuous night with Greek dreams'. Homosexuality was not something you could be open about in Germany at the time. It was against the law. But the implication is clear.

Travelling in Italy later that year, Schumann wrote to his mother to say he had 'found it frightfully hard to leave Leipzig – a girl's soul, beautiful, happy, and pure had enslaved mine'. But in Milan, he met 'a beautiful English girl, who seemed to have fallen in love not so much with me but my piano playing; for all English women love with the head[!] – I mean they love Brutuses or Byrons, or Mozarts or Raphaels.' She was 'very proud, and kind, and loving, and hating; hard, but so soft when I was playing'. Her voice, it seemed to him, was the whispering of an angel.

'If ever I marry, it will be to an English girl,' he said. But it was not to be. 'Alas, my heart is heavy,' he noted in his diary. 'She gave me a spray of cypress when we parted. Accursed memory.'

But soon there was 'a beautiful Dutch girl' who had 'a Greek profile and is vivaciously seductive' and she 'makes eyes like nobody's business'. There was local beauty too. 'Just now I saw a most beautiful Italian girl,' he wrote and commented on the 'big, beautiful fiery, seductive eyes' of Italian women. And there were some jolly goings-on. He noted in his diary a 'voluptuous scandal during the night with the naked tour guide and naked waitress'. Even this was not undiluted pleasure. 'A homosexual thrust himself on me,' he wrote. 'Hence my sudden departure.'

At the same time, he said he had 'a real fear of ladies', and back in Germany he was less inhibited and enjoyed 'the jolly goings-on in the bath-houses' of Leipzig and Heidelberg, as well as 'finger games under skirts' and 'smiling whores'. In his diary he also talks of 'ordinary girls [prostitutes] who can usually love two at a time' and visits to the Hotel de Pologne, one of Leipzig's better known brothels.

Schumann fell for a Ernestein von Fricken. She was the daughter of a nobleman from the town of Asch on the border of Saxony and Bohemia. It was fate, Schumann declared. The letters of her home town appear in his name – SCHumAnn – though not in the right order.

She was sixteen; he twenty-four. And they were both studying under the noted piano teacher Friedrich Wieck, Clara's father. Schumann wrote to his mother describing Ernestine as one of 'two glorious beings of the fair sex who have lately appeared in our set'. Who was the other? The young Clara perhaps.

However, for now, Ernestine was the apple of his eye. Her musical talent was 'just such a one as I might wish to have for a wife'. Clara was not to be overlooked in that department though. In 1830, two years before Schumann had even thought of being a composer, Clara published her *Four Polonaises* and dedicated them to Henriette Voigt, another of Schumann's girl-friends.

Ernestine's father got wind of his daughter's romance and she was summoned home to Asch. Meanwhile, Schumann found comfort with Christel – who he sometimes calls Charitas – a maid in the Wiecks' house. His diary is full of references to having sex with her – 'Christel in one minute', 'Charitas came completely and was bleeding', she was 'full of fire and flames'.

It is clear that Schumann already had the syphilis that would kill him. He referred repeatedly to a 'wound', probably a syphilitic chancre. In sex, he experienced a 'biting and nervous pain'. In his diary, he says that 'sin gives birth to Nemesis'. And when he told Christel about it, she 'turned pale'.

SCHUMANN AND HER TWO MEN

He began bathing his sore penis with 'Narcissus water', a distillate of daffodil bulbs used since ancient times to treat minor skin irritations. Sex continued, against the advice of his doctor, 'with fear and little enjoyment'. He began a play based on the tragic romance of *Abélard and Héloise* (see *Sex Lives of the Popes*).

Already, during piano lessons, his hands began to shake, possibly as a result of the mercury he was taking. Mercury was then the common treatment for syphilis, though it probably killed more than it cured. Schumann was suffering bouts of intense pain and began to exhibit the mental instability that would mark his decline.

At the same time, he began to have homosexual affairs with his roommate Günther and the pianist Ludwig Schunke, who he later moved in with. Christel visited him there and he had her 'one and a half times'. Then came good news. 'Ernestine has written to me in great happiness,' Schumann told a friend. 'Through her mother she has sounded out her father, and he gives her to me.' But her happiness was to be short-lived. Schumann discovered that Ernestine was not as classy as he had imagined. She was the illegitimate daughter of Baron Ignaz von Fricken's sister-in-law Countess von Zedtwitz by a lowly wire manufacturer. Schumann quickly dropped her and she was quickly replaced in his affections by Clara Wieck. After all, he told Clara, 'You are my oldest love.'

Long before, Schumann's mother had picked Clara out as a potential daughter-in-law. 'You must marry my Robert one day,' she had told the thirteen-year-old Clara when she had visited Schumann's home town of Zwickau.

Heinrich Dorn, a young composer who often visited the Wiecks' house, left a vivid description of Clara at thirteen: 'Graceful in figure, of blooming complexion, with delicate white hands, a profusion of black hair, and wise, glowing eyes. Everything about her was appetising, and I have never blamed Schumann for being carried away by this lovely creature."

Reciprocating after a fashion, Schumann said he found both Dorn and Dorn's young wife physically attractive. With

Schumann's growing interest in Clara came an outburst of music and songs that were very sexual in nature. 'About the songs,' said Clara, 'isn't there perhaps a young nightingale inflaming you?' 'I was completely inside you while composing them,' Schumann replied. 'You romantic girl, you follow me everywhere with your eyes, and I often think that without such a bride one cannot make such music.'

Clara revealed that she had yearned for Schumann secretly for years. In a letter to him, she wrote: 'I must tell you what a silly child I was then. When Ernestine came to us, I said: "Just wait till you learn to know Schumann; he is my favourite out of all my acquaintances." But she did not care to know you, since she said she knew a gentleman in Asch, who she liked much better. That made me angry. But it was not long before she began to like you better. And soon it went so far that every time you came I had to call her. I was glad to do this since I was pleased that she liked you. But you talked more and more with her and cut me short. That hurt me a great deal, but I consoled myself by saying it was only natural since you were with me all the time. Besides Ernestine was more grown up than I was. Still, queer feelings filled my heart, so young it was and so warmly it beat even then. When we went walking you talked to Ernestine and poked fun at me. Father shipped me off to Dresden on that account, where again I grew hopeful. I said to myself: "How pretty it would be if he were only my husband." '

Now in Schumann's eyes Clara became 'one of the most glorious girls the world has ever seen'. Not that he kept himself exclusively to her, you understand. Baron von Fricken adopted Ernestine and Schumann renewed their affair. He also renewed his aquaintanceship with Clara von Kurrer and the glorious Nanni, and he paid frequent visits to a Julie.

He had a fling with the Scottish beauty Robena Laidlaw, the eighteen-year-old court pianist to the Queen of Hanover. They met in the rose garden at Rosenau and established a 'quick understanding'. They took a boat trip together and he dedicated his *Fantasiestücke* opus 12 to her. And when she died in 1901, a rose was found that he had given to her in 1836. Meanwhile,

Schumann was caught in the basement being 'wicked' with a country girl. Plenty of other chance encounters are scattered throughout his diaries, including one affair carried on entirely through the two lovers' windows.

Nevertheless, Schumann and Clara became secretly engaged. Her father found out about it and threatened to shoot Schumann if Clara ever spoke to him again. He took her to Breslau. When Schumann found out, he wrote to a music journalist there, a complete stranger, and asked him to act 'as a messenger between two parted souls'. He assured the man that Clara 'loves and is loved' but her father 'forbids any sort of intercourse on pain of death'.

Schumann was a cunning lover and managed to find a way to spend five whole days with Clara. Her father, however, encouraged the attentions of her singing teacher, Carl Banck. She grew interested, but Banck spoilt it all by speaking ill of Schumann, though he probably just told the truth. After all, Christel was still visiting Schumann in his rooms every day and on 17 January 1837 he noted in his diary that she had had a baby. Whether it was his, he did not say.

Whatever Banck said to Clara, it backfired. She sent a letter to Schumann via her maid Nanny – who Schumann describes affectionately as 'cunningly ingenious, discreet'. In it, Clara said of Banck: 'I was astounded by his black heart. He tried to betray you, but he only succeeded in insulting me.' A secret meeting was arranged.

'The moon shone so beautifully on your face when you lifted your hat and passed your hand across your forehead,' Clara wrote later. 'I had the sweetest feeling that I have ever had. I had found my love again.'

Schumann tried writing to Clara's father. He tried speaking to him man to man, but nothing worked. Schumann and Clara were already stars in the world of music and great allies rallied to their cause. Liszt, who was a friend of Clara's father, refused to speak to him, and both Chopin and Mendelssohn denounced his inhumanity. Herr Wieck responded with a campaign of vilification. He published a pamphlet pointing out that

Schumann was a drunk and a syphilitic, which was true. Schumann's syphilis had now reached the stage where he was prescribed 'animal baths'. He had to sink the afflicted parts into the flesh of a freshly slaughtered animal.

Schumann took his prospective father-in-law to court. His ex-wife, Clara's mother, turned up, taking her daughter's side in the case. Herr Wieck promptly lost his temper. The judge overturned all the accusations Wieck had made against Schumann, except one. Schumann was, officially, judged to be a drunk. Clara now wrote to her father.

'My love for Schumann is, it is true, a passionate love,' she told him. 'But I do not love him solely out of passion. I love him because I think he is one of the best of men, because no other man could love me as purely and nobly as he does, or so understandingly. I believe I can make him wholly happy through allowing him to possess me and I understand him as no other woman could.'

Her father responded by spreading slanderous rumours about Clara too, but it did not matter because the courts granted them a licence to marry. Schumann's pure and noble love could hold back no longer. When she was in Weimar for a concert, he turned up at her hotel room unannounced. Three days later they returned to Leipzig together. 'I cannot describe my joy,' Clara wrote in her diary. A week later, they married, and to put her father's nose further out of joint they tied the knot on the day before her twenty-first birthday, when she would have been free to marry without her father's consent anyway. The night before, Schumann gave Clara his song cycle *Myrtles* as a wedding present.

A year later their first child was born. Clara became pregnant nine more times in the next twelve years. Eight children survived. Despite having two incomes – Clara became an internationally famous concert pianist – their large family caused them financial problems. So in the household accounts books, Schumann wrote an 'F' every time they made love.

In those days, condoms and spermicidal pessaries were available, but they were unreliable and expensive. The cervical cap had just been invented by a German gynaecologist, but they had to be custom–made and were difficult to obtain. Schumann's careful record of the times they made love was an attempt at a primitive rhythm method, but plainly it was unsuccessful.

The frequency of intercourse varied from once every two days to once every five. There would be a gap after she had given birth, but the 'F' would reappear with the remark 'slept with Clara for the first time'. Their diaries record his continued drunkenness and his steady decline, but there are no periods of sexual abstinence. Whatever his condition, the Fs kept on coming.

Schumann was in the grip of terminal insanity brought on by tertiary syphilis when Brahms turned up and promptly fell in love with Clara, who recognized in him the genius her husband had once possessed.

Brahms had begun his musical career at the age of nine as a pianist in the brothels of Hamburg. Sailors who had been at sea for months, Brahms recalled, would land like rabid beasts looking for women, and girls would use the young Brahms to excite the punters further.

"These half-naked women would try to drive the men even wilder,' he said. 'They would cuddle me on their laps between dances, and kiss, caress and excite me. This was my first impression of the love of women.'

Goethe said: 'Let no one imagine that he can overcome the first impressions of youth.' Indeed, Brahms himself confessed: 'Whatever I took to my heart when I was young stayed there, firmly embedded.' Not only did he work with prostitutes, he grew up with them in the red-light district popularly known as *Ehebrechergang* or Adulterers' Alley. They were known as the Singing Girls of Hamburg and worked from the tenement block where he lived and he played at their orgies in the lowest dives around the harbour.

Staying up all night took a toll on his health and when he was fourteen a his father's friend, Adolf Giesmann, invited the young Brahms to visit him in the countryside to recuperate.

There Brahms could teach Giesmann's daughter Lieschen the piano. Lieschen was just one year younger than Brahms and shared his love of reading the fashionable romantic writing of the day. They fell in love. Later she came to stay with him in Hamburg, but gradually they drifted apart. She married and went to live in Wihelmshaven, but Brahms never forgot her.

Years later, in 1888, when Lieschen was a widow, she wrote to Brahms asking for his help to secure a scholarship for her daughter at the academy of music in Berlin. Brahms got her a place, but a scholarship was impossible. So he paid for her tuition, secretly, out of his own pocket.

Brahm's 'puppy love' for Lieschen was an exception rather than the rule. 'I never knew of his having an affair with a lady,' his pupil Robert Kahn said, 'but he often went with prostitutes.' Long before he became a resident of Vienna, he knew most of the prostitutes there by name. As he walked down the Kärnthnerstrasse they would call out: *Guten tag, Herr Doktor!* If they were short of money, they would seek him out in the cafés and he would given them a gulden or two, maybe more if they needed it. He was a connoisseur of the ladies of the street and would recommend to friends girls who would fulfil their specific needs. He was proud that he fulfilled his own sexual needs without hurting others. He boasted to a woman friend: 'I have never made a married woman or a *Fräulein* unhappy.'

Simply paying for his pleasures had its advantages too. 'I always have plenty of time because I never fritter it away on cards and women,' he said. Once he submitted an itemized bill for his B flat string quartet to his publisher Franz Simrock which included the item: 'For models for the tender movement, 2 florins each.' The 'tender movement' was the *Agitato* which certainly has a sexual rhythm to it. How many 'models' were required for its completion Brahms does not say.

Elsewhere in Europe, remaining a bachelor would have raised eyebrows. In 1877, he turned down an official position in Düsseldorf, saying: 'In Vienna one may remain single without any ado, but in a small town an old bachelor is a caricature. I no longer wish to marry and have certain reasons to fear the fair sex.' Certainly, there was no secret about Brahms' preference for prostitutes. After the mayor of Leipzig offered him the post of cantor – a position once held by Bach – he began having misgivings about what he called the composer's 'dissolute way of life'. Brahms dismissed his reputation as the result of tom-foolery on his behalf.

'For years now, when I have left the tavern before the others, it has been my custom to remark: "I must visit the Schwender or the Sperl [two notorious brothels flourishing then]",' he said. 'In fact, I only go there once a year – and then with two old friends.'

He once told a friend, Frau Flegmann, that it was a good thing for a man to visit such houses of entertainment in his youth because 'in his manhood similar dives disgust him'. But Brahms never lost his taste for them completely.

When he was young they were a necessary outlet. He was short, his beard was late in coming and his voice remained shrill and girlish until he was twenty-four. It was hard for him to get any girl he did not have to pay for to take him seriously. There was only one, Clara Schumann. When she met the twenty-one-year-old, she was immediately impressed by his genius, but she was old enough to be his mother. In his letters he would even address her as *meine liebe Frau Mama* – my dear Madam Mother. But there was always more to it than that.

'What have you done to me?' he wrote, like a forlorn lover. 'Can you not release me from this magic?' And there can have been no doubt in Brahms' mind what he felt for the thirty-five-year-old Clara. After sending her a collection of songs, he told a friend: 'I can never love a girl again. I've quite forgotten them all. They merely promise the heaven that Clara opens.'

Robert Schumann was still on the scene at the time. But on 14 February 1854, his household account book records what would be his final 'F'. He made love to his wife one last time, then on the 27th he ran from the house in his dressing gown and threw himself into the freezing Rhine. His suicide bid failed, however, as two fishermen saw him jump and hauled him into their boat. He was taken to the lunatic asylum in Endenich where he remained until he died. Brahms promptly moved in with Clara. From that very day, 27 February 1854, the household account's book is kept in Brahms' hand.

Brahms soon began to address Clara as 'my most beloved Clara' and they called each other by the intimate *du*. He wrote: 'Everyday I greet and kiss you a thousand times.' While Robert Schumann was still alive, Brahms and Clara went on holiday together, a walking tour of the Rhineland. It has been suggested that Clara's last child was fathered by Brahms. When Robert died in 1856, things became more problematic. A mother of seven living children could hardly be seen living with a roguish young composer fifteen years her junior. So Clara went to live with her mother in Berlin. She took another holiday with Brahms in Switzerland, but when she went on a concert tour of England, he did not accompany her in case they were taken for a couple.

While she was away, Brahms fell in love with Agathe von Siebold, the plain but charming daughter of a professor in Göttingen. He wrote songs for her, which she sang. Then Clara suddenly turned up in Göttingen. 'I must walk with her for a bit,' Brahms told Agathe. 'Otherwise she will grow jealous.' But one evening, Clara caught Brahms with his arm around the young girl's waist. Clara packed and left town in high dudgeon. Agathe and Brahms exchanged kisses and rings, but Brahms left town believing himself to be only half engaged.

Agathe was upset by his equivocation and a mutual friend wrote to Brahms, telling him that he must make up his mind whether to marry Agathe or not before he returned. Brahms hardly answered the maiden's prayers when he wrote to Agathe, saying: 'I love you. I must see you again. But fetters I cannot wear. Write to me and tell me whether I can come back to fold you in my arms, to kiss you and to tell you that I love you.' Agathe got the message. He liked the physical side, but commitment was out. She 'wrote her parting letter and wept, wept for years over her dead happiness', and never saw him again.

Although Clara had won him back, she upbraided him: 'Poor Agathe ... would not leave my mind. In spirit I kept seeing the poor abandoned girl, and lived all her sufferings with her. Dear Johannes, you should not have let things go so far.' Clara's admonition sounds disingenuous but, whatever the relationship between the two women, appearances had to be maintained.

'I saw her in person at my concert,' Clara wrote to Brahms two years later. 'I marvelled at her strength in coming, for it is impossible that she could have enjoyed it.'

Brahms did not come off unscathed either. 'I have played the scoundrel towards Agathe,' he told a friend. But he knew the cure. He threw all his feelings of guilt and self-recrimination into his G major sextet, or the Agathe sextet as it was known to friends. 'Here I have emancipated myself from my last love,' he said when he delivered it.

As Agathe pined into middle age, she was far from being his last love. A few months after their break-up, he fell for the beautiful and charming young Austrian singer Bertha Porubszky. After he first set eyes on her, he fell on his knees in front of a friend of hers and begged for an invitation to meet her. When they met, their attraction was mutual. But, when push came to shove, once more Brahms refused to commit himself to marriage. They broke up and Brahms feared she would go through a reprise of Agathe's agonies. But Bertha soon bounced back.

'B.P. is engaged to a rich young man,' Brahms wrote excitedly to a friend. 'When I first saw her she was pallid and ailing; and my conscience felt more healthy when I presently received the announcement in question.' She married one Herr Faber and on the birth of their second child Brahms sent her a cradle song which he dedicated to her.

Next came Ottolie Hauer, a singer who had recently arrived in Vienna, and this time Brahms did not hold back. On Christmas Day 1863 he went to her lodgings to ask for her hand in marriage, only hours after she had accepted the proposal of Dr Edward Ebner.

Then there was Luise Dustmann, whose Leonora in Beethoven's *Fidelio* was the Vienna Opera's current sensation. She was a divorcée and rather forward. When they met, she suggested they get together, privately, the next day. In her letters, she signed herself '*Fidelio*' and addressed him as 'Hansi', a common diminutive of Johannes, but she was the only one to use it with the gruff and bearded Brahms. She invited him up to play her piano and afterwards she wrote: 'One day I will invite that fellow from Hamburg for me, not for my piano. Perhaps he will succeed in making my untuned strings twang.' Perhaps not; as according to the pretty young maid of a concert manager who knew him at the time, Brahms was 'a passionate but awkward lover' and the affair was soon over.

The next was the lovely Baroness Elisabeth von Stockhausen. She was just sixteen, beautiful, blonde, charming and gifted. She sought Brahms out to get him to give her music lessons. Her former teacher, Julius Epstein, wrote to Brahms saying that if he could keep from falling in love with her he would be breaking the laws of nature. He was right. After two lessons, Brahms sent her back to Epstein, but he kept her picture on his desk for years. She married the composer Heinrich von Herzogenberg, but Brahms continued to see her. He wrote: 'You must know this, you are one of the few people I love so much that – as your husband is always there – I cannot tell you.' She died young and, at first, Brahms refused to give up her letters for publication. But her husband eventually persuaded him to.

In 1869, Brahms fell deeply in love with Julie, Clara Schumann's third daughter, who looked just like her mother. A friend told Clara of Brahms, feelings and soon after Julie got engaged to Count Marmorito. Brahms was livid. 'Now I suppose I shall have to compose a bridal song,' he said bitterly. When he sent it to his publisher, he enclosed a note: 'Here I have written a bridal song for Countess Schumman – but I do this sort of thing with concealed wrath – with rage.'

At fifty, he fell for the pretty young singer Hermine Spies who, like his other loves before her, he called 'my songstress'. He also called her 'Hermine without an o', which may explain why the affair did not last long.

In later life, Brahms dismissed this affair, saying that 'after middle age' the only woman he really wanted to marry was Alice Barbi, the celebrated Italian singer who he met in 1892. He proposed, but she refused him on the grounds that, at fifty-nine, he was too old. She wanted children.

Whether Brahms was ever sincere in his desire to have a wife and children is not clear. He claimed sometimes that he was 'missing out on the best things in life'. But when a middle-aged friend was fortunate enough to marry a pretty young thing, he declared his disbelief that the man should willingly give up his freedom. Brahms himself celebrated his silver jubilee of bachelorhood in a bridal suite, alone.

Perhaps he was afraid of rejection, and suffered it even in the lowest quarters. Once when Brahms visited a friend in Rome, his host called his unmarried cook from the kitchen and told her that he had found her a husband, indicating the great composer.

'Who is he?' she asked.

'This famous German composer here,' said the host. 'He ought to satisfy you. You are always singing like a lark.' The cook looked Brahms up and down.

'I am a Roman,' she said with the utmost hauteur, 'born on the Ponte Rotto, near the Temple of Vesta. I shall never marry a barbarian.'

Brahms was certainly highly sexed. His music bears testimony to that. He never wore his glasses in the streets, explaining that way he saw more beautiful women than those whose keener sight destroyed the illusion.

It is notable that all his serious lovers were singers. Perhaps these singing girls reminded him of the Singing Girls of Hamburg he had known in his youth. The singing girls of the streets always looked after him much better though. The only respectable women he was sexually intimate with who was not primarily a singer was Clara Schumann. He visited her one last time in 1895 at Interlaken, where she had rented a large chalet. The following year she died, and Brahms followed her to the grave the year after that.

8

NOCTURNAL
EMISSIONS

Chopin's name, like Byron's, conjures up an image of a quintessential Romantic artist. He wrote passionate music and died tragically young. But a glimpse at any portrait will show you that he was not a handsome man. Even his famous lover, the French novelist and poet George Sand, complained that he was 'emotionally versatile' – that is, flighty – when it came to matters of the heart. On stage, though, he was another being altogether. The emotional intensity of his performances would make grown women swoon. He said he would always rather play to a small audience of women than to a packed house of men.

Then there were his famous nocturnes. These were instrumental compositions deliberately designed to put young women in the mood for love as night drew on. It was not that men could not appreciate him too. Berlioz told the critic Legouvé to go and see Chopin play 'for he is something which you have never seen and someone you will never forget'.

Liszt said that his whole appearance made the beholder think of 'the convolvuli which, on the slenderest of stems, balanced divinely coloured chalices of such vaporous tissue that the slightest touch destroys them'. He also had long hair – luxuriant, silky, chestnut tresses that flew about when he played. He was a snappy dresser too, always 'very correct in the matter of studs, walking sticks and cravats'. His delicate physique, his refined, aristocratic manners and his poetic temperament made him the perfect ladies' man.

From early childhood in Poland, Frycek Chopin felt at home in women's company. As a child prodigy, he mixed in genteel society where there was no segregation of the sexes. As a reward for his playing, the Grand Duke Constantine would let him romp in the Belvedere gardens with little Alexandrine, the daughter of his son's French tutor.

Although he was sent to a boys' school in Warsaw, he was soon disappearing behind the bushes with other boys' sisters and he would be seen taking girls for a walk in the park and picking them flowers.

'In 1824', when he was fourteen,'I was in love with a young girl from the convent school,' Chopin recalled. 'Her father was annoyed with me for trying to arrange a secret rendezvous with his daughter. Our go-between was a Jewish boy called Leibush, son of a shopkeeper who supplied us with pens and writing paper. Leibush had a good ear. He would not accept payment for his services. He only wanted to have lessons with me and would listen under my window for hours when I was playing. This messenger of love was a very important person in my life at the time.'

He dedicated his '*Rondo à la Mazur*', published in Warsaw in 1828, to the Countess Alexandrine de Moriolles, who had retained an affection for the boy who had been her childhood playmate in the Belvedere gardens. Then there was Emily Esner, the gifted daughter of a professor, who would listen to his latest compositions and copy them for him. He dedicated two early compositions to her.

After Chopin had taken a brief holiday at the country house of Countess Pruszak, the children's governess was found to be pregnant. The Countess dashed back to Warsaw, burst into the Chopin family's drawing room and accused the eighteen-year-old of being the poor girl's seducer. Far from being offended by the accusation, the young Chopin took it as a compliment. Amorous adventures were something his contemporaries bragged about. But eventually, the real culprit owned up. The governess was dismissed and Chopin, now fully exonerated, was employed to give the children lessons until a new governess was found.

It is not surprising, for a boy of Chopin's delicate nature that his first true love should be another boy. Chopin became deeply attached to his classmate Titus Woyciechowski. Titus was the strong silent type who lived on a farm, but he liked Chopin's music. Chopin wrote him passionate letters, begging him to write back. He longs to kiss his 'faithful friend' but notes: 'You do not like to be kissed.'

On 12 September 1829, Chopin ended his detailed account of his first triumphant concerts in Vienna with 'I kiss you heartily, right on the lips if I may.'

One morning he wrote: 'Don't kiss me now for I have not washed yet.' Then adds poignantly: 'How silly of me! You wouldn't kiss me even if I were to bathe in all the perfumes of Byzantium, unless I forced you by some supernatural power. I believe in such powers. Tonight you shall dream you are kissing me.'

There are kisses all over his letters, both to women and to men, it is true. But Titus was something special. Chopin dedicated his *Variations* to him.

His time in Vienna had set him on another path though. It was said that, in those days, he could fall in and out of love in a single evening. He met the gifted Leopoldine Blahetka, the seventeen-year-old daughter of a Viennese journalist. She was a beauty and encouraged him by describing him as 'an artist of the first rank, and worthy to be placed beside Moscheles, Herz and Kalkbrenner'. Chopin was flattered.

When a tearful Chopin left Vienna, Leopoldine presented him with signed copies of her own piano compositions. But the memory of her soon faded when he got back to Warsaw. Indeed, shortly before he had left for Vienna he had seen a women he told Titus Woyciechowski was his 'ideal'. Her name was Constantia Gladkowska. She was a student at the Warsaw Conservatoire, on the brink of a brilliant career. Liszt described her as 'sweet and beautiful'. Chopin himself talked of an occasion when he had seen her at a concert where she 'wore a white dress and roses in her hair, and was entrancingly pretty'. He was aware of her other talents too.

'Her low B,' he wrote, 'came out so magnificently that Zielinski declared it alone was worth a thousand ducats.' He was completely smitten. He thought of her constantly while he was away in Vienna. When he returned to Warsaw he must have seen her often at the Conservatoire, but he could not pluck up the courage to speak to her.

'God forbid that she should suffer in any way on my account,' he wrote. 'Let her mind be at rest and tell her that so long as my heart beats I shall not cease to adore her. Tell her that, even after death, my ashes shall be strewn beneath her feet.' He neglects to say what he might do to make her suffer. Maybe it was a good thing that he could not summon up the courage to talk to her, because he poured all the fervour of his undeclared love into composition. He wrote to Titus about his plight.

'I love, but I must keep my unhappy passion locked in my own breast for some years longer,' the tormented romantic confided. But his tortured passion did not blind him to other delights. He wrote late one night to Titus that he had just been to party where 'among the other guests was a very beautiful girl who vividly reminded me of my ideal', and that thoughts of her were keeping him awake.

He went out to dinner with another woman simply because she had 'the inexpressibly dear name' Constantia. The mere glimpse of that name embroidered on her handkerchief set his heart aflutter.

At the same time as unburdening himself to his friend, Chopin was making new overtures to Titus. 'I love you to distraction,' he wrote, and he tied a pretty ribbon around a bundle of Titus's earlier letters and carried them about with him, so he could read them whenever he felt dejected.

The wilting Chopin received an invitation from Prince Radziwill to spend a few days in his country house. There the

Prince's two young daughters would scarcely leave him alone. They liked to dance the mazurka. Chopin posed for Princess Eliza who sketched him, and he helped Princess Wanda practise his *Alla Polacca*. She was a keen student and he enjoyed the sensation of guiding her hands over the keyboard. He liked both sisters equally and imagined himself in the Garden of Eden with two beautiful Eves, not an uncommon male fantasy.

Back in Warsaw once more, Chopin performed at the National Theatre, to rapturous applause. Alexandrine de Moriolles sent him a crown of laurels and an anonymous groupie sent him a sonnet. Eventually, the inevitable happened. He was formally introduced to Constantia Gladkowska. The problem was that she had a constant companion, Panna Wolkowa, and went nowhere without her. Chopin could not bring himself to speak of love in front of a third party, but Constantia must have guessed at his feelings.

Constantia Gladkowska and Pannu Wolkowa were selected to sing at the Tsar's state visit in 1830. Chopin rehearsed them relentlessly. 'Gladkowska leaves nothing to be desired,' he told Titus. But he was annoyed that the audience cheered Wolkowa more loudly. Then the young romantic got a little confused. When the twenty-four-year-old singer Henrietta Sontag – the idol of Vienna, Prague, Paris and London – turned up in Warsaw, Chopin fell completely under her spell. Her slender figure, her delicate features, her large eyes and auburn hair were, he said, simply incomparable. He became a regular visitor to her apartments and could not take his eyes off her.

One day he turned up to find Constantia and Panna in Henrietta's rooms. This threw the young composer into terrible confusion. He grew sickly. The concealment of his love had, it was said, like a worm in the bud, fed on his pale cheeks.

He was well overdue for another trip to Vienna, but he kept putting it off. His family suspected that he was having an illicit love affair and threw an eligible but totally unattractive woman in his path. He did not take the bait. 'You are the only one I love,' he wrote to Titus, as if he needed reminding.

Chopin spent a week with Titus on his farm, indulging in

manly pursuits – sports, practising the crossbow, playing the piano together. But back in Warsaw, Chopin continued to procrastinate about his return to Vienna. He felt he had good reasons to stay in Poland. 'I know you love me,' he wrote to Titus. 'But I'm afraid of you as if you were some sort of tyrant. I don't know why I'm afraid of you, God knows you are the only one who has power over me, you and ... well, no one else.'

He arranged another concert for Constantia and Panna. This time he insisted on putting Constantia on second, guaranteeing her the greater applause. He only left Warsaw after Titus promised to meet him in Dresden or Vienna that autumn. A few days before he left, Constantia wrote in his album a patriotic poem.

> The time for change has come
> And you must follow your destiny
> But wherever in the world you are
> In Poland you will be loved.
>
> To keep your laurels green
> You renounce both family and friends
> Though strangers may honour you more
> None could love you better than those here.

She also gave him a ring. But soon after he left, Constantia began courting a Warsaw merchant and she married him fifteen months later. When Chopin's sister wrote to tell him about the wedding she noted disparagingly that Constantia had married 'for the sake of a palace'. She gave up her musical career, settled down in the country and had five children. At the age of thirty-five she went blind. Otherwise she was in good health and survived her bashful young lover by forty years.

After he left Warsaw Chopin never wrote or communicated with Constantia again. But eight years after their parting, he read again the poem she had written in his album. And after the line: 'None could love you better than those here', he wrote plaintively: 'You could'. Not that Chopin had been pining for her all that time. In Dresden, he met Countess Delphina Potocka.

NOCTURNAL EMISSIONS

Born Delphina Komar in 1807, she had married at eighteen Count Mieczyslas Potocki. Delphina's father, Count Komar, was rich, but the Potockis were one of the oldest families in Poland. Count Potocki was considered quite a catch. He was also seven years her senior and an inveterate rake. She bore him five children in six years, but they all died. The rumour was that the Count was spent. He was a man of many vices, some of which were said to be 'unspeakable'. The marriage had been unhappy from the start. Delphina packed her bags and moved to Dresden.

The Count eventually gave Delphina a generous allowance of 100,000 francs a year and she set up home in Paris. That same year, another estranged wife, Baroness Dudevant, arrived in Paris. She was soon to become known as George Sand.

High spirited and avid for pleasure, Delphina threw herself into a merry-go-round of amorous adventures. She changed lovers, it was said, as often as she changed dresses. They always came from the *crème de la crème* of Parisian society. She bedded the middle-aged Count Flahut, the young Duke of Monfort, the Duke of Orléans, who was Dauphin of France, and the painters Delacroix and Delaroche.

Delacroix said that he had never encountered anything more perfect. After bedding her, Delaroche painted her, inappropriately, as the Virgin Mary. And the novelist Balzac raved over her grace and beauty. At twenty-five, she was statuesque, with dazzling white shoulders and generous breasts. Her eyes were dark blue and she wore her golden hair in cascading ringlets or piled up in a bun. She was well read, with an ear for poetry. She played the piano, composed and delighted private audiences with her singing. Her salon was the place to be seen if you were rich or talented.

When it came to making love, she was inexhaustible. New lovers overlapped with old. They vied with each other for her favours and pandered to her every whim. When a friend boasted of her conquests, Delphina dismissed her as a mere *ingénue*. 'She is the greatest sinner of them all' was the poet Adam Michkiewicz's testimonial.

When Chopin arrived in Paris, he dined with Countess

Komar, Delphina's mother. Shortly after, Delphina – who was accomplished on the keyboard – invited him over to give her piano lessons. Their affair quickly became the talk of the Polish community. But when news got back to his family, it was presented as if he were wooing an eligible young maiden and they were delighted. But Delphina was not about to give up her way of life for one young Pole and she continued taking other lovers. Although he was tormented by jealousy, everyone agreed that the sophisticated Delphina was just the person to give young Frycek a wonderful *éducation sentimentale*. Soon he became an uninhibited lover.

Chopin's pet name for Delphina was the anagram Phindela and he addressed her in his letters as 'my one and only beloved'. Throughout their affair, they had a running joke. Robert Schumann had written an article analysing Chopin's *La ci darem variations*. He compared a passage in the third variation to the scene in Mozart's *Don Giovanni* where Giovanni pressed Zelina and 'kisses her on the *des-dur*'. *Des-dur* is D flat major in German, but a Polish friend remarked: 'On which part of her anatomy is the *des-dur*?' In Polish, *des-dur* is *des durka* and there was a well-known artists' café in Warsaw whose name sounds much the same. It was called the Dziurka, which means the Little Hole. Chopin would write to Delphina, telling her how he longed to 'kiss your *des durka* very, very hard.'

Clearly the piano lessons were coming on a treat as he used to write to her about the use of the pedal, of which he was the acknowledged master. 'Treat it carefully, for it is not easy to win its intimacy and love,' he said. 'Like a society lady anxious about her reputation, it won't yield just like that. But when it does yield it can perform miracles, like an experienced mistress.' He added a little PS to one letter: 'I would like to plonk something down your little hole in D flat major again. Do not refuse me. F.C.'

Chopin was hurt when she went off with other lovers, but he was also grateful. It gave him time to work. 'Inspiration and ideas only come to me when I have not had a woman for a long time,' he wrote. 'When I have emptied my fluid into a woman so much I am pumped dry, inspiration deserts me and no new musical ideas come into my head. Think how strange and beautiful it is, that the force used to fertilize a woman, creating new life in her, is the same force that creates a work of art. It is the same life-giving fluid, yet man wastes it on one single moment of pleasure.

'The same is true of science. Those who make great discoveries must stay away from women. The formula is simple enough. A man must renounce women, then the energy accumulating in his system will go – not from his cock and balls into a woman – but into his brain in the form of inspiration where it might give birth to a work of art. Think of it, the sexual desire that drives men into women's arms can be transformed into inspiration. But only for those who have talent. A fool who lives without women will go mad with frustration. For the genius, unrequited love and unfulfilled passion, sharpened by the unattainable image of their beloved, is an endless source of inspiration.

'Oh my sweetest Phindela, think of how much of that precious fluid I have wasted on you, ramming away at you to no good purpose. I have not given you a baby and think how many musical ideas have been squandered inside you. Ballads, polonaises, perhaps even an entire concerto have been lost forever up your little D flat major. I cannot tell you how many. I have been so deeply immersed in you I have hardly created anything. Everything creative went straight from my cock into your *des durka*. Works that could have seen the light of day are forever drowned in your D flat major. You are now carrying so much of my music in your womb that you are pregnant with my compositions ... The saints were right when they said women were the gates of hell. No, no, I take that back. You are the gates of heaven. For you, I will give up fame, work, everything.'

Chopin had to resort to poetry to express himself further:

Fucking you is my favourite occupation
Bed beats inspiration
I long for your lovely tits
So says your faithful Fritz"

Chopin was torn between music and sex, though they were clearly intertwined. 'I know you like my cock and balls. And after this dissertation, you ought to respect them more because they are not only the source of pleasure. They are also source of my artistic achievement. Supreme pleasure, the creation of life, of art, of science – everything stems from them, the all powerful, so long as they may live.'

Chopin was certainly in love and, no matter how much he wanted to conserve is precious fluid, he longed to see her.

'Oh Phindela, my own little Phindela,' he writes. 'How I long to be with you. I am trembling and shivering as if ants were crawling all over me, from my brain down to my cock. When the coach brings you back to me, you won't be able to get me out of your *des durka* for a whole week. Let inspiration go to hell. Let my works vanish up that black hole forever.'

When Chopin tires of his *des durka* and thinks up a new musical term instead.

'I have invented a new musical term instead of *des durka*. From now on we will call it a 'rest'. Let me explain. In music a 'rest' is a pause, a hole in the melody – an apt way to describe your D flat major. My pupils arrive soon, so I must stop. I kiss you all over your dear little body and inside.' The letter is signed: 'Your faithful Frycek, your gifted pupil who has mastered the art of love.'

Chopin got upset when he heard gossip that Delphina could not have children because she had had too many lovers. 'Grass won't grow on a well trodden path,' it was said. 'My own beloved,' he wrote, 'when you come back please stop refusing to become pregnant, let me give you a baby and silence the wagging tongues.'

The affair did nothing to diminish Chopin's reputation as a fop and a ladies' man. His compatriot Anthony Orlowski wrote home how everyone in Paris was wearing gloves *à la Chopin* and that he was 'turning the head of every woman he meets and making every husband jealous'.

He was particularly taken with one of his pupils, Josephine or 'Jusa', the daughter of Count Thun. Chopin could never resist a pretty musician and he dedicated a waltz to her. Nevertheless, he was still fiercely jealous of Delphina. When he heard that she was giving music lessons to a young man, he wrote fuming: 'For him it is only an excuse to be with you. He has no talent for music and is not worth bothering about. Don't take me for a fool, I can see clearly what's going on. The lessons are only an excuse for an amorous adventure. If you want to break up with me, say so. Don't talk to me about so-called music lessons.'

Her music student was a trifling amour. But Chopin really did have a serious rival, an unexpected one, her husband. Beneath her promiscuous veneer, Delphina was deeply conservative. She believed in marriage. She was no longer young, nearly thirty. And when her husband asked her to come back to him, she sold her house in Paris and went.

By this time Chopin was twenty-six. He had sown more than his share of wild oats and his thoughts turned to marriage. Searching for a wife, he considered all the Polish girls he knew and decided that the best of the bunch was Marie Wodzinska. He had known her as a baby, but recently he had seen her again while holidaying in Dresden. She was now sixteen, tall, slender and graceful, with 'fiery black eyes, long, luxuriant, silky, ebony-black hair, and a talent for music and painting'.

Chopin set off back to Dresden immediately. When he got there, he found that the family had left. Count Wodzinski had returned to Poland, but the ladies had gone to Marienbad to take the waters. Chopin set off in hot pursuit. The Wodzinska ladies were staying at the White Swan in Marienbad. Chopin registered there as a landowner from Paris, so not to be looked down on by the hotel's titled clientele.

The Wodzinskas were surprised to see him – and shocked to see the state he was in. Exhausted from the journey, he was coughing badly and too weak to move. He had tuberculosis. The doctor ordered complete rest and Marie nursed him day and night, intercepting all visitors and refusing to allow him to play even a single mazurka.

After four weeks of pampering, Chopin was strong enough

to return to Dresden with the Wodzinskas. There he and Marie became secretly engaged, but no announcement could be made until they had the count's approval and he was still away.

Count Wodzinski, although he liked Chopin well enough, decided that the social gulf between them was unbridgeable. The Wodzinskis were gentry. They had 50,000 acres of land, a country seat near Torun and an elevated position in society. Chopin was famous. But that did not make up for his humble background. His father was a retired schoolmaster and the Chopins lived in a rented flat in Cracow.

Chopin was not so much heartbroken as humiliated. He had only known Marie for a few weeks and he only wanted to marry her because he needed to settle down. Since he had been a child he had been fêted and pampered by the upper classes, but now, suddenly, he found he did not belong. He put all Marie's letters and notes in a single envelope, tied a ribbon around it and scribbled on the package *Moja bieda* – My misfortune – and that was the end of that.

Two years later, Marie married someone of her own class, Count Joseph Skarbek. The marriage was a disaster and had to be annulled. Some years later she married a second time, to a Pole named Orpis Zewski, and lived happily until 1896.

In October 1836, Chopin paid a visit to Liszt, who had just moved to Paris with his mistress the Countess Marie d'Agoult. They had a friend staying with them. Chopin wrote home: 'I have just made the acquaintance of a great celebrity, Mme Dudevant, known as George Sand. I did not like her face, there is something disagreeable about it. There is something about her that puts me off.' Perhaps it was the trousers she wore, or the cigars she smoked. She addressed everyone in the familiar *tu*. Chopin had never seen such unladylike behaviour.

'What a repulsive bitch that Sand is,' he said to the pianist Ferdinand Hiller. 'Is she really a woman? I am inclined to doubt it.'

Delphina was feminine enough to pay lip-service to convention and had returned to her husband when called. Marie d'Agoult had also abandoned her husband and children, but her fidelity to Liszt had redeemed her in many people's eyes. But George Sand heaped outrage upon outrage. Her name alone was an incitement. The publication of her books never ceased to provoke a furore. Her stormy affairs with the writers Prosper Mérimée and the young Alfred de Musset were the talk of the salons. She had numerous other affairs, and had even tried to seduce Liszt while making amorous advances to his mistress. But for Chopin, there was no escape.

In his delicate frame, Sand believed she had found something approaching perfection in a man. She homed in on him. A few days after they had first met, Chopin answered the door to find Liszt with Marie d'Agoult on one arm and George Sand on the other. She made it clear immediately that there was no place to run and no place to hide.

George Sand's real name was Amandine Aurore Lucie Dupin, Baroness Dudevant. Up to this point her love life had been a hit-and-miss affair. At eighteen she had escaped her mother's caprices by marrying the eligible Casimir Dudevant. Within a year she gave birth to a baby boy. But life at their country seat at Nohant bored her. She began a number of platonic relationships with young free-thinkers, and soon it was not just the thinking that was free, but the loving too. Her second child was fathered by a thrusting intellectual.

She sought creative outlets in playing the piano, painting and writing. But her free-thinker was a free-wheeler as well, so she took up with Jules Sandeau, a young law student, and ran off to Paris with him. She became friends with Henri Latouche, the director of *Le Figaro*, and began writing articles, in collaboration with her lover, under the name Jules Sand. Within eighteen months she had written and published *Indiana,* a novel about a woman who abandons her marriage to find love. Realizing the controversy this book would stir, she decided to publish it under a man's name, George Sand. And to further prime her notoriety, she took to wearing men's clothes and swearing and smoking in public. The American novelist Henry James said: 'She may be a man, but she's no gentleman.'

As she gained literary fame, she jettisoned her lover and

began a series of well publicized affairs. When Liszt refused her, she fell for the brilliant republican lawyer Michel de Bourges who conquered her intellectually, then abandoned her. She was sharing her bed with the writer Charles Didier when she first spotted Chopin and laid siege to him. Sand managed to wangle an invitation to every dinner party and *soirée* he attended. She even wormed her way into the affections of the homosexual Marquis de Custine, who had lavished so much attention on Chopin that it had caused gossip.

Sand's divorce case, with its juicy allegations of lesbianism and assault as well as old-fashioned adultery, ended in victory. She won control of the family home at Nohant. She had to return there to look after the children but kept writing to Chopin, inviting him to stay. He refused. When Liszt agreed to visit her, he was pestered to bring Chopin with him. 'Tell him I adore him,' wrote Sand. 'Tell him I worship him.'

True to the romantic ideal, Chopin had TB and was coughing badly. A rest cure might have seemed to be a good idea. The Marquis de Custine, between protestations of love, offered to look after him. 'You must allow yourself to be taken in hand like a child,' the Marquis said. A week in the country with George Sand looked inviting compared to that. Chopin seriously considered it, but instead headed off to London, which was hardly the place to go if you've got tuberculosis. 'Big urinals but nowhere to pee' was his evaluation.

Back in Paris, Sand continued to pester him to visit her at Nohant, and so this time Chopin did go to stay with the Marquis de Custine.

After a triumphant tour of France, Chopin returned to Paris to find George Sand there. She turned up at one of his concerts with an actress friend, and rumoured lover, Marie Dorval. After the concert, Sand sent him a note saying: *'On vous adore'*, Marie Dorval added: *'Et moi aussi, et moi aussi, et moi aussi'*. Chopin had always been a sucker for flattery. After sixteen months of pursuit, he finally consented to a tryst with Sand, but then failed to pounce on so willing a prey. Sand was perplexed and frustrated. Men did not usually hold back when she was so obviously amenable. Worse, the state of inactivity continued.

'Until recently I thought it was beautiful that he should abstain, either out of respect for me, or timidity, or even fidelity to someone else,' she wrote to Count Grzymala, a Polish *émigré* who had been taking a paternal interest in his young compatriot. 'I thought it was a sacrifice that indicated strength of character or chastity. It charmed me and endeared him to me all the more. But the other day, as we were leaving your house, he said something about resisting temptation ... I do not remember his exact words but I think he said something about "certain acts" that might spoil beautiful memories for him. Surely this is nonsense. He can't believe this, can he? Who is this woman who has given him such ideas about physical love? Has he had a mistress who is unworthy of him? Poor angel. Women who degrade the most heavenly moments of ecstasy, the most exalted act in creation, should be hanged.' The woman, of course, was Delphine.

Beauty was always important to Chopin, but once he dropped his aesthetic standards, he was overwhelmed by her force of will. He wrote in his diary: 'I have seen her three times now. I played for her and she looked deep into my eyes. Our hearts beat as one. Her extraordinary, dark eyes held mine. She bent down to the piano keyboard. Those eyes set me on fire and overwhelmed me. My heart was taken. Since then I have seen her two more times. She loves me. Aurore – what a bewitching name.' It is not known whether he called her Aurore in company. Few people dared to. But out of deference to his sensibilities she stopped smoking in public, put away her drag and resumed wearing women's clothes. She doted on him, calling him *mon petit* and 'Chip-chip'.

'I remain as enchanted by him as I was at our first meeting,' she wrote to her former lover Delacroix. 'Not the tiniest cloud darkens our skies, not a drop of vermouth adds bitterness to our wine. I am beginning to think that angels come down from heaven disguised as men ... If God chose to take me this minute, I could not complain as I have had three months of perfect bliss.'

However, George Sand was a woman of the world. She

knew that even the leading romantic of the day was prey to the failings of mortal men. 'You think such happiness cannot last?' she wrote. 'If I consult my memory and my reason, I know it can't. But if I ask my heart and my emotions, they tell me this happiness can never end.' But end it did, though not until Delacroix had painted the couple together at their happiest, with Chopin playing the piano and Sand looking admiringly at him.

The beginning of the end, as is so often the case, was a vacation which turned out to be the holiday from hell. In 1838 they had to get away from Paris. Sand's fifteen-year-old son Maurice was ill. Chopin was coughing up a storm and her recently discarded lover, Maurice's tutor Lucien Mallefille, was out for blood. On one occasion he had burst into the house and tried to kill them both, and on another he had taken a pot shot at her in the street.

Sand took Chopin, Maurice and her daughter Solange on a winter break to Majorca. It was a disaster from the very beginning. The weather was cold and wet. The locals shunned them because of Chopin's TB. They ran out of money. The only place they could afford to stay was in a Carthusian monastery at the top of a mountain, which extended hospitality to political refugees. It was accessible only by donkey. When they reached it, they had to fork out 1,000 francs for furniture which would have cost 100 francs in France. The food was awful and the locals jacked up the prices for the tourists.

There they sat in a dank cell, on the top of a mountain watching the rain come down. George Sand recorded every miserable detail in the delightful little tome *Un Hiver à Majorque*. Read it and you will never want to leave home again. To cap it all, Sand's daughter Solange developed an adolescent crush on Chopin, and the old consumptive reciprocated. The forty-two-year-old Sand struggled desperately to compete with her daughter's eighteen-year-old freshness.

When they got back to Paris Sand got out the big guns. In direct contradiction to her own proto-feminist ideas, she set about marrying her daughter off. Chopin grew fiercely jealous. Although Sand and Chopin continued living together, she began taking other lovers, notably the prominent journalist Victor Borié. To add insult to injury, she chronicled her conquests, thinly disguised, in her fiction.

Chopin took up with Pauline Viardot, a woman of distinguished sexual achievement. She was married to the critic Louis Viardot, who was considerably older than her, and she captivated every man she met. For forty years she was the mistress of the Russian novelist Turgenev. She was so devoted to him that she even took in the illegitimate daughter he had sired by a serving girl.

When Chopin and Sand finally parted, Delacroix's portrait of the happy couple was cut in two. Chopin's half hangs in the Louvre. Sand's has been relegated to a museum in Copenhagen. Sand tried to maintain some form of friendship, but Chopin was bitter and called her Lucrezia, after the Borgia poisoner. 'In his love affairs there was no friendship,' said Pauline Viardot. 'That passion cannot diminish and is the most beautiful of all.'

Having nursed him through his consumption, Sand naturally remained concerned about his health. 'Have you seen Chopin?' Sand asked Viardot. 'Is he well? I am unable to match his hatred and fury. I think of him as an ill child, bitter and lost.' Then Delphina Potocka, her marriage in ruins once more, came back in Paris. Her salon was open for business again and she began lining up new lovers. Chopin joined the queue.

Even though he lived only a few steps away from her in Paris, he wrote to her, explaining about his affair with George Sand. He addressed Delphina as 'my own sweet life' and reminded her of her promise that 'if my explanation is satisfactory you will forgive me and grant me your supreme favour'. What could he mean?

People had been lying about his relationship with Madame Sand, he said. His sexual liaison with her lasted less than a year, and now it was all over. 'I swear on my love for you and for my mother that this is the truth.' Chopin laid it on with a trowel.

'Apparently I could not satisfy her,' he wrote. 'She wanted it five times a night. My illness was her excuse to finish with me. She claimed that my ill health meant I could not make love, so she went off and found herself another lover.' From then on, he said, she only gave him maternal love. She nursed him devotedly.

'You cannot imagine how kind she has been. But to say that I have been her lover all these years is a lie. Everyone who goes to Nohant knows about her lovers there and everyone in Paris knows who her favourites are here. At Nohant she writes all night and locks herself in the bedroom with a lover all day. Even the strongest men grow weak she is so demanding. That is why she changes lovers so often. She is insatiable. It's really an illness you know.

'After our break-up I still loved her. I wanted her. I was still attracted to her. But when I saw her with other men, it turned me off. Today I feel only friendship towards her. I love her like a mother.'

There had been others, he went on to explain. 'After I finished with Madame Sand, I had some brief affairs. They were just physical, barely worth mentioning. People say I am quick to fall in love. Don't believe them. You have known me for a long time and I have not changed. I always look admiringly at pretty women. And if any of them arouses me, I pull them into bed. But I do not give my heart easily. Only you and Madame Sand have taken my heart. And it belongs more to you than to her. I loved you with more passion because you know me and understand me like nobody else can. You are a Pole like me, while she is a foreigner. I could not bare my soul to her because she could not possibly understand.' And the others?

'The other women in my life were youthful dreams long since buried, or winds of passion which swept over me for a short time. I gave them my bed, my body and a little of my life-giving fluid. They never possessed my heart.'

But poor old Chopin was powerless in the face of sexual passion. 'When a violent love gets hold of me temptation and desire tear at me like wild dogs,' he explained. 'The whole world ceases to exist, as it was with you. I am ready to give up everything for a woman, even sacrifice my life and my creative power.'

Of course, it was not like that with those other women. He never lost his head and conserved his strength and his 'life-giving fluid'. 'Except for Madame Sand, there has been no other love and passion in my life.' And he could prove it.

'My work shows it best. When you and I were together I could only revise old works or prepare ones I had already written for the printers. I could only write new ones when you were away from me for a long time. Otherwise I was sucked dry by lovemaking. But for the last few years I have created many masterpieces, so you see my energy has not been taken up making love.'

Chopin thought that he had explained everything so clearly that a child could understand. And now they were even. While they had been parted, he had had one big affair and some small affairs that hardly counted. She too had one big affair, and at the time she was having a well publicized affair with the poet and playwright Sigismund Krasinski – and 'no doubt several smaller ones'.

'I have told you everything. I repented of my trespasses and await to be restored to your favour.' Then he reels out the litany that we have all used when we want to get back into the bed of a lover who has found us out.

'I never loved anyone as much as you.

You always remained in the tenderest spot in my heart.

I always wanted you. Even when I was in Madame Sand's arms, I would rather have been in yours.

Forget the evil lies and gossip you have heard about me. I have changed.

In future I will be better.

I will never again torment you with my jealousy.

I have never loved anyone as deeply as you.

You will be my first mistress and my last.

There will never be another after you.'

By this time Chopin is sure that he is winning. 'I hope I have convinced you,' he writes, 'and you will let me come to you tonight.' But Chopin is the consummate artist. He still has one more card up his sleeve.

'If this clumsy letter, sincere as it is, fails to move you, let me soften your heart with music. Tonight, when I ask your forgiveness, I will lay a new work at your feet. Remember how you used to say that I was a virtuoso in the art of lovemaking, I knew how to satisfy. Well, my romance with Madame Sand has taught me more. Now you will be the pupil and I will teach you love games that are totally new and exciting.'

If that was not enough of an incentive, he resorts to emotional blackmail. 'Don't refuse me. I want you so much my desire will drive me insane. Then you will have that on your conscience.'

Next he adds just a hint of self-pity. 'My poor heart has known more sorrow than happiness. The tears I have held back for so long, I should like to shed them on your bosom.'

Then he dangles the music bonus again. 'I feel like playing and crying. I shall play for you as I have never played for anyone in my life.'

More tears. 'Tears fill my eyes when I think you might say no.' Then he pulls all the stops out for the big finish. 'You, the first and last love of my life, forgive me. My tears stain the paper as I write this. I beg of you! Answer me. I await your call like a dying man awaits the sacrament. With all my heart until death ...' and he signs it '... your Fritz.'

The letter is a romantic *tour de force*. How could she refuse him? Was her heart made of steel? The letter came at just the right time too. Her liaison with Krasinski was coming to an end. He was five years her junior and the affair had been a passionate one. Their love letters filled volumes. But he was about to be married off to the young and attractive Countess Eliza Branica, so Delphina needed another string to her bow.

Good to her word, Delphina granted Chopin her 'supreme favour' again. Chopin showed his gratitude by dedicating his *Waltz in D flat major* – the Minute Waltz – to her. There was that 'little D flat major' again. But she was not to be his alone, naturally. She continued to see Krasinski even after he was married. Chopin said nothing, but was heard sobbing behind the closed doors of his study.

NOCTURNAL EMISSIONS

In 1844, Chopin found a new distraction. A young Scottish woman named Jane Stirling came to him as a pupil and developed a crush on him. He dedicated his *Two Nocturnes* to her. She began doing household chores for him. Soon this domestic arrangement flowered into love, and Jane aimed to marry Chopin. The first part of his plan was to lure him from his home territory. She arranged to take the consumptive Chopin to London. As if that had not damaged his health enough, she took the wheezing composer on to Scotland. It was late autumn and he found himself billeted in cold highland castles. Soon he was coughing up blood.

Chopin hated Britain at the best of times and fled by stagecoach, leaving his beloved behind. By the time he got back to Paris he was so weak he could barely get out of bed. Jenny Lind, the Swedish nightingale, came and sang to him. Delphina Potocka rushed back from Nice to be near him.

'God has spared me so that I might see you again,' he told her. She wanted to sing for him but found her voice was choked with tears. Jane Stirling, presumably out of guilt, sent money. A lot of it. George Sand wrote, but decided against a visit. 'She promised I would die in her arms,' he is supposed to have said. Fortunately, the family provided a stand-in – George Sand's ever-loving daughter Solange.

9

LISZTOMANIA

'That so many women want his love and threw themselves at him so passionately does little credit to our sex,' wrote Adelheid von Schorn, one of Liszt's most dedicated groupies. 'Men, naturally, complained about him terribly. This was envy pure and simple. But Liszt respected honest women. Once, towards the end of his life, he told me in a moment of seriousness: "I never seduced a young girl." '

Adelheid confirmed that this was true. He had never seduced a young girl. He did not have to seduce anyone. Women simply threw themselves at him. 'I saw women importuning him often', she said. 'You would think that the normal roles had been reversed. That Liszt was uniquely attractive to women, I have often witnessed, to my horror. Nor did these cease as he got older. It was painful to see that there were still young women who regarded the old man, much in need of rest as he was, as desirable prey.'

However, despite all this, in Adelheid's eyes, Liszt could do no wrong. 'In spite of everything Liszt only saw the best side of women. He never allowed himself to be misled when they forced themselves on him. His chivalry was one of the traits that drew women to him. It was evidence of his noble nature.'

Liszt had a number of world-class mistresses: Marie Duplessis, the high-class courtesan immortalized by Alexandre Dumas as *La Dame aux Camélias*; the outrageous Lola Montez, who danced naked at the unveiling of the Beethoven Memorial; Princess Cristina Belgiojoso; the poet Bettina von Arnim; Beethoven's lovely Karoline Unger; Princess Caroline Sayn-Wittgenstein; the actress Charlotte Hagn, who Liszt boasted was also the mistress of two kings; the pianist and nymphomaniac Marie Pleyel; Countess Marie d'Agoulet, his long-term and long-suffering *maîtresse en titre*, and many many more.

When the Russian composer Borodin visited him in Weimar, he found Liszt was taking fifteen pupils a day, invariably young ladies. Lessons always ended with a kiss – and not on the forehead. 'Evidently Liszt had a weakness for the ladies,' Borodin said. Evidently.

Born in Hungary in 1811, Liszt was a child prodigy and was thus fawned on by society women from an early age. But he was a deeply religious child and yearned to become a priest.

I dreamed myself incessantly into the world of saints,' he wrote. 'Nothing seemed to me so self-evident as heaven, nothing so true and so rich in blessedness as the goodness and compassion of God. Nothing and nobody has ever been able to shake my faith in immortality and eternal salvation.'

Something shook his ambition to become a priest though – a terrible temptation in the form of the beautiful blue-eyed Caroline Saint-Cricq, the daughter of the Comte de Saint-Cricq, the Minister of Commerce. She was one of his early pupils and pretty enough to tempt a saint.

'Caroline was lithe, slender, angelic and with a complexion like a lily flushed with roses, impressionable to beauty, to the world, to religion and to God,' he told a friend. They were both sixteen and the sweet innocent Liszt found her 'a maiden chaste and pure as the alabaster of holy vessels'. But not for long.

Their lessons became more frequent and prolonged. Liszt was caught creeping out of the house late one night. The Comte got to hear of it and banned him from the building. Heartbroken, Caroline turned to her mother, who was on her deathbed. She begged with her husband to let Liszt back in the house and back into the arms of Caroline. 'If she loves him, let her be happy,' the dying woman said.

LISZTOMANIA

The Comte gave his promise that the two of them could be wed. But when his wife died, he went back on his word. No daughter of his was marrying a penniless musician. Instead, he arranged a good marriage to a nobleman with interests in cattle and land. In grief, Liszt fell dangerously ill, so ill that his obituary mistakenly appeared in the newspapers. On his sick bed, he tried desperately to reconcile his deep religious belief with his now fully awakened sexuality. Why, he asked the local abbé, was the blissful expression of true love condemned as mortal sin? He still harboured a desire to join the priesthood, but was beginning to realize that celibacy was beyond him.

The beautiful Caroline never forgot her young piano teacher. They met again in later life, and when she died, he wrote: 'She was one of the purest revelations on Earth of the blessing of God.' She remained for him the model of his ideal woman.

But there is only one cure for a broken heart, and he set about it with a will. Having reconciled his growing sexual appetite with his religious scruples, he embarked on what he called 'exercises in the lofty French style', meaning the prevailing fashion for clandestine extra-marital affairs. These came easily to him. He was witty, talented, attractive and was constantly surrounded by beautiful women. But his letters dwell particularly on a certain Hortense and a Madame G, and he took a trip to Savoy with Mademoiselle de Barré.

Liszt was only twenty when one lover, Countess Pauline Plater, said of the three great pianists of the day that she would choose Ferdinand Hiller as a friend, Chopin as a husband, but Liszt as a lover. The elderly Comte Laprunarède made the mistake of inviting the hot-blooded Hungarian as a house guest. They were snowed in and Liszt passed the time by making free with the Comte's 'sparkling, witty, young, beautiful' wife, Adèle. But her silken fetters did not hold him for long, and when the snows melted he made off to Paris, though he continued to write to her – something he would later regret.

When he was twenty-one, Liszt's mother and a Madame D tried to arrange a marriage with a Mademoiselle Charlotte Laborie, 'in order to calm my excited nerves'. Liszt resisted, but found himself so much in demand by the daughters of the aristocracy that he grew pale, thin and weary. Countess Dash, who lived in the same building as Liszt, remembers him 'coming down the stairs like a ghost'.

Amateur Swiss composer Caroline Boissier came to Paris to arrange music lessons for her eighteen-year-old daughter Valérie. Only Liszt would do. As soon as they met him, both mother and daughter were captivated. Madame Boissier paid him over the odds and insisted that he cut down on his other teaching commitments. He used his free time to play to a woman in an insane asylum who had become fixated on him. He also played in hospitals and prisons for those condemned to die, and at the mass funerals of victims of the 1832 cholera epidemic.

One of Liszt's select coterie of students was Charlotte Talleyrand. She was being brought up by her elderly aunt, the Marquise Le Vayer, who ran a salon for writers, artists and 'women of the world' – one of whom was the Comtesse Marie d'Agoult.

The Comtesse was born Marie Flavigy in Frankfurt-am-Main, daughter of the Viscount de Flavigny and Marie-Elisabeth Bethmann. At sixteen, she was sent to the Covent of the Sacré Coeur in Paris to finish her education. She came out at eighteen and plunged directly into a torrid affair with the thirty year-old poet Alfred de Vigny. She married the Comte Charles d'Agoult, a lame war veteran, fifteen years her senior. Although they were not in love, they had two children and conducted a largely 'open' marriage. Marie did the rounds of the fashionable salons. She was beautiful and elegant with 'a profusion of blonde hair that fell over her shoulders like a shower of gold'. But beneath her cool beauty, boiled seething emotions. She was described as 'six inches of snow covering twenty feet of lava'.

She became a leading light among the romantics and began to suffer from the fashionable *mal de siècle,* the creeping feeling among the Romantics that they would never achieve their ideals.

The Marquise Le Vayer invited Marie d'Agoult to join the

women's choir she was organizing to perform Weber's Hunting Chorus. The guest of honour was to be Liszt. Marie arrived late; Liszt even later. When he arrived, she remembered the door opening, then 'a wonderful apparition appeared before my eyes'.

'I use the word "apparition",' she wrote in her *Memoirs,* 'because I can find no other word to describe the sensation aroused in me by the most extraordinary person I had ever seen. He was tall and extremely thin. His face was pale and his large sea-green eyes shone like a wave when the sunlight catches it. His expression bore the marks of suffering. He moved indecisively and seemed to glide across the room in a distraught way, like a phantom for whom the hour when it must return to the darkness is about to sound.'

They sat together and he enchanted her. 'Franz spoke with vivacity and with an originality that awoke a whole world slumbering in me.' She was twenty-eight; he was twenty-one. 'The voice of the young enchanter opened out before me a whole infinity, into which my thoughts were plunged and lost. There was nothing of the coquetry or gallantry that usually characterizes the conversation of fashionable people of opposite sexes. Between us there was something at once very young and very serious, at once very profound and very serious.'

The next day, at the Marquise Le Vayer's prompting, Marie wrote to Liszt, inviting him to visit her. Soon they were meeting for secret trysts at his mother's apartment, which he called *Ratzloch* – the 'rat hole'. It was not long before they were making open declarations of love, and he managed to spend an idyllic week with her at her country home at Croissy. After he returned to Paris, he wrote: 'How ardently the flames of your last kiss burn on my lips.'

Their correspondence is passionate. 'Marie! Marie!' he writes. 'Let me repeat that name a thousand times. It lives within me, burns me and threatens to consume me. I am not writing to you; I am with you. Oh for an eternity in your arms. There is heaven and hell, and everything else, inside you, yes, inside you. Let me be wild and crazy. I am beyond help.'

Marie was flattered by his passionate love letters, at first. But somehow some of the love letters he had written to Adèle Laprunarède and others came into her hands, provoking the first of many jealous rows. She forced him to confess in intimate detail all his previous affairs. His previous entanglements meant nothing to him, he assured her. Now he belonged to her alone, 'neither God's or an angel's, but thine,' he said. She accepted this, but never completely forgave him.

Her eldest daughter Louise fell ill and died. Marie was suicidal with grief. Liszt wrote saying that he intended to leave France and wanted to see her one last time. There was a passionate reunion. Nine months later their first child was born.

When Marie discovered she was pregnant, the lovers decided to elope to Switzerland. The arrangements were made in secret. On 26 May 1835, Marie wrote to her husband telling him their marriage was over. It was not his fault, she said. He had been loving and devoted, and although he was justified in blaming her, it was not entirely her fault either.

'When fate has joined two people as different as we are in mind and temperament,' she wrote, 'the constant effort and sacrifices made on both sides only serve to deepen the abyss between. I ask for your forgiveness on Louise's grave. Your name will never leave my lips except when uttered with the respect and esteem which your character deserves. As for me, I ask only for your silence in the face of the world which is going to overwhelm me with insults.'

She knew what she was about to face, but she welcomed her fate. 'I believe in my love and thirst after martyrdom,' she wrote elsewhere. She never lost her respect for her husband. He never blamed her for the breakdown of their marriage, nor did he blame Liszt who he said acted 'like a man of honour' throughout.

By early June, Marie was in Basle with Liszt, 'clinging about his neck, and overwhelming him with caresses and words of burning love'. They could not be married, but Liszt gave her the ring from his finger. Marie wrote: 'Ramparts of granite, inaccessible mountains now arose between us and the world, as if to conceal us in those dark valleys, among the shadowy pines, where the only sound was the murmur of waterfalls, the distant thunder from unseen precipices.'

They had made no plans beyond the elopement, but they soon settled in Geneva. When the baby was born, Liszt freely admitted it was his and registered the birth under his own name. But for the sake of her reputation, a false name was used to conceal Marie's identity.

There were other clouds on the horizon. One of Liszt's pupils, fifteen-year-old Herman Cohen, turned up and stayed a year. Known as 'Puzzi', he had long hair like the masters and was often mistaken for a girl. Then George Sand arrived with her travelling companion Major Adolphe Pictet, who brought with him 'poetic cigars' obtained from an obscure source in the Middle East. They all travelled to Chamonix together. When filling out the hotel register, Liszt wrote: Place of birth – Parnassus; Profession – Musician-philosopher; Coming from – Doubt; Journeying towards – Truth. Not to be outdone, Sand wrote: Occupation – Loafer; Date of passport – Eternity; Issued by – Public opinion.

Their wild antics created a stir at the staid hotel. The major brightened the proceedings by giving them all nicknames derived from Sanskrit literature. Sand, he said, was 'Kamporoupi', a goddess who could change sex at will. Despite Marie's presence, Sand did little to conceal her amorous intentions towards Liszt. But that was not all. It was widely rumoured that she and Marie had a friendship *à la Dorval*. They were, Sand said, 'galley-slaves of love who don't know the value of any chain'.

After the holiday, Marie and Liszt went to stay with Sand at Nohant. Liszt, Sand said, was 'wanting love, young, untamed, overflowing with vitality'. Soon Marie was expecting another child. She went to Italy with Liszt and waited at Como to have the child while he visited Rossini in Milan. Their relationship was reaching the point where they were unhappy together and unhappy apart. He began touring and she suspected he was being unfaithful.

In Frankfurt, he met the young Clara Wieck, who was to become Clara Schumann. There he heard about the terrible flood in his native Hungary. He went to Vienna to earn money for the flood victims, leaving Marie in the care of Count Emilio Malazzoni.

From Vienna, Liszt wrote home enthusiastically about the various Austrian ladies who were giving fund-raising parties for him. One day a letter was delivered with the coat of arms of a well known Viennese lady on the envelope. The arms were repeated on the note paper. It had clearly been written in the lady's boudoir. Marie tore it up. She wrote to Liszt imploring him to come back to her. When he did, she accused him of being unfaithful to his face. He admitted that women had thrown themselves at him in Vienna, but he could hardly brush them off without appearing rude. After all, he was no Don Juan. She called him a 'Don Juan *parvenu*'. This, he said, hurt him deeply. But he must have got over it quickly as Marie was soon pregnant once more.

Once the child was born, Liszt was out on the road again, supporting his growing family by his performances on the concert platform. Marie wrote warning him to take care of her love. 'I fear that trouble will come from the way you can no longer willingly submit to any restraint,' she said. 'I cannot believe that a man ought to surrender himself so completely to his instincts.' He continued to surrender, however, and she asked him to take back the ring he had given her.

'I don't know why,' Liszt wrote, 'but in putting this ring back on my finger I felt as if I were recovering from a long illness. I rediscovered all the confidence of my early youth. It was as if we had just met.' But the sensation did not last long. He did not want it to. 'Sometimes, in the morning, I deliberately forgot to put the ring on,' he wrote. 'I felt a curious pleasure in abandoning this symbol of our union to chance.' In October 1839, they parted in Florence. They were both blinded by tears. Liszt bought her a lovely bouquet of flowers. She knew it was essentially all over between them. 'I am willing to be your mistress, but not one of your mistresses,' she wrote.

LISZTOMANIA

Marie went by ship from Livorno to Genoa, while Liszt travelled to Trieste where he spent a great deal of time in the company of the singer Karoline Unger. He wrote to Marie explaining that he and 'La Unger' were 'just good friends'. From Trieste, he went back to Vienna, ostensibly to earn money for the children. She went back to Paris, where she met the British diplomat Henry Bulwer-Lytton. He proposed to her. She wrote to Liszt, jokingly, asking for *'une petite permission d'in-fidélité'*. She was shocked and hurt by the reply:

Dear Marie,
You do not give me a name, but I suppose it is Bulwer. It does not matter. You know my way of looking at this kind of thing. You know that for me the facts, the deeds, are nothing. The feelings, the ideas, the shades of meaning are everything. I want you to have complete freedom because I am convinced you will use it nobly and tactfully until the day you say to me: 'This man has understood me more fully, more intimately what I am and what I can become, than you have.' Until that day, there will be no infidelity between us ... If you feel the need, or if it gives you pleasure, to talk to me about Bulwer, do so. I shall be flattered. Otherwise, I will never mention it.

Marie was naturally upset that Liszt's letter betrayed no hint of jealousy. She wrote back saying 'your way of looking at things will always be incomprehensible to me'. It was 'as impossible for me to understand as it is for a fish to fly'. She went on to tell him that she had been ill since she had returned to Paris. Her condition made it impossible for her to be having an affair with Bulwer. But the Polish expatriate Bernard Potocki had also asked her to marry him. She also spelt out in detail her relationship with George Sand. They had begun seeing each other again, driving Chopin mad with jealousy. Liszt, though, was unmoved.

Marie's friend Delphine de Girardin introduced her to her husband Émile, the editor of the influential newspaper *La Presse*. Émile immediately fell for Marie and persuaded her to write for him under the pseudonym of Daniel Stern. She also began an affair with him. But Marie and Liszt still exchanged passionate love letters. In one, he admitted to having a trifling affair – 'a passion of forty-eight hours'. She no longer minded. Indeed, she was even pleased that he had told her about it, rather than lying about his infidelity as he had done so often in the past.

When Liszt returned to Paris, the flirty Princess Belgiojoso set her cap at him. She asked her confessor for permission to 'tell a little lie' to prosecute the affair. Marie even took it in good part when the Princess visited their apartments and Liszt went out with her. She simply dismissed her rival as *La Comedienne*.

Marie took one final trip with Liszt to London, where they argued. Afterwards she went back to Paris, then on to Fontainebleau. He went on a concert tour of Germany. In her letters, she thoughtfully kept him up to date with the development of her affair with Émile de Girardin. He feigned interest, claiming he felt little or no sexual jealousy and using it as an excuse for his own sexual licence. Just because he was being physically unfaithful to her did not mean he did not love her.

'In the loveliest days of my youth,' he reminded her cruelly, 'I had similar feelings for Piff [George Sand] and I spoke of an eternal bond between us.' But Liszt could not help himself. His constant touring had sent the whole of Europe into a state known as 'Lisztomania', which was decried at the time as a manifestation of 'women's idolatrous worship of men of genius'.

In Moscow, a friend noted: 'The ladies flocked around him like peasant boys on a country road around a traveller inquisitively examining him, his carriage, his cap.' While in Rome, at a reception at the Villa Medici, a guest said: 'It is impossible to count the ravishing celestial women who came to fall trembling, like poor little larks, at the feet of this terrible enchanter.' Women fainted when he played. Once he left a glove on the piano which was torn to pieces and shared out like a religious relic in the salon of two beautiful princesses. In St Petersburg, princesses and court beauties fought over the rind of an orange he had sucked and thrown away. Female fans stole his cigar butts and tucked them down their cleavages. The phallic symbolism was not lost on them. One fan grew unaccountably smelly in her old age and when she died one of his cigar butts was found hidden inside her corset.

Four noted beauties of the Prussian court dressed themselves as caryatids, the pillars of Greek temples carved as bare-breasted maidens, and carried a bust of Liszt. Again in St Petersburg, an aristocratic lady stopped him on the steps of his hotel and crowned him with flowers. A Polish countess received him in her boudoir ankle-deep in rose petals. One young woman spoke for them all when she cried out: 'If Liszt would only love me for a single hour – that would be joy enough for life.' Indeed, a certain Charlotte von Hagn, who was a beautiful and talented actress, and just twenty-one when she met Liszt in Berlin, seduced him after writing a love poem to him on the corner of her fan. Seven years later, after she married, she wrote to him, saying: 'You have spoiled all others for me. No one can stand the comparison.'

At the same time he had been with Charlotte, Liszt had been seeing the formidable Bettina von Arnim, an intimate of both Beethoven and Goethe. Marie got wind of his scandalous affairs, the drunkenness, the women, the wild parties. Nevertheless, in 1841, she arranged a romantic holiday with him on the tiny island of Nonnenwerth on the Rhine, near Bonn. He did not turn up.

'My brain is spinning again and I cannot stand it,' she wrote to him. 'I cannot live in this state of perpetual agitation ... I shall be more use to you as a friend than as a lover ... I am suffering and if I stay I shall make you suffer, eternally. So goodbye. This is not a break but a postponement. In five or six years, we will look back on this and laugh.'

But even this was not the end. He had his grievances too. In 1842, he wrote to Marie saying: 'You have made me suffer, you have wounded me blow on blow. But I feel that from these wounds there will one day spurt beautiful harmonies.'

Although his rampant infidelity continued – Marie said his god of love had been defeated by the devil of concupiscence – they finally had that holiday in Nonnenwerth in 1843.

Afterwards, she went back to Paris, while he stayed in Germany where he met the adventuress Lola Montez.

Lola was born plain Eliza Gilbert in Limerick. When her mother tried to marry her off to a sixty-year-old judge, the eighteen-year-old Eliza eloped with British Army Captain James who was posted to India. The marriage was a disaster and her husband ran off with the wife of an adjutant. On the ship home she met a Captain Lennox. When they docked in London, they checked into the Imperial Hotel together. This disgraceful behaviour resulted in the spectacular court case *James v. Lennox,* reported in *The Times* of 7 December 1842.

Eliza then decided to become an actress. She enrolled in a drama school run by Fanny Kemble, who persuaded Eliza to try dancing instead. In June 1843, she appeared on the stage of the Haymarket Theatre in London as Doña Lola Montez and dressed as a flamenco dancer. Unfortunately, Doña Lola seemed to know few of the steps of her country. She was a flop. But her bust wasn't. It brought her to the attention of a number of Continental impresarios. Doña Lola toured Europe, taking a series of theatre managers as her lovers to help keep her career afloat.

While exploiting her natural assets, she dreamt of capturing a great man, a poet or a prince. When she met Liszt in Dresden in 1844, she figured he would do. By this time in his career Liszt craved nothing more complicated than a one-night stand. Soon he found that Lola was a pain and had difficulty shaking her off. She pursued him around Germany. She would turn up at his hotel and persuade the manager to let her into his room while he was out performing at a concert. He returned to find her naked in his bed. Once he bribed a hotel porter to lock her in the room for twelve hours while he fled town. But she caught up with him at the dinner following the memorial concert in honour of Beethoven in Bonn. Liszt was the star of the show. Berlioz, Hallé and a handful of other great composers were there, along with King Friedrich Wilhelm IV and his Queen. Lola elbowed her way through the crowd, declaring that she was 'a guest of Liszt's'. Once inside, she leapt on a table, stripped off and gave an uninhibited display of her talent as a dancer. It is not recorded whether it was her nudity or her terpsichory that caused the guests to flee the banqueting hall. Once outside a thunderstorm came rolling in and everyone got drenched in the downpour.

This sort of behaviour bored Liszt, but King Ludwig I of Bavaria seemed to enjoy it. After she flashed her boobs at him, he bought her a house in Munich and installed her as his favourite 'sultana'. Rumour had it that he enjoyed spanking her naked bottom, at least, that's how cartoonists depicted the happy couple at the time.

Plain old Eliza Gilbert dropped her stage name, became Countess von Starhemberg and ruled Bavaria by her lover's side. She fancied herself as a stateswoman and social reformer. But her intrigues brought disaster. King Ludwig was deposed and she was banished. She went to America where she quickly ran through the huge fortune she had amassed. She was 'saved' by the Methodists, but died in penury at the age of forty-three.

Liszt's affair with Marie d'Agoult was not well and truly dead, and they continued writing to each other. Lola's antics were a source of constant amusement to both of them. Liszt also began owning up about his other affairs and gave detailed explanations of his encounters with Charlotte von Hagn, Balzac's Polish mistress Eva Hanska and the insatiable pianist Marie Pleyel.

In November 1845, Liszt met the beautiful courtesan Marie Duplessis, *La dame aux camélias*. He was the last great love of this beautiful but doomed girl. Among the meagre possessions found in her squalid room at 15 boulevard de la Madeleine was a portrait of Liszt. He settled her doctor's bills after she died.

When Liszt heard about her death, he was in Poland. On 1 May 1847, he wrote to Marie saying: 'This poor Mariette Duplessis has died. She was the first women I fell in love with, and now she has been laid to rest in an unknown cemetery, where worms will eat her body. Fifteen months ago she said to me: "Take me, take me with you wherever you want. I will not be a burden to you. During the day I will sleep. In the evening

I will go to the theatre. At night you can do anything you want with me." I have never told you what a strange attraction I felt for this charming creature when I last stayed in Paris. I told her I would take her to Constantinople with me. Now she is dead. I do not know what strange, mournful note vibrates in my heart at the memory of her.'

Mariette Duplessis was just twenty-three when she died and was one of the greatest beauties of the century. Although she was a high-class prostitute, she somehow never lost her innocence. 'I would have saved her at any price,' said Liszt, 'for hers was a truly enchanting nature and practices generally thought to be corrupting – perhaps rightly so – never touched her soul.'

His next great love was no great beauty, but she was rich, titled and pious. Princess Carolyne von Sayn-Wittgenstein had been born Carolyne Ivanovska in Poland. At seventeen she had married Prince Nicolas von Sayn-Wittgenstein, a Westphalian, who had huge estates in the Ukraine. She met Liszt in Kiev where he was giving a charity concert. She sent him her card, attatching a hundred rouble note. The next day he went to thank her and she invited him to visit her estates on his way to Russia.

The Princess was short and dumpy, with small, dark, saturnine features, which were often described as 'Jewish' by people who did not like her. She puffed cigars stronger than the ones George Sand smoked and rode horses astride. She lived in an enormous castle with a staff of one hundred, and ruled over thirty thousand serfs. The Prince had long since gone his own way.

Liszt took up her offer and fell for her immediately when he saw her bedroom. Like him, she was a religious nutcase and her bedroom was of grey stone like a monk's cell and positively groaned with crucifixes. He considered her to be a saint. He was also a snob and loved her title. Her youth was equally attractive – she was eight years younger than him – and would not concede that she was pulchritrudinously challenged. When people told him that she was ugly, he replied: 'I, who can claim to be a connoisseur in such matters, maintain that she is beautiful, because her soul lends her face the transfiguration of the highest beauty.'

He wrote to Marie from Carolyne's castle in Woronince that he had met 'an extraordinary and eminent' woman in Kiev. Marie wrote back: 'If this woman is of noble character, she will certainly not want to share you with anyone else. She will not want to be just one of your mistresses. During these past four years, you must have reached satiation and have become disgusted with loveless pleasure. You must grasp this thread, so that it can pull yourself out of the labyrinth. My only regret is that Woronince is so far from Paris, for the greatest joy of my heart would be to see you straightened out.'

Liszt did not need her advice. In Russia a string of new lovers awaited him, including one called, intriguingly, the Snow Queen. Nevertheless Princess Carolyne was still waiting on her knees, with her Bible, when he headed westwards again.

Liszt and Princess Carolyne settled in Weimar, where he had been appointed musical director by Grand Duke Karl Alexander. His wife, the Grand Duchess Marie Pavlovna, was the sister of the Tsar and Liszt hoped that she would use her influence to get Princess Carolyne's marriage annulled. But Carolyne, a devoted Catholic, would have nothing to do with his plan and alienated the Grand Duchess by smoking in court.

Meanwhile, in Paris, Marie was achieving literary success with her scandalous novel *Nélida* – an anagram of her *nom de plume* Daniel – and her tract on atheism and free love; *Essay on Liberty*.

When the young pianist Amy Fay – '*une blonde et piquante Américaine*'– turned up in Weimar to study under Liszt, she was immediately smitten. 'Women still go perfectly crazy over him,' she wrote. Plainly, she was one of them. When he lost all his money in a stockmarket crash, Amy urged him to go and play in America. He would make a fortune there. 'My dear,' he said. 'If you needed a fortune, believe me, I would go.' But he had Carolyne and her millions to bail him out.

Carolyne's husband wanted to marry again and she agreed to a divorce, after she had obtained a satisfactory property settlement. Once she was free, Liszt planned to marry her. But she got cold feet and procrastinated over the property settlement. He found the wedding repeatedly postponed. In pique, he took holy orders. Marie, now a full-fledged atheist, was shocked. But even though he was now an abbé it did not reduce his attraction to women. They still quarrelled over him. 'Does the cassock make no difference?' asked a friend. 'On the contrary, it excites them all the more,' he was told. 'He now has the added attraction of being forbidden fruit.'

Another cigar-smoking proto-feminist, the 'Cossack Countess' Olga Janina; fell for him in 1869. She was never a Countess nor a Cossack, but the daughter of a boot-polish manufacturer from Lemburg. She was one of his pupils and highly unstable. When he dropped her, she tried to commit suicide. Then, when she failed as a concert pianist, she achieved notoriety with three highly fictionalized accounts of an affair between an abbé and a Cossack.

One Russian Countess took such violent exception to the fact that he would not bed her that she burst into his study with a loaded pistol. Liszt folded his arms, looked her in the eye and said: 'Fire.' The woman wavered for a moment, then dropped the gun and ran from the room in tears. Women were mad about him to the end.

Liszt himself explained that once the commandments had been explained to him he broke them all too willingly. 'Still,' he said, 'I shall never abjure love, for all its profanations and false pretences.' And he never did.

10

WAGNER'S RING

Richard Wagner was a macho composer. He was a swaggering would-be revolutionary and anti-Semite. Never before had anyone so successfully set sexual intercourse to music and many of his compositions are brimful of testosterone. But there is another side to him. He had a passion for silk underwear. He completed his famous *Ring Cycle* for Mad King Ludwig of Bavaria, who called him: 'My beloved, my own one', hugged him a lot and with whom a homosexual relationship may have occurred.

At the age of eleven, Wagner found himself turned on by the contents of his five older sisters' wardrobe. 'Their clothes exercised a subtle charm over my imagination,' he wrote. 'Nay, my heart about beat madly at the very touch of their dresses.' But his early love of all things feminine was repressed when, soon after, he met the castrato singer Sasaroli.

'The Italian male-soprano horrified me,' he wrote in his autobiography *Mein Leben*. 'On account of this dreadful person, the sound of Italian, spoken or sung, seemed to my ears almost diabolical ... I conceived so strong a dislike for everything connected with that nation that, even in later years, I used to feel myself carried away on an impulse of utter detestation and abhorrence.'

At thirteen, he began to fancy girls, but in a curious way. 'I remember a very beautiful young girl, whose name was Amalie

Hoffmann, coming to call one Sunday,' he recalled in *Mein Leben* (her real name was Malchen Lehmann). He spent most of his time with her shyly stroking her hair, and would blush whenever she entered the room. 'On other occasions I recollect pretending to be too sleepy to move, so that I might be carried up to bed by the girls. I found, to my surprise, their attention under these circumstances brought me into closer and more gratifying proximity with them.'

He was fixated on his mother and, from an early age, drew comfort from caressing soft fabrics such as silk, satin and velvet. He found they had an all-encompassing maternal warmth. He admitted that certain silky fabrics had an 'electrifying' effect on his skin. They were his great fetish. In later life, when composing, he would sit at his desk dressed up in fantastic outfits of silks and satins and furs, and drenched in expensive perfumes. He especially liked silk underwear.

On a journey to Prague, he became acquainted with two of the great beauties of Bohemia, Jenny and Auguste Raymann, who were the illegitimate daughters of Count Jan Pachta of Pravonin. Crammed in a small carriage with them, he could not help but appreciate the feel of their soft fineries. They took little notice of the fourteen-year-old frotteur.

He lost his heart for the first time at fifteen to Leah David, the impossibly beautiful daughter of a Jewish banker. She was, of course, unattainable, but he remained besotted with her until her future husband came along. Sadly, this youthful love for a Jewish girl did not staunch his later anti-Semitism.

At sixteen, Wagner became 'most intimate' with a strange musician called Flachs. They were seen everywhere together. Then Flachs became ensnared by 'a woman of dubious character'. 'I found his house closed to me,' Wagner said. 'Jealousy was the cause.'

At nineteen, he caught up with Jenny and Auguste again. This time he stayed on their father's estate. Jenny particularly attracted him. 'Conceive of Jenny as an ideal of beauty. Add that to my ardent imagination and you know all,' he wrote. One day, when he sat beside her at the piano, Wagner found himself overcome with tears. He dashed outside and, at the sight of the evening star, found himself transported into a mysterious ecstasy. This was all very romantic, but he could not cope with Jenny in reality. His 'glorious apparition' liked cheap novels and flirting with aristocratic beaux. 'She is not worthy of my love,' he wrote to a friend.

When he became chorus master in Würzburg, he fell in love with a young member of the chorus called Thérèse Ringelmann. He gave her private singing lessons by 'a method that has remained a mystery to me ever since'. She was the uneducated daughter of a lowly gravedigger, so he would not introduce her to his friends. She gave him cause for jealousy, then pressed him to marry her. He broke off the affair.

Next he temporarily suspended his hatred of all things Italian when he fell for Friedrike Galavani, another singer who was engaged to the oboist in a local band. Wagner went to a country wedding and danced with Friedrike so wildly that they lost all self-control. 'We embraced each other, while her real lover, who was playing the dance music, looked on.'

The young Wagner quickly supplanted the oboist in her affections. He would go around to her house where 'intimate intercourse' took place. Wagner insisted that their relationship never 'degenerated to the level that might cause suspicion or concern', but after a 'touching and tearful' farewell she was left pregnant. Although her oboist took her back, there was no possibility of them marrying. Wagner himself was too busy writing an opera, thanks to the support of his loving sister Rosalie, to bother with such trivialities.

Wagner was offered the musical directorship of the Magdeburg Theatre Company, which was spending its summer season at the seedy spa town of Bad Lauchstädt. When Wagner arrived there, he was greeted by the company's director Heinrich Bethmann, who was dressed in his dressing gown and night-cap. He introduced Wagner to his second wife, a cripple, who was snuggled up on the sofa with her lover, an elderly baritone.

The company was planning to put on Mozart's *Don*

Giovanni that Sunday. But they had a problem, the local bandsmen refused to come over for rehearsal that Saturday. Given the impossibility of the situation, Wagner turned the musical directorship down. However, he needed somewhere to stay that night and was taken to a nearby lodging house, where he bumped into one of the other guests, Minna Planer. She was the company's juvenile lead and an exceptionally pretty girl. Wagner took a room on the floor below hers. The next day he told Herr Direktor Bethmann that he had changed his mind and he would take the job after all.

Minna – short for Wilhelmina – was a woman on the make and four years older than Wagner. Her voice was mediocre, her acting mannered and she badly needed to secure her future. Once her looks were gone, there would be nothing for her in her chosen profession – and slim pickings on the next rung down the ladder.

At fifteen, she had been seduced by a captain in the King of Saxony's guard. When she fell pregnant, he abandoned her and Minna's daughter, Natalie, was brought up, in the custom of the time, as her sister. When Wagner met Minna, she was engaged to Herr von Otterstadt. But he married another woman for money, leaving the way open for Wagner. Minna soon granted him her favours, though she was not in love with him. 'How can I resist when you are stronger than me and kiss me half to death?' she said.

Wagner was tormented with jealousy when other men paid court to her and they often rowed. He got his own back by openly succumbing to the advances of the actress Christiani Wunsch, who was, he admitted, a young women 'of not unblemished reputation'. He squandered money on her and fell into the hands of moneylenders. But suddenly he became jealous again. Where was Minna? Why was she avoiding him? Was it because of his extravagant behaviour? Or was she enjoying the attentions of sundry young aristocrats?

On New Year's Eve, he invited all the leading members of the company to a party. Minna was on her best behaviour and shunned other admirers. Christiani went into a fit of jealous rage when Wagner ignored her. Everyone got drunk and Wagner ended up in Minna's bed. The next morning, hungover, they had breakfast together and Wagner, for the first time, found himself relishing the domestic comforts of bourgeois marriage.

The Madgeburg Theatre Company found itself in financial difficulties and collapsed under the weight of its debts. Wagner went home to Leipzig. When Minna came to stay for three days, his sister Rosalie teased him relentlessly for being so obviously in love. Later, accompanied by his mother and another sister, Amalie, he went to Dresden to see Minna, and the four of them went for a holiday in the mountains.

Minna took a job at the Königstadt Theatre in Berlin. Wagner fired off a passionate love letter begging her to marry him. 'Open your heart,' he pleaded. He would take care of everything. She would never have to worry about money again. When there was no response, he rushed off to Berlin, but Minna had moved on to Königsberg. During his frantic search for her, he ran into a Jewish businessman named Schwabe who had been her lover. Wagner wrote to Minna saying that he was addicted to her. She wrote back begging him not to come to Königsberg. Their relationship must remain a secret there. But he pursued her anyway.

He had trouble finding a job and they argued constantly about Schwabe. Wagner still insisted that they get married anyway, and eventually Minna consented. They both lied about their ages on the marriage licence. He added a year to his, otherwise he would still have been considered a minor under Prussian law. She tactfully shaved four years off hers, making her a blushing twenty-three-year old.

Wagner became musical director of the Königsberg Theatre. Minna's daughter moved in and soon their cramped apartment was a living hell. Wagner was often violently jealous, and not without good reason as Minna was spreading her favours far and wide. He confronted one of her lovers, a businessman named Dietrich, only to find a few days later when he got home from rehearsals that Minna had run off with him. Wagner followed her and caught up with her, alone, at her parents' house in Dresden. He threw himself on his knees at her bedside, begged her forgiveness and implored her to come back to him. If she did, he would give her the financial stability she craved. Her father threw him out.

Soon after, he managed to secure the musical directorship of the prestigious theatre in Riga. Although Minna had removed her wedding ring, she joined him at his lodgings just outside Dresden. She was noticeably agitated when she arrived, but soon grew calmer. After a couple of days, she said that she had to visit her parents, but in fact she ran off with Dietrich once more – this time to Berlin. Wagner set off after them with a horsewhip and a brace of pistols. Fortunately, he did not catch up with them and had to abandon his search and head for Riga where he was overdue. There he got a letter from Minna, openly admitting her infidelity but begging his forgiveness. It was the only time that she had expressed such sentiments, he said later, and it softened his heart. Minna arrived in Riga and they managed to patch things up.

It was always a make-do-and-mend relationship and Wagner sublimated his need for erotic love into opera. Minna, now denied any healthy sexual outlet, became sickly and spent much of her time naked in the mineral baths.

For most of his life Wagner was plagued with financial problems, but women often helped him out. In 1843, he gave himself to the seemingly insatiable Wilhelmine Schröder-Devrient. She was the star of the Berlin opera and creator of the role of Senta in *The Flying Dutchman* who consumed lovers at an extraordinary rate. She paid Wagner 1,000 thalers for the privilege. Privately, he considered her too 'played out' and, when he sought to lecture her on her other amours, she snapped: 'What do you know about it you, marital cripple?' Their liaison ended when Lieutenant von Döring, a Prussian guards officer, made off with all her money.

He then turned to Alwine Fromann – 'already past her first youth and no great beauty, except for her penetrating and expressive eyes which showed the greatness of her soul'. Not to mention the greatness of her bank account and her influence at court. He also had a fling with the famous singer Henrietta Wüst, while borrowing considerable sums of money from her husband which he somehow 'forgot' to pay back.

The great composer further neglected his marital duties by throwing himself into revolutionary politics. Minna stood by him through all his philandering and financial misfortunes but, after twelve miserable years, his marriage now stood on the brink of collapse.

In 1849, Wagner was involved in the failed Dresden uprising and had to flee the city to avoid arrest. Minna wrote a chiding letter. He wrote back thanking her for her concern and the purity of her love, and that he had decided that he was not really cut out to be a revolutionary. It made no difference. Dresden, she said, was her home and he was no longer welcome there. But eventually she weakened and followed him into exile in Zurich, where she found he had surrounded himself with slim, big-eyed boys with girlish features.

There was one female fan on the scene, too, nineteen-year-old Jessie Laussot. Her mother, the widow of a wealthy English lawyer, had had an affair with a Bordeaux wine merchant Eugène Lassot, then forced her daughter into a loveless marriage with him. Jessie's escape was music. She had first heard *Tannhaüser* in Dresden when she was sixteen and Wagner's blatant eroticism touched a deep need in her.

In 1848, Jessie heard that her hero had fallen on hard times. As incompetent in money matters as he was in politics, he was constantly hounded by creditors. Jessie persuaded her mother to help him and arranged a subsidy of 3,000 francs a year. Jessie was an accomplished pianist and identified herself with Wagner's romantic heroines. Her husband was bored by the intellectual conversations and was happy to leave them alone together, preferring the company of Jessie's mother. The flames were fanned further by Minna who complained constantly that she did not want to be with a man who supported her thanks to the charity of others.

Wagner and Jessie both yearned to throw off the chains of their respective marriages. Wagner told her that he intended to assign half of his allowance to Minna, then 'seek oblivion' in Greece or Asia Minor. Jessie sighed and she said she was ready to follow her Siegfried to Valhalla. As a first step, Wagner took a room in a small inn run by a Monsieur Homo – a name that seemed to amuse him. Meanwhile Jessie wrote to Minna, tactlessly assuring her that as 'your husband's admirer' she would do everything in her power to help him 'live and write as his heart bids, and work towards his great goal unhampered by external considerations'. Minna got the message.

Wagner wrote to Jessie saying that they should take an English ship from Marseilles to Malta on 7 May. Then he wrote to Minna bidding her farewell. In response, he got a letter from Minna looking back over their years together as if they had been full of blissfulness and contentment. Then disaster struck. Jessie sent a note saying that she had confided in her mother, who had naturally spilt the beans to her husband. Eugène was now threatening to put a bullet in the great composer's head and mummy dearest was going to cut off his allowance.

Using his pupil, the young homosexual Karl Ritter, as a go-between, Wagner wrote to Monsieur Laussot, telling him that it was a mistake to hang on to a wife who no longer loved him. He responded by forcing Jessie to pledge that she would not see Wagner for a year. So Wagner set out to Bordeaux to resolve the situation, but he did not have a valid French visa and was deported. Wagner was bitter. His great love, he said, had been destroyed by human cowardice. Jessie's mother and husband had good reason to be 'proud of themselves. What a beautiful corpse they have acquired'. However, there were understandable reasons for Jessie to play safe.

'The woman who wanted to bring me salvation has proved herself with child,' Wagner wrote to his other patroness, Karl Ritter's mother Julie. 'She was all love and we had consecrated our lives to the god of love. Then suddenly she saw happiness in conventional respectability. The depth of her fall breaks my heart. Mother! Dear faithful woman, if you could only have seen the instinctive, clear and naked revelation of her love. Her kisses were the richest delight of my life. No honours, no splendour, no glory can ever match their delight. Farewell, my beautiful blessed Jessie. You have been dearer to me than anything in the world. I shall never forget you.'

In his evident confusion he wrote to Minna, giving a very different spin on the story. It was all Jessie's fault. She was married to this 'very handsome young man', taking a keen interest in him as an artist and helping him out financially, when ... 'she suddenly wrote to me that she was determined to leave her family and throw herself under my protection. Her words were full of burning, desperate passion. I was alarmed and deeply moved. I replied, describing my circumstances in discouraging terms and reminding her of the dangers she faced. I urged her to consider if she was ready to die in cold blood, for that is what she would have to face.' So he had decided to go to Greece to escape from Jessie. That is why he had written the farewell. He then decided he had better go to Bordeaux and sort things out, but now he wanted to return to her 'unconditionally'.

Minna wrote in the margins of his letter comments like 'downright lie', 'outrageous' and the ironic 'so that's why'. But they got back together and the affair with Jessie was never mentioned again. Jessie later left her husband and went to live in Florence with the essayist Karl Hillebrand and after her husband's death they married.

Minna believed that it was the strength of her love that brought her husband back to her. Wagner wrote to Julie Ritter and another friend in glowing terms about his 'new wife'. But he plainly had other romantic intentions. 'Women are life's music,' he mused, and he was about to experience a huge spurt of musical creativity.

In 1852, he had met twenty-two-year-old Mathilde Wesendonck, the wife of a wealthy businessman, Otto Wesendonck. Five years later the Wesendoncks asked Wagner to come live in a house on their property at Asyl. Minna was keen to go because she had noticed Emilie Heim, wife of the conductor Ignaz Heim, making eyes at her husband at their musical evenings.

At Asyl, surrounded by costly tapestries, luxurious curtains and subdued lights, and pampered with perfumes and, of course, silk undergarments, Wagner underwent the most musically creative period in his life. In just sixteen months he wrote a large part of *Siegfried*, began *Tristan and Isolde*, composed five romantic songs, which were settings of Mathilde's words – the *Wesendonck Songs* – and he conceived *Parsifal* there.

It came to an end when Minna intercepted a love letter Wagner sent his muse. 'The day before yesterday, an angel came to me at noon, blessed and comforted me,' he wrote. 'That made me feel so wonderful and serene that I greatly longed for the company of friends in the evening. Then I heard that they had not dared deliver my letter to you personally because De Sanctis' – Mathilde's hot-blooded Italian teacher –'was with you.' This had provoked a jealous tantrum.

'Forgive my childish behaviour,' he wrote. 'Now I have come to my senses and am able to pray to my angel with heartfelt emotion. This praying is a prayer of love. Love! Profound joy in this love, it is the source of my salvation.' Then he lays on the romantic stuff: 'When I look into your eyes, there is nothing more to say. Everything becomes meaningless... Everything is then so clear to me ... I feel so sure of myself when this wonderful, sacred gaze falls upon me and envelops me ... The distinction between the subject and the object ceases ... All is one and at one, profound, infinite harmony...There is peace, and in that peace the perfect realization of life ...What a fool is he who would gain the world and his peace from elsewhere ... Blind is he who, gazing into your eyes, did not find his soul in them...'

Minna was jealous. She had not received a letter like that for some time. She was so impressed that she showed it to Mathilde and her husband. Afterwards Minna decided to leave and bid farewell to her hostess in a letter. 'You have succeeded in alienating my husband's affections after nearly twenty-two years of married life,' she wrote disingenuously. 'May this noble deed add to your comfort and joy ... You repeatedly incited my husband against me and even made unjust and indiscreet accusations about me and your good husband.' On the other hand,

Wagner had been dishing it out and she was willing 'to discuss the matter as between friends'. But Wagner would not sanction any accommodation. He had been caught with his hand in the cookie jar, and shamefacedly, he went off to Venice where he finished *Tristan and Isolde*.

To keep his muse alive in his mind, he penned thirty-three fantasy love letters to Mathilde in his diary, and it worked. 'The most subtle and mysterious fluids seep into the finest pores of sensibility and penetrate to the very marrow of life,' he reported, 'leaving only that strangely sublime sigh.' But it is more profound than common, vulgar sex. Wagner explained that the Delphic wisdom was imparted by the priests. 'But they themselves got it from the priestess Pythia, who, seated on the tripod of inspiration, passed through the wildest convulsions of ecstasy. She pronounced the utterances of the gods with ecstatic moans, which the priests merely translate into the language of the world. I believe that he who has sat on the tripod can never more be a priest, for he is closer to a god.'

Wagner then headed for Berlin, where he wrote to Mathilde of the new women in his life. One of them warned of the uncontrollable passion in his music and 'thought it risky to take her young daughter to see *Tannhäuser*'. After a quick visit to Paris, Wagner decided to settle in Biebrich, a small town across the Rhine from Mainz. Minna turned up unannounced. The atmosphere was quickly soured after letters and belated Christmas presents turned up from 'that dirty bitch' – as Minna called Mathilde. After 'ten days of hell' Minna left.

This left the field free for the actress Friederike Meyer. But she got sick and, while Wagner was nursing her better, her lover the theatrical director Herr von Guaita turned up. He proposed to stage one of Wagner's operas in Frankfurt, but, after a jealous row, the offer was withdrawn.

Friederike and Wagner headed for Vienna where the actress hoped to make some guest appearances, but she failed the audition. Wagner tried to soothe her with a holiday in Venice, but afterwards she returned to von Guaita.

In Mainz, Wagner met twenty-nine-year-old Mathilde

Maier. She was a Germanic beauty, blonde-haired, blue-eyed – the living embodiment of his Aryan ideal. Twenty years his junior, he called her 'my child' and 'my good little girl'. At first, her letters to him are stiff and formal. She finds him 'patronzing' and warns him that he could easily hurt her pride. But he revs up the romantic engine one more time.

'Fear nothing, my child,' he wrote back. 'Everything that can make a person dear to me is within you. It is your whole being that I love, your loveable, stalwart and yet pliable nature. You are so many-sided and always so secure and true, that I could not wish to take any one part of you. All of you is mine, even though I may never possess you. You are my last source of sublime purification. If you are that to me and if I may find fulfilment through you, then you too will not feel wholly unblessed for having encountered me on your journey through life.'

He asked her to find a place to live close by. When she has difficulties, he writes: 'One does not ask much from you women, but in the end all you do is cause us grief and pain ... Adieu, wicked child.' However, he does not mean it and when he moved to Vienna he wrote asking her to come and be his 'housekeeper', explaining: 'Marriage is out of the question, as long as my wife is alive.' Minna was ill with a heart condition and the strain of a divorce might kill her. Nevertheless, 'if I am to survive, I want a loving woman by my side, even if she is also a child.'

He begins to call her 'my child (or wife)', describes his modest apartments and spells out her household duties. Naturally, at the end of a day of cooking and acting as social secretary, 'the child comes to my bed'. She declined the position, and so he wrote to her mother, explaining of course that in the event of his wife's death – 'I cherish no frivolous hopes, God forbid!' – he would ask for her daughter's hand in marriage. In the meantime, he says perfidiously: 'I wish, chastely and profoundly, for a dear woman by my side.'

Fortunately, he did not send this letter directly to Frau Maier, but to Mathilde who he asked to pass it on to her mother. She wisely did not do so. Mathilde had already been treated to an insight of Wagner's domestic arrangements the year before when he was looking for a maid.

'A modest young girl has been recommended to me,' he wrote. 'I shall take her in and try her out. Perhaps she will be able to fulfil my needs.' A week later, he wrote to Mathilde again saying that he has decided not to hire the girl after all: 'As I grow older, I grow more weary about entering into any sort of relationship.' Two weeks later he changes his mind and finds the girl's looks nice and her manner 'undemanding'. But he quickly tires of her and gets rid of her, only to replace her with her older sister, Mariechen.

'The older sister moved in yesterday and turns out to be a pleasant, clever and warm creature,' he told Mathilde. 'She keeps me company at breakfast and in the evening, and pleases me not so much by talking but by being there.' He even took to writing to the girl while he was away on a concert tour, informing her that he is on his way home. 'Now my sweetheart,' he tells Mariechen, 'make sure the house is in good order.' He tells her to spray his study with perfume: 'Buy the best and make it smell beautifully. God, how I long to relax with you at long last. (I hope the pink panties are ready too.) Just be nice and sweet. I deserve a really good time again.' He neglects to mention that while on the concert tour, in Budapest, he had met a young and beautiful Hungarian soprano, who sang excepts from *Lohengrin* and fell passionately in love with her 'awakener'.

On his way home from awakening his Hungarian soprano, Wagner had stopped off in Berlin to lunch with the conductor Hans von Bülow. In the afternoon, while von Bülow rehearsed, Wagner took von Bülow's wife Cosima on a carriage ride. Cosima was born Cosima Liszt and was Liszt's illegitimate daughter with Countess Marie d'Agoult. Her husband was a long-time friend and patron of Wagner's. The couple had even come to stay with him in Zurich on their honeymoon.

Von Bülow seduced the teenage Cosima to the strains of Wagner. He was conducting the overture to *Tannhäuser* when she first heard it. The music, she said, 'overwhelmed' her. She stayed the night and they got engaged. They married and had two children. As her husband regularly collaborated with Wagner, they were often in each other's company. But that afternoon in the carriage, things were different. 'We gazed mutely into each other's eyes,' he recorded in his autobiography. 'A fierce desire to acknowledge the truth seized us … With tears and sobs we sealed the pledge that we belonged to each other alone. It came as a relief to both of us.' That night, he slept at the von Bülows' home.

The carriage ride with Cosima was another thing that he neglected to tell poor little Mariechen, who was at home perfuming her - or perhaps his - pink panties. He also forgot to tell Mathilde, who he was still imploring to come to Vienna to be his housekeeper and warm his bed. But things were about to come to a head. Wagner had invited the von Bülows to come and stay, and Cosima was arriving a week before her husband.

When Cosima turned up, Wagner came clean, well, almost. He wrote to Mathilde telling her not to hand his letter on to her mother. He had changed his mind. 'I beg you with all my heart not to give that letter to your mother,' he wrote. 'It seems I have been too hasty. I was mistaken. A change in our mutual relationship is now out of the question. Adieu, and look after yourself. Love me in spite of everything. My heart is true.' Mmm.

What happened to Mariechen and the pink panties is, sadly, lost to history, but just nine months later Cosima gave birth to Wagner's daughter Isolde. Von Bülow stood by his wife and gave the child his name. He seemed to be flattered that the great composer deigned to share his wife. As the bond between Wagner and Cosima grew closer, she moved in with him as his secretary. They had another child, Eva, whom Wagner acknow ledged as his own. When Minna had a heart attack and died, Cosima pushed her husband for a divorce so she could marry the great man. 'He [von Bülow] would never have lost me if fate had not led me to the one man who it became my purpose in life to live or die for,' she confided to her diary.

Before the divorce was finalized, she had another child, this time a son, Siegfried Wagner. Meanwhile, Wagner was involving himself with King Ludwig II of Bavaria, grandson of Ludwig I who was brought down by Liszt's friend; Lola Montez. Wagner's luxurious house in Vienna, and the staff, was costing him a fortune. Debts were piling up and, for the second time in his life, he was threatened with the debtor's prison. To escape his creditors, he fled back to Switzerland. But then he was saved by Ludwig.

On his accession, the pretty nineteen-year-old King summoned Wagner to Munich. Ludwig instructed him to complete *The Ring* and put all worries about money from his mind. Wagner bowed low in gratitude. King Ludwig sank to his knees, clutched the composer to his bosom and swore an oath of eternal fidelity. He showered Wagner with expensive gifts – diamond rings, sumptuous textiles, precious ornaments, expensive furniture and, of course, paintings and busts of himself. Wagner responded with poetry, sycophantic to the point of insanity. In their letters they called each other 'Beloved', 'Embodiment of my Happiness', 'Supreme Goodness', 'Source of Light in my Life', 'My One and All', 'Saviour of my Happiness' and 'Dearly Beloved Adored One'. Their correspondence was so passionate that Cosima, still only officially his secretary at the time, grew jealous.

Wagner's interminable private audiences with Ludwig set tongues wagging, not least because Wagner was a Protestant and a noted revolutionary. Wagner's high camp mode of dressing in silk and furs, and his addiction to perfume were a gift to satirists. The King, a notorious homosexual, preferred thigh boots, tight breeches and army uniforms. Ambitious courtiers circled. One faction tempted Wagner with a young women called Agnes Street to persuade him to use his influence with the King on their behalf. Meanwhile, with all Wagner's talk of Siegfried, Brünhilde and the joys of Valhalla, the chronically unstable King was losing grip on reality.

When King Ludwig discovered the true nature of Wagner's relationship with Cosima, he accused the composer of 'adultery' and 'betrayal'. Wagner grew so unpopular that he was forced to leave Bavaria. The King consoled himself by building magnificent castles, but gradually went mad. After being forced to abdicate, he drowned himself.

Wagner's marriage to Cosima has been portrayed as the perfect match, the sublime union of the master and his muse. But soon Wagner's head was turned by the beautiful nineteen-year-old Judith Mendès-Gautier, daughter of the poet Théophile Gautier and wife of the novelist Catulle Mendès, when she came to stay.

'Her nose continues the line of her brow, as in the days the gods walked the Earth,' it was said. 'Her dark hair curled softly, as if dishevelled. Her complexion was dark ivory; her teeth white, small and not too close together; her lips red as coral. Her eyes were brimful of mischief and lit up with laughter. Her eyebrows were fine and straight; her ears entrancing. Every feature could have been taken from a god-like Sphinx or a female warrior of Thyatira. Her flawless, ideal beauty could have served as a model for the *Comédie Humaine*'.

When Wagner met her at the station, he told her on the ride home: 'We are united by a single emotion.' In other words, he fancied her.

He saw her again at the first Bayreuth festival. By then he was sixty-three, but he used the busy festival to set up a secret rendezvous with her. Behind the scenery he smothered her with kisses and fondled her shapely breasts. Cosima turned a blind eye. She must have known what to expect. Before they had married Wagner had already had an affair with her own sister Blandine Ollivier, the wife of a prominent republican who had helped Wagner in Paris. Cosima dismissed Blandine as 'a rather dissolute creature'. Her husband, Emile, went on to become prime minister of France.

'Was it for the last time that I put my arms around you this morning?' Wagner wrote to Judith at the end of the festival. 'No, I shall see you again. I want to because I love you.' He suggested that they elope together. She refused, but his letters show that the passion continued. 'Precious soul, sweet friend. How I long to kiss you once more, dearest sweetheart,' he wrote in 1877. 'Love me and let us not wait for the Protestant kingdom of heaven. It will be terribly tedious. Love me. Love me forever.' In another letter: 'I embrace you, my beautiful love, my precious adored soul, my child, my Judith.'

His letters are a shopping list of perfumes and soft fabrics: milk of iris, ambergris, *rose of Bengale,* white rose powder, balm of Arabia and 'yellow satin, pale as possible, sprinkled with plaited rosebuds', pink silk to match her complexion, chamois and Turkish slippers without heels. She must buy these things in Paris and ship them to him. Then, with all the regret of an ageing man, he wrote in 1878: 'My precious love, why in heaven's name didn't I find you in my Paris days, after the failure of *Tannhäuser*? Were you too young at the time?' She surely was. But she was Wagner's one last love.

11
PATHÉTIQUE

Pyotr Ilyich Tchaikovsky was the Sugar Plum Fairy, but this could not be admitted in Tsarist Russia. The punishment for being gay was loss of civil rights, public disgrace and exile to Siberia. His preferences seem to have been the cause of his premature death. 'My whole life has been a chain of misfortunes because of my sexuality,' Tchaikovsky once said.

Pyotr was a mother's boy and clung to her skirts. Screaming with terror, he had to be forcibly parted from her on his first day at school. His mother died of cholera when he was thirteen. He never got over it. He was also close to his nanny, Fanny Dürach, and wept copiously when she returned to Switzerland. For consolation, he turned to music, and found comfort in the company of other boys.

One of his school friends was Prince Vladmir Meshchersky, a lifetime confidant whose promiscuous gay lifestyle earned him the sobriquet 'Prince of Sodom and citizen of Gomorrah'. Another friend was Alexey Apukhtin, a long-term lover whose poems Tchaikovsky set to music. But it was a keen amateur musician; Vladimir Adamov, who later became the head of the Justice Ministry, who first stirred Tchaikovsky's adolescent desire. 'Their mutual attraction was so strong that they remained intimate until death separated them,' said Tchaikovsky's younger brother Modest, who was also a homosexual.

117

SEX LIVES OF THE GREAT COMPOSERS

The School of Jurisprudence, which Tchaikovsky attended, was a paradise for a young homosexual. It was an exclusively male establishment with communal baths, public floggings for those into S&M and dance classes where boys naturally had to dance with each other, one in each couple taking the role of the lady. Mutual masturbation and buggery were tolerated. Tchaikovsky is pictured in his graduation photograph holding another boy's hand. But society at large was not so tolerant.

When Tchaikovsky left the school to become a lowly civil servant, he had to hide his sexuality from his colleagues. The only tell-tale sign was that he was clean-shaven, which was not the fashion of the time.

Only in homosexual circles did he feel entirely at home. Along with Apukhtin, he became an active member of the homosexual underground in St Petersburg. Apukhtin papered the walls of his apartment with pictures of dashing young officers. Tchaikovsky was known for his impersonations of female dancers, which he performed even in heterosexual company. 'He had a gift for making the unacceptable acceptable,' said Modest.

He was also seen at the camp extravaganzas of Prince Alexey Golitsyn, a high-born homosexual who could get away with flaunting his orientation. Tchaikovsky wrote to his sister of being 'unhappy in love', spending all his money on 'idle pleasures' and being 'constantly broke'. After a while, according to his brother, he 'grew weary of this life of idle dissipation'. He wanted to start afresh.

While still a teenager, Tchaikovsky had struck up what Modest called 'an intimate friendship' with a Neapolitan voice coach named Luigi Piccioli which had a great influence on him. Nobody knew how old Piccioli was because he dyed his hair, rouged his cheeks and had, hidden under his collar, a device that stretched the skin of his face and smoothed out the wrinkles. At the very least, he was fifty. He had a passion for Italian music and regularly took the young Tchaikovsky to the theatre to hear the Italian masters, such as Rossini, Verdi, Bellini and Donizetti.

PATHÉTIQUE

Tchaikovsky quit the civil service to accompany a friend of his father's on a trip around Europe, where he hoped to broaden his musical education. Soon after, when Tchaikovsky was asked what his duties in the civil service were, he said that he was 'quite unable to remember'. In Hamburg he attended dances with 'women of dubious reputation' and was delighted by the sight of mixed bathing at Ostend. In London, he was over-whelmed by a performance of Handel's *Messiah* at the Crystal Palace. But then in Paris he fell out with his employer, partly because he was running up huge bills and partly because he had become attracted to an old school friend, Vladimir Yuferov.

Soon Tchaikovsky and Yuferov were having a 'high old time'. But then Tchaikovsky began to have misgivings. 'How shall I wind up?' he wrote. 'Sooner or later (probably sooner), I shan't have the strength to cope with the "problem" side of my life, and it will smash me to pieces.'

He returned to Russia and became a lecturer at the Conservatoire in Moscow. He was a handsome young man and found himself constantly the victim of unwanted female advances. But he was not yet entirely gay. Tchaikovsky wrote home about his 'preoccupation' with one girl, Elizaveta Dmitrieva. His contemporary Nikolay Rubenstein, who had already enjoyed her favours, teased him relentlessly about it. Tchaikovsky's father, a serial womanizer, wrote that 'she must be so pretty, so lovely, and of course so clever, I have quite fallen in love with her myself and can't wait to meet her when I come to Moscow.' However, within six weeks Tchaikovsky's preoc-cupation was dead. 'My feelings have completely cooled,' he wrote. 'I am completely disillusioned with her.'

This did not, however, put him off trying to be heterosexual. He wrote piano pieces dedicated to Vera Davidova, who had hopes of marrying him and talked of the farm house where they would end their days together. Tchaikovsky clearly regarded his homosexuality as an abnormality that could be corrected if he found the right woman. Vera was patient.

He wrote to Modest, lamenting his continuing dependence on the shameful and abominable habit of masturbation. He

119

urged his younger brother to cure himself of his sexual leanings before it was too late. Tchaikovsky himself continued the struggle. But then he took as a pupil the fourteen-year-old Vladimir Shilovsky, stepson of the director of the Moscow Imperial Theatres, the rapacious Vladimir Begichev. According to Modest, they soon became 'intimate' and the three of them went on holiday together, along with Konstantin de Lazari, a baritone at the Bolshoi.

Tchaikovsky attempted another heterosexual foray with the Belgian soprano Désirée Artôt. In person, he did not think she was up to much, but when he saw her on the stage, he admitted to Modest that he was 'very, very smitten'. They acted like two lovelorn teenagers, gazing deep into each other's eyes. Désirée was thirty and boyish, frequently playing 'trouser roles'. Tchaikovsky had hopes and they got engaged. But he soon realized that marriage to Désirée would be a disaster for him professionally.

As a struggling composer, nothing could be worse than being dragged around Europe as the appendage of an opera star. No one would ever take him seriously again. Désirée's mother was against the match too, especially when Nicholay Rubinstein told her that 'Tchaikovsky was not fitted for the part of husband' – that is, he was gay. Tchaikovsky's father, ever optimistic, was all for the match. Désirée resolved the situation by going off with and marrying the Spanish baritone Mariano Padilla y Ramos, without even informing her fiancé. Tchaikovsky was devastated by the rejection, but his friends rejoiced. The marriage could never have worked. Besides, Russia needed him. In gratitude that she did not broadcast the real reason for the failure of their relationship – his homosexuality – he dedicated his Six French Songs, ironically named *Romance*, to her.

In 1869, Tchaikovsky attended a masked ball in Moscow dressed as a woman, which led to certain complications. Vladimir Begichev, as always, was skirt chasing and pointed out the object of his latest attentions to what he took to be Tchaikovsky in drag, but in fact was his wife.

PATHÉTIQUE

At that time, Tchaikovsky was having an affair with his fifteen-year-old pupil Eduard Zak. He always liked them about that age. Four years later, Zak killed himself. Tchaikovsky admitted that he never loved anyone as much as he loved Eduard – 'the sound of his voice, the way he moved, the way he used to look at me'. It was Eduard who inspired the love theme in Tchaikovsky's overture *Romeo and Juliet*. After Zak's death, Tchaikovsky tried to shun homosexuality because of the 'tragedies' it might lead to, and urged his brother Modest: 'If there is the remotest possibility, try to be straight. At your age, you can still force yourself. Try it at least once. It may work.' He was now beyond such experimentation. He took a three-room apartment and a servant named Mikhail Sofronov who would procure little boys for him.

'I am very satisfied with him,' Tchaikovsky wrote to Modest, 'and even more so with his younger brother.' The younger brother, Alexey, soon replaced Mikhail in Tchaikovsky's household as he 'well understands all my needs and more than satisfies my demands'. By eighteen though, in Tchaikovsky's eyes, Alexey had lost his looks but he remained 'as dear to my heart as ever ... I will never let him go'.

Meanwhile, Modest had given up the struggle to be straight and took over Mikhail as his manservant and procurer. Tchaikovsky now addressed Modest as Modestina and signed his letters Petrolina instead of Pyotr. This camping around was all well and good, but to others Tchaikovsky maintained that he was upset that his brother was 'the same as me'.

Tchaikovsky also took in an effete lodger by the name of Nikolay Bochechkarov, who catered for his more exotic needs. Rent boys and rough trade were paraded through the apartment while the great composer entertained them all in drag. He had a more robust affair with an architect named Ivan Klimenko, who later married and had children. But according to Klimenko's own account, he 'succumbed to Tchaikovsky's seductive invitation and lived with him for some time'. In Tchaikovsky's seductive invitations he addressed Klimenko as 'Klimenka' and the affectionate 'Klimenochka'. In one of them, Tchaikovsky

121

played the Turkish Sultan and ordered his subject to return to his divan – under threat of punishment which, in this case, was 'death by impalement'.

Occasionally, this monstrous self-indulgence left him with a 'disgust for life and a yearning for death' and he longed to swap Moscow for 'life in a monastery'. But in 1875, his spirits were raised by the visit of the French composer Camille Saint-Saëns, who was also gay. In a private performance in the Conservatoire, with Nikolay Rubinstein at the piano, the forty-year-old Saint-Saëns and the thirty-five-year-old Tchaikovsky danced the *Pygmalion and Galatea,* a ballet with two women's parts.

Soon after, Saint-Saëns returned to France and married the teenage Marie-Laure Truffot. They lived unhappily with his mother. They had two sons. One fell out of the window of their apartment at the age of two and was killed. Six weeks later, the other one, who was just seven months old, died of a childhood illness. Saint-Saëns blamed his wife and left her. With his faithful manservant Gabriel, he travelled to North Africa and Uruguay, whose national anthem he composed. In these out-of-the-way places, he practised his perversion – doing unspeakable things with little boys.

When Modest became a tutor to his nine-year-old nephew who was a deaf-mute, Tchaikovsky became deeply concerned. He fired off salvos again urging his brother to 'be as other men'. But in his letters, Tchaikovsky even hints that sex with the child was not beyond his scope. However, Tchaikovsky was to put such terrible temptations behind him.

'I have decided to get married,' he wrote. That is, he had decided to get married in principle. 'I have made a firm decision, starting today, to enter into lawful matrimony with anyone who will have me,' he told Modest. 'It seems to me that our inclinations are the biggest and most insurmountable obstacles to our happiness, and we must fight against our natures with all our might.' The marriage, he said, would not just be to silence the gossips, it would be for his own peace of mind. It should take place within a year. Even if he lacked the courage, he said he would 'abandon forever my previous habits' and avoid the company of homosexuals.

At the same time, he was writing to other friends, boasting of his latest homosexual encounters. In moments of reflection, he expresses his commitment to marry some 'unknown, beautiful woman' but says that it is impossible just to cast off his old ways and tastes like a glove. Besides, he tells a friend, 'since my last letters to you I have already given way some three times to my natural compulsions'. Tchaikovsky continued to urge his brother to conquer his passions, while he indulged himself daily. At the Conservatoire he was getting a reputation for favouring his male students over his female students, and for taking some of them home with him. One of them was the young violinist Yosif Kotek, with whom be quickly became infatuated.

Socially, his sexual orientation was causing him problems. But he was grateful that there were 'some who cannot despise me for my vices because they began to love me before they came to suspect that I was a man who had lost his reputation ... they pity and forgive me' but they are 'ashamed of me'. Consequently, he needed a marriage or 'an open affair with a woman' that would 'shut the mouths of those contemptible creatures whose opinions don't bother me, but cause pain to my loved ones'.

With all this in mind, Tchaikovsky began working on the opera *Eugene Onegin*; an adaptation of Pushkin's masterpiece in which the heroine Tatyana is cruelly spurned by the eponymous young gallant. Tatyana writes a passionate love letter to Eugene and Tchaikovsky was working on the *Letter Song* when he received an equally emotional letter. It was from a former student at the Moscow Conservatoire, twenty-eight-year-old Antonina Ivanova Milyukova, who professed undying love. He wrote back telling her to master her feelings. But she wrote again saying that this was impossible. No one else would do.

'After seeing you, I no longer wish to even look at another man,' she said. He did not reply, so she dashed off another missive saying that she was going to commit suicide. But first 'let me see you and kiss you so that I can remember that kiss in the other world'. At this point, Tchaikovsky seems to have confused Antonina with Tatyana, the passionate heroine of *Eugene Onegin*. He stated his dilemma clearly: 'To preserve my own freedom at the cost of this girl's life, or to marry.' He went to see Antonina and tried to put her off. He said he was happy to be her friend and warned her that he was irritable, moody and generally anti-social. But he neglected to mention that he was as bent as a nine-bob note. 'Then I asked her whether she wanted to be my wife.' Antonina wet herself and 'Naturally, she said yes.'

Without actually spelling out that he was gay, he did his best to explain that there were going to be problems in the general area of the bedroom. He said that he was 'too old to fall passionately in love'. The best he could do was offer her 'the love of a brother'. She said she would take whatever she could get. Then he offered her his cheek to kiss. She threw her arms about his neck and smothered him in wet ones. Cringing, he struggled out of her grip and out of the door. It was only then that he began to look into the background of his bride to be. When he asked her piano teacher at the Conservatoire about her, his reply was a torrent of 'unprintable profanity'.

Tchaikovsky probably did not remember, but he had met her once before, twelve years ago at a friend's house, which is now the site of a McDonald's in Moscow. The sixteen-year-old Antonina had developed a schoolgirl crush on the handsome young composer. But as he was a promiscuous homosexual at the time he paid her no mind. She saw him regularly in the corridors of the Conservatoire and her teenage infatuation soon matured into a full-scale obsession. By the time she was twenty-four, she was deeply in love with him.

Something had to be done. But what? She began to believe that if she prayed every day for six weeks outside one particular chapel in Moscow, he would be hers. In the rain and the snow, she would be there, on her knees, but still no Tchaikovsky. 'I could tell that he liked me,' Antonina said. 'But he was too shy to propose.' So she had taken matters into her own hands.

Despite his evident distaste for her physical advances, Tchaikovsky crossed his fingers and hoped everything was going to be okay. Antonina would be a neat and compliant housewife who would give his life the veneer of respectability while he bedded his other male students. This was not wholly unreasonable. He had a married friend, Nikolay Kondratiev, whose wife tolerated a male servant who doubled as her husband's lover. What could be cosier? But Antonina was not about to see it that way, especially after she heard *Eugene Onegin*. 'He is Onegin, I am Tatyana,' she wrote, and she was fired with passion.

Tchaikovsky's father was delighted that his son was getting married. Tchaikovsky's sister only worried that he might be marrying the wrong woman. Modest said that any woman would be wrong. Tchaikovsky himself was confident because he was marrying a woman 'who loves me like a cat'. But come the day of the wedding, things were very different. During the service, Tchaikovsky said he was in a daze, like he was not really there. Then came the moment when he had to kiss the bride. 'At that point, I felt a stab of pain through my heart, and such anxiety gripped me that I began to weep,' he recalled. Afterwards he went back to his bachelor pad to lie down, leaving his bride alone at the reception. He turned up briefly but the atmosphere was like that of a funeral. Even Antonina felt a shiver of foreboding.

At 7 p.m., the bride and groom met up at the station to take the train to St Petersburg for their honeymoon. On the platform Tchaikovsky said he stifled a scream and held back the sobs to the point he thought he would suffocate. He had made up his mind that he must at least talk to his bride until they reached Klin, some sixty miles down the track. Then, duty done, he could go to sleep. But fortunately his old friend Prince 'Sodom' Meschersky was on the train. The old school chums withdrew and Tchaikovsky poured out his heart amid copious tears. Antonia spent her wedding night unmolested.

In St Petersburg, she made a fumbling attempt at consummation. When Tchaikovsky could not rise to the occasion, she became hysterical. He managed to calm her down and explain the exact nature of the problem. Finally, she agreed to a sexless marriage and told Tchaikovsky 'she will never want more than to love me and take care of me'. Tchaikovsky was deeply relieved. He felt he had won this battle against her. His victory, he said, was due the to fact that she was a woman of limited intelligence and he was immensely superior.

Antonina tried to be a good wife, but they had nothing in common. She had little understanding or appreciation of music – and no taste. Although in her letters she had claimed to be a fan, she did not know a note of her husband's music. When he had staged concerts at the Conservatoire she had not bothered to attend. Just five days after the wedding, he wrote to his brother: 'My wife has become physically repulsive to me. Yesterday, when she had a bath, I had to go to St Isaac's Cathedral. I felt the urgent need to pray.' When that did not work, he hit the bottle. Friends who knew of his sexual proclivities were shocked at news of his marriage. But they rallied around and invited him out, on his own, so that he could escape from his bride.

Two weeks after the wedding, he told his family: 'I would be lying if I said I was swimming in an ocean of ecstasy.' Three weeks after the wedding he left his bride and set out to spend the summer on his sister's estate. Within a month, he was attempting suicide. 'It seems to me that I am irretrievably lost,' he wrote. And Antonina? 'Far from feeling the slightest fondness for her, I hate her in every sense of the word.'

The only reason he did not kill himself was, ironically, the love and support of another woman. Her name was Nadezhda Filaretovna von Meck. She was the wealthy widow of a railway tycoon. Married at the age of sixteen, she had had eighteen children before her husband died of shock – when he discovered that the last one was fathered by his secretary Alexandr Yolshin. Madame von Meck was a music lover and, as a wealthy widow, was in the position to help struggling musicians. One of her protégés was Yosif Kotek, Tchaikovsky's young friend. Kotek was installed in the von Meck household and interested his patron in Tchaikovsky's work. After hearing one of his concerts at the Bolshoi, Madame von Meck was blown away. She wrote to Tchaikovsky in such passionate terms that made Antonina's missives seem shy and retiring.

Madame von Meck, however, was more passionate about the music than the man. Although she maintained an insatiable curiosity about Tchaikovsky, she felt that she would not be able to control herself if they ever met. She wanted him to keep on composing so that he would speak to her of his great passion through his music. Tchaikovsky wrote back in a similar passionate vein. They were lovers on paper only, often exchanging letters daily. Tchaikovsky even wrote to her about his marriage. She was sympathetic, but later confessed that she had found the news 'bitterly unbearable'. Thankfully, her pain was soon over.

After Tchaikovsky's summer break with his sister, he went back to Moscow and tried to put a brave face on things. But he had never been much good at hiding his true feelings. He found it difficult to get any work done with his wife around and their evenings together were intolerable. He was too embarrassed to invite friends home, but when they did meet her the general opinion was favourable, though some complained that she was 'not quite real'.

Tchaikovsky had a simple choice to make, either get rid of Antonina and face public humiliation, or get rid of himself. But he did not want to draw attention to himself with any dramatic suicide attempt. So, while out cruising the streets of Moscow one cold night, he waded into the freezing Moskva River and stayed there until he found the cold unbearable. Convinced that he would die of pneumonia, he struggled out of the river and dragged himself home. He told Antonina that he had had a fishing accident. His constitution was so strong though, that he did not even go down with a chill.

Once more, he tried to get away. He arranged for his brother to send a telegram summoning him urgently to St Petersburg. When he arrived, he was in a state of nervous exhaustion. His brother took him to a nearby hotel and called a psychiatrist. He prescribed total rest and never, under any circumstances, should Tchaikovsky see his wife again. Rubinstein broke the news to Antonina in Moscow. She accepted the inevitable stoically, then started flirting with Rubenstein. While she was telling him how many famous men had fallen for her, he made a bolt for the door.

The marriage had lasted three months from beginning to end. They had spent less than half that time under the same roof together. Tchaikovsky was terrified that the rejected Antonina might spill the beans about his homosexuality. The only way to ensure her silence was to pay her off, but she had already plunged him into debt. Madame von Meck rode to the rescue. She suggested an annual stipend of 6,000 roubles, paid in monthly instalments. She wanted to see the back of Antonina too. 'I thought she had robbed me of what should have been mine by right and mine alone,' she wrote, 'for I loved you and valued you more than anyone else in the world.'

But that was not the end of Antonina by any means. She kept the prospect of divorce dangling before Tchaikovsky for three more years. One of Modest's more unsavoury friends offered his services to prove her guilty of adultery. Then 'the spawn of hell' fell pregnant of her own accord and had an illegitimate child. Tchaikovsky considered divorce, but he was up to his old tricks again and decided that he could not risk it. He tried to cut her maintenance payments, but she threatened to expose his homosexuality so he backed off. For the rest of his life he lived in constant fear of her. He told friends he considered himself already ruined. 'She can divorce me on the grounds of adultery, impotence, anything she likes,' he said. But in the back of his mind he rehearsed the closing speech he would make if he were charged with sodomy.

He never managed to free himself of her. After the opening night of *Eugene Onegin,* she tracked him down at his brother's apartment, burst in and flung her arms around him, claiming that she could not live without him. She sent him heart-rending letters. 'Come to me. I am yours, body and soul. Do with me anything you wish,' she wrote. Her grip on reality had obviously come loose. Three years after his death she was committed to a lunatic asylum, where she spent the remaining twenty years of her life until her death in 1917. In 1913, she published her memoirs. Touchingly, she said that she never forgot his 'extraordinary, wonderful eyes'. And although there is mention of his homosexuality in her letters, in her memoirs, mad as she was, she kept quiet.

Meanwhile, Tchaikovsky had proof, if proof were needed, of his true nature. There was no escaping the fact that he liked men and he did not like women. This preference became the central tenet of his life. To recuperate, he took a villa on Lake Geneva with his manservant Alexey, Modest and his deaf-mute ward. Alexey appalled Tchaikovsky by seducing their landlady's daughter and the night air was rent by their noisy lovemaking. Tchaikovsky remarked bitterly that, henceforth, his beloved 'Alyosha' or sometimes 'Lyonya' would be 'nothing more than a servant to me' and the young Kotek was invited to join the party.

Tchaikovsky went to Florence, where Madame von Meck invited him to visit her villa – when she wasn't there – so he could picture her domestic life. She also sent him a young pupil, Vladislav Pakhulsky, but he resisted this temptation. With Madame von Meck around, he dare not get up to any hanky-panky. He even resisted the temptations promised by a gay pimp called Napoleon, who had procured for him on his last trip to Italy. Because of his behaviour in Switzerland, Alexey had fallen from grace. Then Kotek caught up with the happy party. But he too proved a disappointment. He had miraculously transformed himself into an obsessive womanizer.

Tchaikovsky therefore found himself ensnared in a long period of enforced sexual abstinence, relieved only by repeated trips to watch a dashing young actor named Boucher, whom he had long lusted after, in Racine's *Andromaque*. At the dénouement of the play, Boucher had to slap another character across the face. 'What I wouldn't give for that precious hand to slap me across the face a hundred times,' Tchaikovsky wrote to Modest.

Back in Russia, Madame von Meck became increasingly puzzled by Tchaikovsky's failure to file for divorce. Then came the moment they both most dreaded. One afternoon when Tchaikovsky was out walking, Madame von Meck, out for a carriage ride with her entire family, rode by. It was a horrendously embarrassing moment for both of them. He sent a note apologizing, but Madame von Meck was secretly thrilled by 'the sweet, enchanting moment' they had come face to face.

He tried to allay his anxiety with a three-day drinking spree in Moscow, headed to Paris where he dressed himself up as a 'French fop', then on to Rome for a thoroughly debauched time with a number of homosexual friends. All of which sapped his energy and his only output from his Roman escapade was the uninspired *Capriccio Italien.*

In Berlin, Tchaikovsky found Wagner's *The Flying Dutchman* 'noisy and boring'. He found cruising the city's gay bars more to his taste. For the rest of his short life he would often, of an evening, go out for a 'stroll'.

Staying with Nikolay Kondratiev, he found Kondratiev's young manservant Shash Legoshin 'most obliging', visiting Tchaikovsky in the morning before his master awoke. Tchaikovsky grew more confident and did not mind being seen out with his old friend Apukhtin and his live-in lover Alexandre Zhedrinsky. He renewed his acquaintanceship with Prince Meshchersky, who lived an openly outrageous lifestyle. But Tchaikovsky did not have the courage to come out and continued his clandestine, hole-in-the-wall sex life, leaving him vulnerable to Antonina's blackmail.

Madame von Meck took up the young Debussy and Tchaikovsky's ardent letters fell on increasingly deaf ears. There were rumours that the von Meck estate was in trouble. Tchaikovsky returned to Russia to find his beloved Alexey had been drafted into the army. Despite the military censor, he wrote to him: 'Every evening, after undressing, I pine for you. I sit sobbing at my desk, knowing you are far away. There will never be another sweet Lyonya. I will never stop missing you.'

The new Tsar extended the length of military service by

three years, depriving Tchaikovsky of his beloved Alexey for six years. So Tchaikovsky headed back to Italy to improve his spirits. There he had another brush with heterosexuality with Kondratiev's daughter's governess Emma Genton, who wrote him passionate love letters. At the time Tchaikovsky admitted to 'a crazy desire to be stroked by a woman's hand' not a young woman's though. He longed to rest his head on the knees of an attractive older woman and smother her hands with kisses. But he could not cope with heterosexuality in reality. While visiting his sister, Tchaikovsky saw his young niece Tanya make love to the family's music teacher, Stanislav Blumenfeld, under a rug during an afternoon carriage ride. The spectacle so appalled him that he fled the country.

At the other end of the spectrum, Modest suffered a painful series of operations on abscesses around his anus. Tchaikovsky cheered him up with a batch of letters full of vivid descriptions of the homosexual nightlife in Paris he was enjoying. He risked more trouble with the military censors by sending Alexey full-blown declarations of love.

Back in Russia, Tchaikovsky became obsessed with his thirteen-year-old nephew Bob. 'All day I feasted my eyes on Bob,' he wrote in his diary. 'How ravishing he looks in his little white suit ... What a perfect being Bob is ... Bob will drive me mad with his unutterable charm.' He spent as much time as he could with his 'little darling Bob', picking flowers, playing duets, reading to him. He was also plagued with 'the feeling' that came on him then passed. His diary also contains coded complaints about 'X' and 'Z'. 'Z is really tormenting me,' he wrote. 'This Z is less agonizing, if more powerful than X, but both are very unpleasant.'

Biographers have struggled to make sense of 'X' and 'Z'. Some have identified Z as his sexual longings, and X as the guilt they bring with them. But X and Z could equally be minor ailments, perhaps symptoms of a sexually transmitted disease. Soon after, his friend Kondratiev died of syphilis.

In Tbilisi, a young artillery officer named Ivan Verinovsky began to flirt with Tchaikovsky. Seeing what was going on,

Tchaikovsky's sister-in-law flirted with the officer until the dashing young man was so torn between them that he shot himself. The composer was inconsolable for months. He headed back to Paris where he fell in love with the young cellist Anatoly Brandukov, who he introduced to the decadent circle of Prince Golitsyn. Although Tchaikovsky and Golitsyn grew close, Tchaikovsky generally preferred lovers from the lower orders. When he met Ivan, a coachman, he wrote 'I have fallen headlong into Cupid's net.'

In Turkey, he fell in love with a fourteen-year-old boy called Vladmir Sklifosovsky and wept when he had to leave him behind in Constantinople. Sklifosovsky was a sickly lad and died nine months later. Tchaikovsky dedicated his *Chant élégiaque* to him.

After fourteen years, Madame von Meck suddenly ended her relationship with Tchaikovsky. The estate was facing financial difficulties and greedy relatives threatened to expose Tchaikovsky as a homosexual unless she cut him off. Naturally, he cursed her treachery, fickleness and her 'female inconstancy'. 'To read her letters,' he complained, 'one might think that fire would sooner turn to water than her subsidy cease'.

He acted like the spurned lover although, in fact, he was now world famous and not badly off. He bought a house and surrounded himself with house guests, languid young men who called themselves, jokingly, Tchaikovsky's 'Fourth Suite'. One of them was his young nephew Bob. Although Bob was now in his twenties and past the age Tchaikovsky usually fancied his boys, Tchaikovsky remained obsessed with him for the rest of his life. Another house guest was Vladimir Napravnik, son of the minor composer Eduard Napravnik. Tchaikovsky got on well with the boy and took him on a binge in Moscow. But it was to Bob that he dedicated his sixth symphony, the *Pathétique*.

There is a mystery surrounding Tchaikovsky's death. The death certificate says that he died from cholera, which it has been suggested he caught from a gay prostitute in St Petersburg. But it is generally accepted that he killed himself either by drinking a glass of untreated water or, more likely, by taking arsenic.

One theory is that he killed himself because of his love for young Bob, which found expression in the *Pathétique*. But it seems, shortly before his death, Tchaikovsky had got involved with Alexandr Vladimirovich, the eighteen-year-old nephew of Count Alexey Alexandrovich Stenbok-Fermor who was a close friend of the Tsar. Outraged, the Count wrote a letter to the Tsar condemning Tchaikovsky as a homosexual, a sodomite and a pervert, and handed it to the Tsar's secretary, Nikolay Jacobi. By chance, Jacobi had been a classmate of Tchaikovsky's at the School of Jurisprudence. He promptly convened a 'court of honour' of distinguished lawyers who had been at the School of Judisprudence and were friends of Tchaikovsky's. Tchaikovsky was present.

This kangaroo court decided that if the great composer's conduct was revealed it would bring dishonour on the School, on Russia and, not least, upon themselves. Even though many of them had gone straight in later years, most had been involved in homosexual practices when at school. Exposure meant ruin. They decided that the only way out was for Tchaikovsky to kill himself. He left the hearing 'white and agitated', having agreed to abide by their decision. Two days later he was dead. He was just 53. But he had been saved from the dishonour that he had feared all his life and for nearly a hundred years his reputation remained intact.

12

DEATH IN VENICE

Gustav Mahler was more than a little confused. Like many a musical genius before him, he acquired an astonishing reputation as a womaniser. But he had intense unconsciously homoerotic relationships with male friends. That is, they were unconscious, until Freud sorted him out. Mahler is widely thought to be the subject of Visconti's film of Thomas Mann's novel about the final fumblings of a closet paedophile, *Death in Venice*. But he did not die in Venice and it was regular heterosexual love that killed him.

Mahler was a prude and a prig when it came to other people's morals, lecturing the singers and musicians who worked for him. The same dizzy standards did not apply to his own behaviour, of course. As a student, he went with prostitutes, but true to his high moral calling, he always gave them a stern telling off afterwards.

In letters to lovers, though, he was the romantic hero. At nineteen, he was sending poems to Josephine Poisl, the daughter of a local postman in Iglau, Bohemia. 'A new name is now inscribed in my heart,' he wrote, that of his 'passionately beloved'. To Josephine herself he wrote: 'I am closer than ever to the goal of my desires when that which we (oh, that I could say we both) so ardently long for will be fulfilled.' He could not say both because poor Josephine wanted nothing to do with him. The only thing she ardently longed for was for him to stop writing to her. Soon Mahler was reduced to begging for it: 'I have never humbled myself before anyone. Look, I kneel before you.' However, when Josephine's father wrote to him saying that the fair Josephine DID NOT RETURN HIS AFFECTION, he took the love poems he had written to her and set them to music.

At Kassel, he fell in love with shapely, blue-eyed soprano; Johanna Richter. He was willing to die for her, but then 'a nameless grief sprang up between us like a wall and there was nothing I could do but press her hand and go'. Again he turned the rejection into music.

The 'nameless grief' that ended the affair could have been that he was Jewish and she was not. Or that she lived with Wilhelm Treiber, Mahler's hated boss at the opera house. Or that he was just plain ugly. 'In spite of his ugliness, he had a demonical charm,' wrote British composer and feminist Ethel Smyth. 'But intercourse with him was like handling a bomb cased in razor blades.'

When Mahler was twenty-six, he had an affair with Marion von Weber – 'the most beautiful person in Leipzig'. She was four years older than him and married with three children. Her husband was the grandson of composer Carl Maria von Weber and a captain in the Leipzig regiment. Mahler was a conductor at the Leipzig opera house and he planned to elope with Marion, but she did not turn up at the station and the train left without them.

The whole of Leipzig knew about their liaison. When it came to love, Mahler was a tyrant. He had no qualms about compromising his mistress and broadcasting the affair. Although the whole city sniggered behind his back, Captain von Weber said nothing. A scandal would have ruined his army career, but the strain proved too much for him. One day, on a train to Dresden, he started laughing manically, pulled out his revolver and started shooting at the head rests. Other passengers overpowered him. The train was stopped and von Weber was taken to the police station. From there he was bundled off to a lunatic asylum. Even though her husband was out of the way, Marion ended the affair.

Meanwhile Mahler was being pursued by Natalie Bauer-Lechner. She had fancied him when he was a student at the Vienna conservatory. Ten years later, when she broke up with her husband, who was a professor at the Vienna conservatory, she turned up in Budapest. Mahler was then musical director at the opera house. Natalie, it seems, wanted an uncomplicated affair. She had taken to wearing men's clothes and had a string of lovers, including several married men. But it was Mahler she really wanted.

By sheer persistence she managed to inveigle her way into the Mahler family. His parents had died and he was left to bring up his younger siblings. Natalie went with them when they went on walking holidays in the Alps. Unfortunately, Mahler treated her like a sister.

For sexual gratification, he turned to the twenty-three-year-old soprano; Anna von Mildenburg. The relationship did not begin promisingly. Mahler had shouted at the young singer at rehearsals when he took over at the opera house in Hamburg, reducing her to tears. But soon Mahler was writing love letters to her, much to Natalie's chagrin.

In a last ditch attempt to incite some jealousy in Mahler, Natalie took him to meet her old heart-throb Siegfried Lipiner, who had just married for a second time. But the meeting, as far as Natalie was concerned, was a failure. The two men got on famously. They ended the day standing outside a café in the teeming rain discussing philosophy.

Mahler lavished all his attention on Anna. He became her personal coach and turned her into one of the greatest dramatic sopranos of the age, especially in Wagnerian roles. Their affair was the talk of Hamburg. 'When love speaks to me, it always talks of you,' Mahler wrote to Anna. 'But love in my symphony is different. It is an attempt to show the summit, the highest peak from which the world can be surveyed.'

Mahler grew tired of Anna's possessiveness and the way she continually gossiped about their sex life. When he converted from Judaism and was baptized as a Catholic, some suggested it was so that he could marry Anna. Actually, it was so that he could get a job in anti-semitic Vienna. Anna went with him, but his name was soon linked with Rita Michalek and Marie Gutheil-Schroder, two singers at the opera.

He started writing passionate love letters to Selma Kurz, a beautiful soprano who made her début in Vienna in 1899 at the age of twenty-four. 'Dearest Selma,' he wrote in one, 'Believe in my love. It is something unique in my life and will remain so. Remember we are at the beginning of a long road and we should travel fresh and unwearied.' The two were soon snatching secret meetings during rehearsals of his orchestral songs. They took a brief holiday in Venice together, but Natalie and Mahler's sister Justine tagged along too. Soon afterwards, the affair cooled. Selma feared that marriage to Mahler would spell the end of her career. It was then that twenty-one-year-old Alma Schindler moved in on him.

Alma was a musical groupie with a thing about older men. She was already having an affair with her music teacher and noted composer Alexander von Zemlinsky, and had a brief fling with the painter Gustav Klimt, who was twelve years her senior. But she had seen the forty-one-year-old Mahler conducting the Vienna State Opera. She had heard about his reputation on the casting couch and was greatly attracted. When she found out that he was going to be at a dinner party, she managed to get herself an invitation.

Alma was known as 'the most beautiful woman in Austria'. She was talented musically and well versed in politics and philosophy. Mahler noticed her from the other end of the dinner table. He looked at her furtively at first, then brazenly. Soon he was chatting her up. She fired his jealousy by repeatedly referring to Zemlinsky and the work she had done under him. Mahler asked if he could see some of this work too. Alma was certainly game. She quickly dropped Zemlinsky who was, she wrote, 'a hideous gnome ... chinless, toothless, always reeking of the coffee house'. She wrote in her diary her only doubt: 'What if Alex becomes great and powerful?'

DEATH IN VENICE

Mahler was smitten at their first meeting. Soon afterwards, he sent her, anonymously, a love poem. He fluttered around her when she visited the opera and took her for a walk in the snow. This cold stroll was followed by a hot kiss in her bedroom. Though his letters are full of love, they have a schoolmasterly tone. In one, he insists, when they get married, she cease composing. 'You have only one job now,' he wrote, 'to make me happy.' When she read this, she cried all night, then agreed to his terms.

Once they were engaged, she decided that the illusion of her virginity need no longer be preserved. According to her diary, their first attempt at lovemaking occurred on New Year's Day 1902. It was a flop. However, a few days later she made an entry of just three words: *'Wonne über Wonne'* – 'Bliss upon bliss.' When they married two months later, she was pregnant.

It was not enough that she had Mahler, she wanted him all to herself. She began to alienate his friends. She did this by showing no respect for the master musician they all admired. She rarely bothered to hide her anti-Semitism and, when asked by Anna von Mildenburg what she thought of Mahler's music, she replied that she disliked what she knew of it. Mahler himself seemed to find this remark amusing.

She was jealous of the women he worked with at the opera, especially Anna von Mildenburg. Alma spied on them. Although she witnessed only the most innocent of encounters, when she came home in the evenings she would berate him and resist his embraces. But she was so hot for him, she could not resist him for long. Soon she was pregnant again.

When Mahler was conducting the Viennese première of Hans Pfitzner's *Die Rose vom Liebesgarten*, Pfitzner took an interest in some of Alma's early composition. Alma was flattered by Pfitzner's attentions. Mahler, normally a jealous man, went out of his way to leave the two of them alone together. And when he caught her in a compromising position with the handsome young pianist Ossip Gabrilovich, he 'was nice about it'. She also had an affair with the artist Oskar Kokoschka, who painted them in bed together. Alma's diaries were full of references to Mahler being a poor lover, if not impotent. 'I knew that my marriage was no marriage,' she wrote, 'and that my own life was utterly unfulfilled.'

It may be that he just did not fancy her anymore. She constantly accused him of sleeping with other women, especially Anna von Mildenburg. Whatever the truth, she took the precaution of keeping her bedroom door firmly locked at night. Mahler slowly went mad with frustration. Alma would find him lying on the floor, weeping at the thought of losing her. He sent her pathetic little notes, trying to worm his way back into her affections. 'I have kissed your little slippers a thousand times and stood yearning at your door,' he wrote. 'But the demons have punished me again because I thought of myself and not of you, dear one.'

He trotted off to Freud in the hope of a cure from this terrible affliction. Freud said that Mahler's troubles stemmed from 'his wife's resentment at the withdrawal of his libido from her'. But it was she who locked the door. Not only was Freud confused, he was puzzled. Why had Mahler not married someone named Marie, which was the name of Mahler's mother?

Mahler was impressed by this insight, as Alma's second name, which he never used, was Maria. But if Mahler had wanted, unconsciously, to marry his mother, why did he not marry someone who was older than him, rather than someone twenty years younger. Freud provided an instant analysis of Alma too. She had been deeply attached to her father, that was why she was attracted to older men. Her real problem, though, was not with older men, but with one four years her junior. She had fallen in love with the architect Walter Gropius. She had always been impressed by anyone famous and Gropius was already a famous designer at the age of twenty-seven. In her letters to him, she refers to herself as 'your wife' and wrote: 'You lie naked against my body and nothing can separate us but sleep.'

In his youthful enthusiasm, Gropius wrote a letter begging Alma to drop everything and run away with him. But he sent it instead to Mahler. Whether this was a mistake has never been fully explained. Anyway, Mahler demanded a meeting with

Gropius, then told Alma she must decide between the two of them. Naturally, she told Mahler that she would give up Gropius, but actually kept him on as her lover on the side.

On a trip to New York, Mahler was diagnosed with heart disease, exacerbated by the knowledge of his wife's infidelity. Knowing he had not long to live, he headed back to Vienna where he died. This left Alma free to marry Walter Gropius. After that, she fell in love with the novelist Franz Werfel, who was twelve years younger than her. Even so, he died a full twenty years before she did. The artist Kokoschka, who was living in London after World War II, suggested that they get back together again. They both regretted not marrying. But she refused to see him. Forty years had passed and she did not want to ruin the image he had of her beauty back in 1914.

The German novelist Thomas Mann was writing *Death in Venice* not far from Venice when he heard of the death of Mahler and he consciously gave his protagonist Aschenbach some of the characteristics of the great composer. But in the book Aschenbach was a writer. In the film, Visconti makes Aschenbach a German composer. He used Mahler's music as the soundtrack, reinforcing the idea that *Death in Venice* is about Mahler and his yearning for little boys. It is not. It is about Thomas Mann's yearning for little boys.

13

ROMEO AND HARRIET

Louis-Hector Berlioz was an incredible romantic. Every Tammy, Dixie and Harriet was Juliet to his Romeo. When he met his first love again, after a gap of fifty years, he declared that she was 'still the embodiment of my earlier adored ideal'. Her name was Estelle Duboeuf – 'the name alone was enough, on account of Florian's pastoral *Estelle et Némorin*, which I have taken from my father's library and had read secretly many times'. This classical love story was the nearest thing to pornography that he could get his hands on at the time.

He admitted that in the half century since he had last seen her he had forgotten the colour of her hair – 'but whenever I remember her I see a vision of great brilliant eyes and pink shoes'. It was those shoes that really turned him on. They were 'rose-coloured lace-up boots – you laugh – but I had never seen such boots before'. Berlioz was just twelve years old at the time; the object of his intentions eighteen. But there was no doubt that this was the real thing.

'The moment I beheld her, I was conscious of an electric shock: I loved her. From then on, I lived in a daze. I hoped for nothing, I knew nothing, and yet my heart felt weighed down by an immense sadness. I lay awake whole nights disconsolate. By day I hid myself in the maize fields or in the secret corners of my grandfather's orchard ... Everyone at home and in the neighbourhood laughed at the spectacle of a child of twelve broken on the wheel of a love beyond his years. Time is powerless: no other loves can efface the imprint of this first love.'

But he suffered more of the pains of a first love than its pleasures. 'One evening her aunt gave a party and they played a game where everyone was divided into two groups,' he recalled. 'The gentlemen chose their ladies. I was purposely made to choose mine first. But I did not dare, my heart was beating so violently. I lowered my eyes in silence. Everyone was making fun of me. Then Estelle took my hand and said: "No, I will choose. I take M. Hector." What misery. She laughed cruelly, looking down on me in all her beauty.'

This early experience did not put him off. In fact, at the age of twenty, he commemorated his youthful infatuation in his first opera. It was about young love and was called *Estelle et Némorin*. Although Estelle's rejection of him left him 'wounded like a dumb, suffering bird', when he was sixty-two, he sought her out. She was then a sixty-eight-year-old widow living in Lyons. But when he saw her he was overwhelmed by passion and collapsed, appropriately, at her feet.

'I recognized the divine stateliness of her step' – those feet again – 'but, heavens, how changed she was,' he wrote. 'Her complexion was faded, her hair grey. And yet at the sight of her my heart did not feel one moment's indecision. My whole soul went out to its idol as though she were still at her dazzlingly loveliest. Balzac, nay, Shakespeare himself, the great painter of the passions, never dreamt of such a thing.' 'I have loved you; I still love you; I shall always love you,' he told the astonished widow. He took her hand and pressed it to his lips – 'my heart melting and every nerve thrilling' – and he 'gazed at her with hungry eyes'. But once again she refused him. 'You have a young heart,' she told him. 'But I am six years your elder and, at my age, I know how to deny myself to you.' Rejected once more, he went on his way.

In Berlioz's autobiography, he is remarkably quiet on the subject of his youthful sexual experiences in Paris. Maybe he did not indulge himself like his contemporaries. He claims he went to confession regularly and said: 'Father I have done nothing.' 'Keep it up, my child,' the priest replied. An instruction 'I followed all too faithfully for a number of years,' he notes. However, at the age of twenty-two, he mentioned to a friend: 'I have just overcome a violent passion which was tearing me in two. It would have done for me if I had not had my music.'

His first recorded sexual indulgence was with the nineteen-year-old pianist Camille Moke. Berlioz was twenty-six and, by that time, hopelessly infatuated with the Shakespearean actress Harriet Smithson. He was struck by Harriet's poise and her serene beauty. He saw her play Ophelia in *Hamlet*, and was 'shaken to the core by the experience'. 'I vowed that I would not expose myself a second time to the flame of Shakespeare's genius,' he noted. But his resolve did not even last twenty-four hours. 'Next day the playbills announced *Romeo and Juliet*. I had my pass to the pit. But to make doubly sure of getting in I rushed around to the box office and bought a ticket for the stalls'.

That night Berlioz saw his Juliet in the flesh. He wrote in the preface of *Symphonie Fantastique:* 'A young musician sees for the first time a woman who embodies all the aspects of the ideal being his imagination had striven for.' After another dose of Shakespeare and another dose of Harriet Smithson, 'my fate was doubly sealed,' he wrote.

He sent a letter to Harriet, declaring his love. She replied coldly that she was 'unable to reciprocate his feelings'. He wrote to the theatre offering to write an overture. His offer was rejected. Berlioz tried to stay away from Shakespeare and Miss Smithson, but they were the toast of Paris. Everywhere he went, people were talking about her. Soon his music was bursting with unrequited love. He set Thomas Moore's *When He Who Adores Thee* to music for his beloved Harriet.

Sometimes his passion for her grew so intense it stopped him working altogether. She got reports that he was epileptic, if not completely mad. Because of Berlioz's blind infatuation with Harriet, his colleague the German composer Ferdinand Hiller thought that he would be the perfect go-between, carrying notes back and forth to his lover the beautiful eighteen-year-old pianist Camille Moke. She lived at home with her mother, who kept an eagle eye on her. But she taught piano at the same girls' school where Berlioz gave lessons. Berlioz was thrilled to be entrusted with such a romantic mission. When Hiller told Camille of Berlioz's hopeless infatuation with Harriet, Camille was impressed with his passion and sought to divert some of it on to herself. She repeated malicious gossip she had heard about Harriet. She even told him that Harriet was having an affair with her agent, who had once encouraged Berlioz by offering to be a go-between with Harriet.

Berlioz was mortified. He struck out from Paris, south-east, walking until he dropped from exhaustion. In all, he was missing for thirty-six hours. But the ordeal had been cathartic. His vision of Harriet as his romantic ideal evaporated and now he saw Camille for the great beauty she was. 'Since my recovery, I loved her,' he told a friend. 'But she loved me long before the hydra left my heart. She loved me even when she was thought to be involved with someone else.'

Indeed, Camille took the initiative. She confronted Berlioz at the school where they both worked and told him to his face that she loved him. This was a bold step, especially in those days. A few days later he told her that he loved her too. They became lovers. Camille would visit him in his garret at 96 rue de Richelieu. Camille wanted to marry him. She told her mother, who was outraged. She had intended a fabulous match for her daughter, who was already making ten or twelve thousand francs a year from recitals. Now she wanted to throw herself away on a penniless composer. In desperation, they eloped, but they only got as far as Vincennes on the outskirts of Paris before turning back. It may not have been much of an elopement, but at least they had one whole night alone together.

Berlioz wrote to his father asking for his backing. His father wrote back saying that he had no intention of increasing his son's allowance if he married. Berlioz had one chance left, he had to win the prestigious *Prix de Rome*, which had a cash prize of 3,000 francs. That and his allowance would give him enough time to sell some of his compositions. That would show Madame Moke – who he called 'the hippopotamus' – that he was a suitable son-in-law.

In preparation for the examination, Berlioz had to lock himself away for three weeks without seeing Camille. So she took another suitor – a rich one. Berlioz won the prize but not by producing his best work. He had to reign in his natural romanticism and make the work more academic. Winning the *Prix de Rome* did not automatically win him the hand of Camille. Madame Moke insisted that he had to have a success in the concert hall first, which he soon had with *The Tempest*.

One of the conditions of the *Prix de Rome* was that the winner had to go to study in Italy. Fortified by Camille's solemn vow and with her ring on his finger, Berlioz set off for the Villa Medici in Rome. Even though he had fulfilled Madame Moke's conditions, the hippopotamus still had other plans. With Berlioz away, she planned to marry her daughter off to the concert pianist; Camille Pleyel. He was twenty-three years older than her, but he was the son of a wealthy family of piano manufacturers. This made him a better bet than Berlioz.

When Belioz heard he had a rival, he did not take it seriously. He said blithely: 'Pleyel's net is made of gold but its mesh is too wide and the little bird he took from me will escape.' However, thanks largely to the persistence of her mother, Camille did not escape. Madame Moke took it upon herself to write to Berlioz in the most brutal terms of her daughter's wedding plans. She told Berlioz that he had caused them nothing but trouble and said she had never consented to his request for her daughter's hand under any circumstances. She also told him not to kill himself, thus planting the idea in his mind. Indeed, suicide was exactly what Berlioz planned, but not before he had killed Camille, her mother and Pleyel. He devised a dastardly plan. He had an outfit of women's clothes run up for him – along with a hat with a green veil – and bought two double-barrelled pistols and some strychnine. He planned to turn up at Camille's house disguised as a lady's maid. Saying that he had brought an urgent note from Countess X, he would be ushered into the drawing room, shoot everyone in sight, then poison himself.

Pausing only to scribble some hasty revisions to the *Symphonie Fantastique*, he headed for France. Unfortunately, he lost his lady's maid outfit along the way and had to have another one made in Genoa. He was so lovelorn that he could not eat and so weak from hunger he fell into the sea. He was rescued, though only just. He spent a long time lying on the beach, vomiting up all the seawater he had swallowed.

The police refused him a visa to travel via Turin. As a Frenchman, they thought he might stir up unrest there. So he set off along the Riviera. He was four days into the horrendous coach ride from Rome to Paris when he realized that the end of his life would mean the end of his music. He stopped in Nice, where his appetite miraculously reappeared. He stayed there for a month, firing off letters slandering Camille and Madame Moke to everyone he could think of. When he ran out of friends, he turned to literature as an outlet for his spite. He wrote the novellas *Suicide with Enthusiasm* and *Euphonia*, in which he portrays Camille as a flirt, a hypocrite and a sadist, and her mother as a whole lot worse. During his sojourn in Nice, he wandered in the orange groves, swam in the sea, wrote the *King Lear* overture and made love to a local girl.

'As I did not want to take my lover back home,' he wrote to friends in Paris, 'I took her to a cave I knew at the edge of the sea. But when we went in, we heard a growl from the back. It was some sailor sleeping – or perhaps it was Caliban himself. We left the cave to him and our union was celebrated without ceremony on the beach, some way off. The sea was raging. The waves broke at our feet. The night wind blew fiercely and I cried with Chactas [hero of Chateaubriand's *Atala*]: "Majestic nuptial rites, worthy of the grandeur of our untamed loves." You see,' he told his friends, 'I am cured.' He even began to think of marriage again, this time to his pretty seventeen-year-old cousin; Odelie.

Berlioz returned to Rome and set to work with a will. Later he praised one Louise Vernet for making his stay in Rome bearable. It can have been little consolation that Camille's marriage proved disastrous. She soon tired of her middle-aged husband and made off with a younger lover.

When Berlioz returned to Paris, he found that Harriet Smithson had just returned, too, after a tour of northern Europe. He staged a concert of his music with Shakespearean and autobiographical themes. Harriet attended, to find the programme notes a hymn to his unrequited love for her. The concert was an enormous success. Harriet sent him a note congratulating him. He wrote back: 'If you do not wish my death, in the name of pity (I dare not say love), let me know when I can see you. I beg you for mercy, and ask you sobbing on my knees for forgiveness. Wretch that I am, I do not believe that I have deserved all I have suffered, but I bless the blows that come from your hand.' She consented. But as lovers, they had a lot of ground to make up. She had been told that he was an epileptic and a mad man. He had been told that she was promiscuous, and he still had to tell her about his engagement to Camille Moke. But soon, they were publicly declaring their love for one another.

Harriet was soon identified as the subject of much of his music. Capitalizing on the notoriety their affair was creating, she appeared in *Romeo and Juliet* once more. Berlioz attended. Many found that Harriet had put on weight and lost the youthful bloom that she had brought to the role five years before. But Berlioz found himself in romantic ecstasy. In private, Harriet was less keen on the physical side of the relationship than Berlioz. This was partially because her mother and younger sister, who depended on her, did not want her marrying a Frenchman who lived in Paris. Berlioz's family were also against the match. Harriet was an Englishwoman, a Protestant, an actress, in debt and three years older than him.

His father refused to give his consent to the marriage. Determind to go ahead, Berlioz took legal action to stop his father disinheriting him. He planned to spend the rest of the grant awarded under the *Prix de Rome* and threatened to kill himself if Harriet would not let him accompany her on tour. But fate intervened. Harriet tripped on the hem of her dress, descending from a carriage. She broke her leg in two places.

Her long convalescence meant that she could not work. She was deeply in debt and, in the face of a campaign of slander spread by her sister, Berlioz arranged a series of benefits. Despite the opposition of both their families, Berlioz was resolute. 'Harriet Smithson will be my wife sooner or later, whatever the cost,' he wrote.

Harriet was not so sure though. In desperation, Berlioz threatened to break with her. She realized then that she could not bear to be without him. A civil marriage was arranged. Harriet's sister tore up the papers and Harriet herself accused Berlioz of not loving her. He responded by trying to OD on opium in front of her. She shrieked. He laughed. She protested her love for him and begged him to live. An emetic was administered and for three days he hovered on the brink of death, but survived. But still Harriet delayed.

She suggested they wait another two months. This was too much for Berlioz. If she did not marry him within a week, he would go to Berlin. A friend, Jules Janin, had fixed him up with a beautiful eighteen-year-old who had just run away from an old man who had bought her as a child. Berlioz offered to take her with him to Berlin and seemed more than ready to fall in love with her. This was enough for Harriet. They married in the British Embassy. The witnesses were the composers Liszt and Hiller, and the poet Heinrich Heine, while Janin took care of the beautiful eighteen-year-old.

They honeymooned in Vincennes, which no doubt brought back memories of the night he had spent there with Camille. Nevertheless, the marriage was happy at first. They had a son, Louis. But having been an actress since the age of fifteen, Harriet was not a natural wife and mother. Her career was on the wane too, while Berlioz's was on the up and up.

He wrote *Roméo et Juliette*, but he dedicated it, not to his wife but to the violinist Nicolo Paganini. It seems that, although he had pursued Harriet with all Romeo's passion, now in her mid-thirties, she could not respond like a youthful Juliet. Ironically, as her beauty faded, her passion grew. But without beauty Berlioz could no longer respond. Harriet's unrequited passion made her ill. Berlioz responded by playing around with actresses, singers, dancers and other women. But he retained his love for romance.

When his father died in 1848, he tried for the first time to look for Estelle Duboeuf, the object of his infatuation when he was twelve. He was forty-five and returned home to Saint-Eynard to look for her. 'I breathe in the blue air she breathed,' he wrote. 'A cry re-echoes from the Saint-Eynard, a cry no human language can convey. I see, I see again, I behold, I worship. The past is before me, I am a boy of twelve. Life, beauty, first love, the infinite poetry of existence. I throw myself on my knees and cry: "Estelle! Estelle!" to the valley and the hills and the sky. And it begins: an access of loneliness, intense, overwhelming, indescribable. Bleed, my heart! Bleed! Only, leave me the power to suffer.'

Back in Paris, he enjoyed the less transcendental and more substantial pleasures of Marie Recio. She was an indifferent mezzo-soprano who insisted that Berlioz use her at his concerts. He admitted that she sang like a cat, but she was his mistress and he could not refuse her. He began referring to her ominously as his 'second wife'. Marie took this appellation seriously and once sent a friend to Berlioz's home in Montmartre. When Harriet answered the door, Marie's friend said: 'I am looking for Madame Berlioz.' Harriet replied: 'I am Madame Berlioz.' Then the friend said: 'No, you are the old abandoned Madame Berlioz. I am looking for the young, the pretty, the adored Madame Berlioz.'

After 1844, Berlioz and Harriet lived apart. He stayed with Marie and her mother, but maintained both households. Harriet drank heavily. Berlioz still visited her and nursed her, but he began to spend long periods abroad. In a bizarre incident, Harriet was shot at. The bullet embedded itself in a tree two inches away from her. Soon after she suffered a series of strokes. Then Berlioz nursed her through cholera. It was a long slow decline. She died in 1854. Seven months later Berlioz married Marie, even though this greatly upset his son Louis.

However, Marie died in 1862. A few months after she was

buried Berlioz was offered a grander plot in Montmarte cemetery. He had her moved and was on hand to witness the exhumation. When the small cemetery where Harriet was buried was closed, he had her dug up too. 'Instead of lifting out the whole coffin,' he wrote, 'the gravedigger wrenched at the rotting planks, which came away with a hideous crack, exposing the coffin's contents. The gravedigger bent down and with his two hands picked up the head, already parted from the body – the ungarlanded, withered, hairless head of "poor Ophelia" – and placed it in the new coffin ready for it at the edge of the grave.'

The two dead women lay side by side in the new vault *à deux* for seven years. In 1869 their mutual husband joined the morbid *ménage à trois*.

14

DEBUSSY, AND PUSSY

Many descriptions of Achille-Claude Debussy portray him as effeminate, but he was feline rather than feminine. There is no mistaking the virility in his music and in his life. Like an old tom cat, he was solitary, sleek and extremely amorous. His feline quality extended to his work. One friend, André Suarès, wrote of him: 'Just as the cat rubs itself against the hand which strokes it, Debussy caresses his soul with the pleasure that he invokes.' Debussy spoke of music as feminine and he sought female beauty in it. He was a hedonist, a sybarite, a sensualist; his music voluptuous, warm, sensuous. And he loved cats. He had a number of Angora cats throughout his life, but each one was called *Line*.

As a child, Debussy learnt that love and music were inextricably intertwined. He was taught the piano by Madame de Fleurville, one of Chopin's many conquests. And he quickly put into action what he had learned at her knee.

At eighteen, Debussy was taken up the fifty-year-old Nadezhda von Meck, Tchaikovsky's benefactor. She told Tchaikovsky that her little 'Bussy' said he was twenty but looked sixteen. And with Bussy, von Meck did not want the remote, hands-off relationship she had with Tchaikovsky. She wanted her 'little Frenchman' to sit next to her on the piano stool, while they played something rousing by Tchaikovsky. 'I cannot play without the fever penetrating my innermost being,' she wrote, 'and I am unable to rid myself of these feelings for days on end.'

Debussy put a little strain on this relationship by falling for Madame von Meck's sixteen-year-old daughter Sonia. He proposed, she turned him down and he left the family home 'crying bitterly'. But love affairs for Debussy were like buses; there was always another one along in a minute.

A top civil servant, Eugène-Henry Vasnier, invited Debussy into his home to teach his daughter the piano. But Debussy preferred Vasnier's beautiful young wife Marie-Blanche. He lost his virginity to her. In gratitude, he wrote her a number of songs and, privately, dedicated them to her. One dedication read: 'To Madame Vasnier, These songs which she alone has brought to life and which will lose their enchanting grace if they are never again to come from her singing fairy lips. The eternally grateful author.'

Monsieur Vasnier tolerated their affair, if not actually encouraging it. He was eleven years older than his wife and, in a Parisian way, had a mistress or two of his own tucked away. He also kept an extensive library of erotic literature, where Debussy would often browse. Under the firm guidance of Madame Vasnier, Debussy won the *Prix de Rome* and headed off to Italy. Separated from his love, he grew restless. He wrote to Monsieur Vasnier, telling him how he was dying of boredom at the Villa Medici. His letters carry touching little PSs, enquiring after the health of Madame and Mademoiselle Vasnier. No letters from Debussy to Madame Vasnier have survived.

But Debussy was not in fact 'dying of boredom' at all. It was a ploy. The other students called him the 'Prince of Darkness' for his amorous exploits on the dark streets of Rome. Music was his principal weapon of seduction. After playing and singing one of his compositions, a 'beautiful young Parisian woman' found her way to his room, naked under a long overcoat. But in many ways, Debussy was still naive in the ways of love. He was puzzled that, when he pursued women, they rejected him. But as soon as he stopped pursuing them, they turned and chased after him.

'Wouldn't it have been better for them to begin where they ended?' he asked one woman.

'There has to be a minimum …', she replied.

'A minimum of what?'

'… a minimum of decency observed, for the woman at least,' she explained.

'Why do you need decency in a thing that fundamentally has none?' he enquired.

'One must know how to make oneself desired,' she said, 'to heighten one's value'.

'What makes you think, that men and women have different values in this thing?' he asked. 'What magnifies love, what makes it divine, is to be the creator of beauty and to put beauty into everything everywhere without distinction of sex or class.'

'To hear you talk,' she said, 'it would be up to the women to do the courting.'

'Here we have it, the big word has come out,' said Debussy. 'It is the idea that shocks you rather than the thing itself? How much simpler everything would be if you got over that.'

'How?'

'Well, imagine a woman who, feeling herself loved by a man whom she finds attractive – you women have such an amazing instinct for these things. Imagine her coming to him without all the superfluous chitchat, insipid compliments that only waste time and often weaken true love. She would simply say: "Take me, you big stupid thing."'

'But what an unflattering opinion he would have of her then?'

'It would be no more unflattering than the one she would have of him, my pretty lady,' Debussy said.

Despite these debates and other amorous distractions, Debussy missed Madame Vasnier terribly. One day, he could stand it no longer. He threw himself at the feet of the director in tears. When this did no good, he brandished a revolver and threatened to commit suicide if he was not allowed to go back to Paris. The following day he was on his way home. But his reception Chez Vasnier was cool. Madame Vasnier had been comforting herself in the arms of other young lovers and her husband advised Debussy to return to Rome. He did and soon salved his broken heart with a brief affair with Madame Hochon, a society lady who was visiting the Villa Medici with her husband. Debussy called her 'Loulou' and told her that she was his muse.

The six years following Debussy's return from Rome are known as his Bohemian period. He continued his affair with Madame Hochon, while at the same time grazing widely in the field of love. Then in 1889, he met the alley cat; Gaby. Her real name was Gabrielle Dupont, or Gabrielle Lhéry. She was the daughter of a dressmaker in Normandy who, at twenty-one, had come to Paris to enjoy her youth and freedom. A friend of Debussy, René Peter, said that he met her in a 'low dive', but others say it was a brothel. She had cat-like green eyes and was the first of a series of blondes whom he immortalized in his prelude *La fille aux cheveux de lin* (The Girl with the Flaxen Hair).

René Peter said that Gaby was the 'least frivolous blonde' he had ever met. She and Debussy lived together in a disorderly garret dominated by a borrowed Pleyel piano. Gaby was pretty and well built and he could not get enough of her in bed. But she also stood sentinel on him, keeping friends at bay, making sure that he worked and took in pupils. When money was short, she would work in a store or scrub floors to support him. They were happy and very much in love. 'If you ever ... you know ... with anyone else,' she told him, 'I will shoot you like a rabbit.' Debussy gave his word that he would never even look at another woman. But, of course, he did. He roamed like a tom cat but, like a tom cat, he always came home to eat, sleep and lick his wounds.

While Gaby scrimped and saved, Debussy gambled and hung out in low dives. He was a particular fan of the singer Jeanne Bloch, who sang bawdy songs in a state of near nudity. With a small cap cocked over one ear, she 'threw at her audience her drunken voice, her big stomach, her large breasts and her fat behind'.

In April 1890, Debussy began his opera *Rodrigue et*

Chimène. He dedicated it to Gaby, but he was already in the throes of another affair. For a while he was happy, but at the end of the year came 'the sadly unexpected end of the story, a banal event with silly little stories and words that should never have been spoken'. Debussy never revealed the name of his lover, but he did spell out the details of the end of the affair to a friend.

'I heard a strange change in her tone,' he said. 'At the very moment harsh words fell from her lips, I heard inside me all the adorable things she had said before. And these false sounds – alas, real – grated against those that sang inside me. They tore me to pieces in a way I could hardly understand. But I had to understand. I have left a great deal of myself caught on the thorns of her love and it will be a long time before I can threw myself back into music – the art that heals everything. What an irony it is. Music contains all one's sufferings, yet one knows those who are healed by it. Oh, but I loved her very much. Sadly my ardour was all the greater because I knew from the beginning that she would never fully be mine. It still remains to be seen if I was what she was really looking for, if it was not all for nothing. Despite everything, I am crying at the disappearance of the dream of this dream. But that is the least upsetting thing. There were days when I felt I should die while, at the same time, watching my own death. Oh! that I shall never relive them.'

This affair had been kept from Gaby and all correspondence referring to it was routed via his parents. He thought of running away to London, but Gaby, as always, got him back to work. He was always on the look out, though, for 'the dream of his dreams' – someone respectable and single that he could marry.

Meanwhile he began work on the opera *Pelléas et Mélisande,* based on the play by Maeterlinck. Debussy may have been drawn to it because it is stuffed full of women with flaxen hair. He had this thing about blondes. The heroine Mélisande lets down her hair like Rapunzel and Debussy incorporated an almost erotic hair-grooming song.

The opera was not well received. The story tells of the ill-starred marriage of a widower to a young girl and *Pelléas et*

Mélisande was quickly dubbed *Pédéraste et Mélisande* by the critics. A bed scene in the Third Act and a scene in the Fourth Act involving a boy and a sheep were cut by the censor.

It was around this time that Debussy fell for Catherine Stevens. She was the daughter of the Anglo-Belgian painter Alfred Stevens and he dedicated the first manuscript of *Fêtes galantes* to her. René Peter described her as 'one of the most radiant and charming figures to whom Debussy ever succumbed'. He asked her to marry him. 'In other circumstances, Debussy would probably have tried to lead matters to some less idealistic conclusion,' Peter wrote. 'But here he was dealing with a young woman of honour with whom there could be no question of lovemaking without marriage. So why not marry?'

Debussy turned on all the charm. He helped out during a family crisis and played her *Pelléas et Mélisande*. She was so impressed by his genius that she was even willing to overlook the gossip surrounding the fact he was still living with Gaby. 'I would have married him, despite everything that was being said about him at the time,' she said, 'if I had not met Henry.' Henry was a charming young doctor. Debussy was heartbroken. He asked for the manuscript of *Fêtes galantes* back and when it was published, Catherine was surprised to find that Debussy had dedicated it to another woman. 'This was his only revenge,' she said.

Once more, Gaby was there to console him. In gratitude, he dedicated the first sketch of *L'Après-midi d'un faune* to Gaby, but he was not going to dedicate much more of his life to her. The critics were outraged by *L'Après-midi d'un faune*. Everyone knows what a faun – not a young deer but a mythological creature, half man, half goat – gets up to on a hot afternoon. It was an outrage to public decency.

Then, after years of poverty and squalor, he had a success with the first performance of *La Damoiselle élue* and the music publisher Georges Hartmann gave him an advance of 500 francs a month for his future compositions. To celebrate, Debussy got engaged to the young singer Thérèse Roger, daughter of a well-known pianist. This cannot have come as much of a surprise to Gaby as Thérèse took the lead role in *La Damoiselle élue* and it is clear that they had been lovers for some time.

However, the engagement did not last long. Thérèse found him fickle. Debussy, it seems, was also engaged to a society woman at the time and, of course, he was still living with Gaby. They were still living together in 1897 when Gaby found a letter in the composer's pocket. It was from Alice Peter, the estranged wife of René Peter's brother. She was a notorious flirt and Debussy had been seen out on the town with her. The letter suggested that he was more than just her escort. It was clear from the letter, Debussy said, that the affair was 'well advanced'. Gaby got a revolver and shot herself. She was rushed to hospital, but her wound was mercifully superficial. 'All this is barbarous, unnecessary and does not change anything at all,' Debussy wrote to a friend. 'Kisses and caresses cannot be effaced with an India rubber. An adulterer's India rubber, now that would be quite an invention.'

Somehow Debussy managed to put things back together again and he continued living with Gaby. He also continued seeing Alice Peter and had time for a passionate fling with the beautiful, blue-eyed sculptress Camille Claudel, a pupil and former lover of Rodin. The affair had ended when Rodin would not leave his mistress-model Rose, with whom he shared his whole life. When Debussy played for Camille, she would touch his icy hands at the end of a piece and say: 'You don't need to explain.' But it was not long before Camille broke off the relationship, scared that any renewed drama surrounding Gaby would damage her reputation as an artist.

Throughout all this, the only consideration Debussy showed Gaby was sonorously blowing his nose before going to bed each night. He considered snoring the height of bad manners. Sleeping around was okay though.

Although Debussy loved women and the company of women, for intellectual stimulation he surrounded himself with men. The homo-sexual writer Marcel Proust was an admirer and more than once drove Debussy home in his carriage.

Debussy's relationships with men were close, often suspicious-ly so. One male friend, Erik Satie, four years his junior, said of Debussy: 'From the moment I saw him, I was drawn to him and wished to live always by his side. I had the pleasure of realiz-ing this wish for the next thirty years.'

Another long-term chum was the wealthy young poet and librettist Pierre Louÿs, who was eight years Debussy's junior. They met in 1893, when Louÿs was twenty-three. They even planned to live together and often embarked on amorous escapades as a twosome. When travelling, Louÿs always report-ed back his erotic adventures in long letters. In Algeria, he seduced the exotic Meriem. 'She is the most beautiful, the most graceful and the most delicate being I have ever seen,' he wrote. 'Unfortunately it is no more possible to drag this little animal along in a civilized city than to present a panther in a drawing room. I beat her like a little dog, but rest assured I will not spoil her for you. I beat her and not with a flower.'

Louÿs returned to Paris with a burnous and endless stories of his erotic discoveries which enchanted Debussy. He pub-lished *Chansons de Bilitis*, 143 prose poems outlining the life of a courtesan in ancient Greece. Debussy wrote a work of the same name years later, after Meriem's younger sister, the volup-tuous Zohra, turned up in Paris.

After the publication of *Chansons de Bilitis,* Louÿs headed off to Seville were he spent three months compiling a list of teenage girls who he had 'exercised in the same art as that of Don José and Carmen in Bizet's opera'. Debussy wrote back that he hoped that these little girls had more original charms than the latest libretto Louÿs had supplied. Later, they had a falling out when Louÿs refused to write the libretto to the opera *Cendrelune* which Debussy had planned, because the theme, the triumph of chastity over love, was an anathema to him.

When Louÿs married in June 1899, he practically apolo-gized to Debussy. But five months later, Debussy married Rosalie Texier, a fashion model; a partnership of fame not dis-similar to rock star–supermodel liaisons of the late twentieth century.

DEBUSSY, AND PUSSY

Mademoiselle Texier was known as Lilly, Lily or Lilo. At first, Gaby thought that Lily was just another of his peccadilloes and befriended her. But soon she was his constant companion in the bars and cafés of Montmartre, and became friends with the other musicians, writers and painters he knew. Debussy left Gaby, after dedicating one last composition to her, and moved in with Lily. Their cohabitation was not a success but nevertheless they got engaged. Debussy threatened to kill himself unless Lily married him. His family was against it, and so were his friends. The witnesses even refused to turn up to the wedding breakfast, which was paid for by a piano lesson Debussy had given the morning of the wedding. But the sex was good. Debussy wrote to his publisher Georges Hartmann saying that his summer had been unhappy, save for 'tender compensations'. 'And I must warn you of my marriage to the aforesaid tender compensations,' he wrote. She was, of course, 'incredibly blonde, beautiful as in a legend'. 'In love,' wrote a friend, 'Debussy is particularly sensitive to the "decorative" side.'

Debussy wrote a play called *Brothers in Art* about a lecherous painter who stifles the career of a talented young pupil by seducing his wife, which was based on his relationship with Lily. It was never performed, but the manuscript was found in a second-hand bookshop after his death.

When Lily became ill, Debussy scarcely left her side. 'What poor little creatures women are,' wrote Louÿs. 'If they don't marry, they become ill because of their chastity, so they say. And when they try to have a child, it's even worse.' Debussy told his friends, when they saw tears in Lily's eyes, that they could not have children. This was another weakness in their relationship. That they were deeply in love is beyond dispute, but essentially Lily was a second Gaby – great in bed but intellectually his inferior.

After five years of marriage, Debussy met Emma Bardac, the wife of a financier. She was another blonde with green, cat-like eyes. She was also a brilliant talker and his intellectual equal – everything Debussy desired in one package. Conversation with her reminded him of all that was lacking in

Lily, whose voice, Debussy complained, now 'froze the blood in my veins'.

Debussy eloped with Emma to Jersey, where he wrote *L'isle joyeuse*. Her husband dismissed the affair, probably because he had his own fish to fry. Besides Emma had already had an affair with the composer Gabriel Fauré, which had started during Fauré's honeymoon. When Emma eloped with Debussy, Bardac simply said: 'She's just treating herself to the latest fashion in composers. But I am the one with the money. She'll be back.'

However tolerant Monsieur Bardac was, the affair did not play well in the papers. Debussy was a famous composer throwing over his working-class wife for a society matron. It was a scandal. Lily shot herself, though not fatally. When Debussy visited her in hospital, she said that she could not live without him. She had been very young when they met and she had built her whole life around him. He told her not to be discouraged 'after all you are still young and pretty'. This remark was seen by the newspapers as 'an exhortation to prostitution'.

To add fuel to the scandal, Debussy's father was accused of stealing 200 francs from Lily's night table in the hospital. 'What of it?' he said. 'She only has a few hours to live.' But Lily did not die and Debussy weathered the storm. Audaciously, he dedicated his latest composition to *la petite mienne* – 'my little one', the five-foot Emma. But Debussy's behaviour towards Lily cost him his friends and Emma found herself disinherited. Her family did not approve of them living together openly. They even had a child.

Emma's husband eventually conceded that she would not be back, despite his money, and granted her a divorce so she and Debussy could marry. The wedding prompted another bout of notoriety. It coincided with the opening of a play *La Femme Nue* (The Naked Woman) by Henry Bataille. Ostensibly, the play is about an artist who abandons his mistress-model for a princess, but everyone knew that it was really about Debussy, Lily and Emma, especially as the artist urges his abandoned mistress to return to prostitution and she shoots herself. It ran longer than the Debussys' honeymoon and was revived regularly throughout their lifetime.

In many ways, the scandal helped promote Debussy to stardom. He was approached by Italian writer and proto-Fascist Gabrielle d'Annunzio, who invited him to collaborate on a musical version of the mystery play *Le Martyre de Saint Sébastien*. Debussy readily accepted. 'How could I not love your poetry?' Debussy wrote to d'Annunzio. 'The mere thought of working with you gives me a sort of fever.' D'Annunzio planned to create a sensation with *Le Martyre de Saint Sébastien*.

'Have the characters in mystery plays ever been played in the nude?' he asked. When told that traditionally all the parts, both male and female, in mystery plays were played by men, d'Annunzio said: 'Then I will take my revenge for the feminine sex and have *Le Martyre de Saint Sébastien* performed by naked women.' He had in mind Ida Rubinstein, the star of Diaghilev's *Cleopatra*. 'Ida Rubinstein will play Saint Sebastian,' he said. 'Tall, slender and flat chested, she is absolutely perfect for this role. Where could I find an actor whose body was so ethereal?'

Debussy's ballet *Jeux* for Diaghilev's Ballets Russes also caused a scandal. It concerned a young man and two girls searching for a lost tennis ball. 'The search for the tennis ball is forgotten and the young man flirts, first with one girl, then with the other,' Debussy said. 'But as the first girl sulks and the young man hesitates, the two girls make love to each other to console themselves. Finally, the young man decides, rather than lose either of them, to have both.' A wholesome enough story, but in the hands of the great bisexual ballet dancer Nijinsky, it became positively risqué. 'Immorality passes through the legs of the girls and ends in a pirouette,' Debussy wrote of the first performance. 'Sensuality is overflowing its banks. These Russians are like Syrian cats.' Nijinsky's wife said: 'Love becomes, not the fundamental driving force, but merely a game, as it is in the twentieth century. Here love is nothing more than an emotion, a pastime, which can be found among three as well as among the same sex.'

When the ballet was performed in London, the critics missed all this naughtiness and their reviews concentrated on the fact that the ball used on stage was bigger than a regulation-sized tennis ball and that Nijinsky's tennis trousers were not cut according to the classic pattern.

Slowly the erotic flame that had fired Debussy's music died. He became an establishment figure – *Le Maître, Le Musicien Français* – mocked by the younger generation of Bohemian composers who came after him. The flame of his life finally went out at the end of the World War I. But cats, it is said, have nine lives and the alley cats of Montmartre in particular know how to fill the nights with their music. And it was in Montmartre that Debussy, the great Bohemian, was most at home.

'Here, even the prostitutes scream out in ecstasy,' he wrote.

15

BIZET'S CARMEN

Georges Bizet was a precocious child. Before he was ten he was accepted as a student by the Paris Conservatoire, where he was taught by the composer Charles Gounod. Gounod was known as the philandering monk and would kiss anyone of either sex at the slightest provocation.

Bizet modelled himself on his mentor who, as a young man, had fallen in love with Mendelssohn's sister Fanny, who was the wife of the artist Wilhelm Hensel and a dozen years his senior. Next he bedded Pauline Viardot, mistress of Chopin and Turgenev and wife of the critic Louis Viardot. He actually lived with Pauline, Louis (or Loulou) and Turgenev for a while in a notorious *ménage à quatre*. The happy foursome gradually became unsettled by Gounod's philandering.

The affair ended in what Louis Viardot regarded as the ultimate act of treachery. Gounod announced his engagement to Anne Zimmermann, the daughter of his teacher at the Conservatoire. At the time, Pauline who was pregnant. Gounod had the good manners to postpone the wedding until Pauline had given birth. But the Zimmermanns snubbed the Viardots by omitting to send them an invitation.

Throughout Gounod's marriage he chased young girls – even schoolgirls, Bizet said. Later, Gounod left his wife to live with the beautiful English singer Georgina Thomas and her husband Captain Harry Weldon.

Gounod immediately took to the young Bizet. Bizet quickly followed his teacher's example and showed that he was precocious not just in music. Naturally, he won the *Prix de Rome*. He did not mind leaving behind his lovers in Paris. They could always be replaced. 'As regards the fair sex, I am less and less the French cavalier,' Bizet wrote. 'I see nothing in that beyond the satisfaction of self-esteem. I would willingly risk my life for a friend, but would think myself an idiot if I lost a hair of my head on account of a woman.' He roundly condemned a cousin who jilted his fiancée to marry a serving girl he had got pregnant, saying that he was 'cowardly to renounce his position in order to wallow in miserable poverty'. He deplored 'all the transports of the thing called love, without understanding them'.

Bizet boasted of carrying on two love affairs at the same time, and he too got a serving girl pregnant. Her name was Marie Reiter and she was the Bizet family's maid, who comforted the young Bizet after the death of his mother. Exactly nine months after Madame Bizet's funeral, Marie gave birth to a son, Jean, who Bizet openly acknowledged was his. But there was no question of Bizet marrying the girl. Instead he again followed in Gounod's footsteps, and married the daughter of one of his teachers at the Conservatoire. But Marie stayed on with the family, becoming Bizet's wife's maid and nursing Bizet himself through his final illness.

In 1865, Bizet met the Comtesse de Moreton de Chabrillan on a train. She had just bought a plot of land adjoining his summer cottage at Le Vésinet and was building a house there. She was no ordinary countess. She was born Céleste Vénard. Her mother was a woman of easy virtue; her father a passing soldier. She left home in her early teens to escape the amorous attentions of her mother's new lover. Beginning her career as a prostitute, she became an actress under the name of Célest Mogador, a circus rider, a novelist and playwright, though she had no formal education, could not spell to save her life and could barely hold a pen. Nevertheless, aristocrats, great composers and great writers, including Alfred de Musset, worshipped at her feet. At the age of thirty, she scandalized Paris by marrying the Comte Lionel de Moreton de Chabrillan, a prominent diplomat. When he died four years later, she returned to the stage to pay off his debts. And at forty, she had a triumph with the dramatization of one of her own novels, adapted for the stage by Alexandre Dumas *père*. She was, naturally, a friend of Lola Montez.

'Moderation is not part of my nature,' she wrote. 'My life has been one long excess. When I want something I am willing to gamble ten or twenty years of my life to get it as quickly as possible. I have always been capricious and proud. Among women who have a tendency to say yes, no one gets more pleasure than I do from saying no. So the men to whom I give the most are those who ask the least of me'.

Bizet must have asked for little, for she certainly did not say no to him. He would knock on her window on his way home from the station late at night. This annoyed Céleste's mother who once emptied the contents of a chamber pot on his head. His music excited Céleste physically, but she warned Bizet not to get serious about her.

'My heart has never dreamt of living in another heart that is more like a lodging house, where one is put up for the night,' she chided.

'I might give my other lodgers notice,' said Bizet.

'But one of them has a lease and she is the wife of your best friend.'

'I think her lease is up,' Bizet replied. 'I don't love her any more.'

'Maybe you simply love her less than you did,' Céleste counselled.

Céleste was fourteen years older than Bizet and took almost a motherly interest in him. Nevertheless, many musicologists believe that the proud and capricious Comtesse de Moreton de Chabrillan was the model for Carmen. However, Céleste was to become a problem for Bizet when he finally fell in love with someone who would make a suitable wife. 'No more parties. No more mistresses. All that is finished, absolutely finished,' he wrote to a friend. 'I am talking seriously. I have met an adorable girl. In two years, she will be my wife.'

The adorable girl was eighteen-year-old Geneviève Halévy, the second daughter of his teacher Jacques Fromental Halévy. But the engagement was broken off not long after it had been announced. The Halévys had heard that Bizet had been entertaining the notorious Céleste in his bed. They denounced him as a 'bohemian and an outsider'. They changed their minds when he had a success with both *La jolie fille de Perth* and *Roma*. But the engagement was only resumed when Bizet promised his mother-in-law to be that he would never allow 'women of the theatre' to cross his threshold and publicly proclaimed his agreement with Dumas *fils'* statement that unfaithfulness is as deplorable in a husband as in a wife.

They married in 1869 and three years later they had a son, Jacques, but the marriage was not a great success. They had a trial separation before patching it up again. An American girl who took piano lessons with Bizet while he was finishing Carmen found him 'as uneasy as a lion in a cage'. Sensibly, his wife went to stay with her cousin Ludovic in Saint-Germain when *Carmen* went into rehearsal. The backstage gossip at the Opéra-Comique was that Bizet was sleeping with Galli-Marié, the singer who created the title role. For the second time, it seems, Bizet was bedding his Carmen.

News of the scandalous nature of Bizet's new work spread and he was quickly created a chevalier of the *Légion d'honneur* before it opened. At the première, the first act was applauded. But the end of the fourth act was greeted with silence. *Carmen* was written off as a flop.

The public was shocked and outraged by the subject matter of the opera, with its fascinating, unscrupulous heroine and her jealous, dependent lover. After a few months, though, it was recognized as a masterpiece, but by then Bizet was dead. Never a well man, he went swimming in the Seine and came down with a fever which triggered an attack of his already weakened heart.

16

THE BLUE DANUBE

Vienna, capital of the Austro-Hungarian empire, was a city of decadent pleasure. With political turmoil all around them, everyone was happy to live for today. At the end of the nineteenth century, half of Vienna's children were born out of wedlock. The narrow streets around the great dancehalls – the Sperl, Mondschein and Apollo – swarmed with prostitutes. The dancing itself often went well beyond being the vertical expression of a horizontal desire. And the men who set the city throbbing were the Strauss family.

The dance they inspired was banned for a time in France. In England, even Lord Byron railed against it. A French tourist described the shocking lasciviousness of it all: 'A young maiden, lightly clad, throws herself into the arms of a young man. He presses her to his heart with such vehemence that they soon feel the beating of their hearts and their heads and feet begin to spin. This is what is known as the waltz.'

Johann Strauss was a lowly fiddle player in the orchestra of the drunken, womanizing bandleader Ignatz Pamer when he met fellow musician Josef Lanner. They lived together and, due to poverty, shared each other's clothes. Lanner was eager to branch out on his own and Strauss joined his ensemble. It was a huge success and Lanner was soon known as 'The Father of the Viennese Waltz'. While Lanner wrote the waltzes and conducted, Strauss lead the string section and occupied himself with an innkeeper's dark-haired daughter, Anna Streim. She was soon 'heavy with child'. They were forced to marry and their first child was duly named Johann.

With a wife and child to support, Strauss needed more than a fiddle-player's wages. He had already written a couple of waltzes but, for commercial reasons, they had been presented as Lanner's. Strauss now wanted money and recognition for his compositions. The two friends fell out. Their partnership ended in a fight in the ballroom of *Zum Bock* (The Ram) when the establishment's famous giant mirror was smashed.

Strauss formed his own band and was soon driving Vienna's dance craze to a new climax at the Sperl, where he became known as 'The Tyrant of the Waltz'. While Lanner stayed in Vienna, living discreetly in the suburbs with his pretty young mistress, Strauss took the show on the road. He toured relentlessly, leaving his wife and children at home alone for months on end. Everywhere he went he was a hit with the ladies. He eventually collapsed with exhaustion after visiting England to play during the coronation of Queen Victoria.

When, after months of convalescence, the gaunt and debilitated Strauss played again in Vienna, the women in the dancehalls openly sobbed. Young Johann was eager to follow in his father's footsteps. But when he picked up a violin, his father grabbed it from his hands and smashed it. He wanted something better for his son than a musician's life, full of drunken brawls, one-night stands and financial insecurity.

Strauss the elder's illness forced him to confine his activities to Vienna. This brought his philandering closer to home and so made his sex life more problematic as he could no longer up sticks and move on to the next city after a *petit amour*. He found himself pursued by a groupie, a hatmaker named Emilie Trampusch. Wherever he played she would be there looking up at him in admiration. She was pretty and young with a nubile body. He took her for midnight rides in closed carriages and late suppers in secluded inns. Soon she was pregnant and all Vienna knew it.

Anna clung on. This was not the first time her husband had succumbed to temptation and she hoped it would blow over. But when he had his bastard son christened Johann, she snapped and confronted him. Either he must leave Emilie, or her. Strauss stared at her without saying a word, then turned and walked out of her life forever. The next day he rented an apartment on the seedy Kumpfgasse for himself, Emilie and his second family. It was to be his home until he died. He had given up a comfortable home for a dingy cramped apartment, which was soon crammed with five illegitimate children. Money was needed to feed this swelling brood and before long Strauss was out on the road again.

With his father out of the way, the young Johann was now free to pursue a musical career. At the age of nineteen, he applied for his first licence to perform music in public. Normally, such a licence would not be issued to a minor. Nor would such a young musician have the capital to put an orchestra together. But all Johann needed was the Strauss name. The whole of Vienna turned out to see the 'new Strauss' and he was a huge success. On one occasion the audience forced him to give nineteen encores of one of his compositions. He was also just as great a hit with the ladies.

Strauss *père* returned to Vienna to go head to head with his son. He still had his fanatical followers. He was playing at the Sperl when he came down with scarlet fever. A messenger came to the Strauss house and told Anna to come quickly. Full of trepidation, she followed the messenger to the Kumpfgasse where she found the naked body of her husband lying on a bale of straw in the empty apartment. In panic, Emilie had packed up everything – children, clothes, furniture – and fled. Despite the younger Johann's efforts to help her, she was reduced to earning a living as a water carrier and there are dubious reports of her stealing the flowers and ornamental lanterns from her lover's grave.

After Johann senior's death, younger brothers Josef and Eduard followed Johann junior into the music business. Josef became renowned as the 'Schubert of the Waltz' and was happily married. Eduard, like Johann, became a favourite of the women in the dancehalls. They called him *Der schöne Edit* ('Handsome Eddy') and would fight over his discarded gloves.

Johann's popularity with women caused problems. At the Russian resort of Pavlovsk, one Russian nobleman challenged Strauss to a duel because his wife had sent the composer a bunch of flowers. Strauss invited the nobleman up to his room. It was filled with flowers. The beautiful débutante Olga Smirnizki who fell for him, but her aristocratic family did not approve of the match. Another family approved of his liaison with their daughter and tried to hijack him into marriage. But he managed to escape from the church and took refuge in the Austrian Embassy.

A succession of beautiful women passed through his life, and by the time he was thirty-seven he had broken off more than a dozen engagements. Then he shocked Vienna by marrying the forty-seven-year-old Jetti Treffz (she only admitted to forty-four). 'She was as graceful as a reed' and had a voice that he compared with Jenny Lind's. Both Berlioz and Mendelssohn had been smitten and dedicated songs to her. She knew George Sand and the Comtesse d'Agoult and made her way as a singer thanks to a number of wealthy 'patrons'.

When Strauss met her, she was the mistress of Baron Moritz Todesco, and mother to his daughters. Jetti invited him to play at a ball in Todesco's palace, and at the ball they fell in love. But they managed to keep their affair a secret until the day of the wedding. Even the best man and the few close friends that were invited only got their invitations the night before. Viennese society was shocked, but Baron Todesco took it in his stride. He thanked her for her love, assured her of his continued friendship and endowed her with a small fortune in recompense.

The imperial court cooled towards Strauss, as it had towards his father after he had left Anna. Nevertheless, they awarded him the title of *Hofkapellmeister*. The Court Chamberlain in Vienna grudgingly noted: 'Since becoming a successful music director, he adopted a prodigal and unseemly mode of life and has only recently shown any tendency towards a more orderly existence.'

THE BLUE DANUBE

Despite the furore caused by their marriage, Strauss and Jetti were the perfect couple. She attended to the mundane chores – paying the bills, looking after the kitchen, copying the music for the orchestra – while he attended to his career. Jetti in effect became his manager and persuaded him to leave the running of the world famous Strauss orchestra to his brothers and concentrate on composition. In 1867 he presented the *Blue Danube* but it was a flop, largely because the timeless charm of the waltz was hidden under a lame libretto. It was only when the accompanying male voice choir was dropped that it became an international hit.

Despite the obvious good she was doing for him, there was a tension between Anna Strauss and her daughter-in-law. Anna looked down on Jetti as the ex-mistress of a *nouveau riche* Jew, and sadly the situation was only resolved in 1870 when Anna died. Eight years later, Jetti died of a stroke brought on, in part, by the reappearance of a long-lost son. Strauss was grief-stricken. He could not even bring himself to attend the funeral, which had to be organized by his younger brother Eduard. Instead he sought consolation in a prolonged bout of promiscuous sex.

In a matter of weeks Strauss had become engaged to Fräulein Ernestine Henriette Angelika Diettrich of Cologne, a pretty young singer. She was twenty; Strauss fifty-three. Some believed that she had been his mistress before Jetti died. The family banker Albert Strauss (no relation) said: 'The situation seems to be dating back some time and seems to have developed already during Jetti's lifetime.'

Angelika 'Lili' Diettrich was blonde and sensual with a slender body. She was said to combine the qualities of Eve and Jezebel. They were married six weeks after the announcement of their engagement. It was not a popular move. Angelika was soon dubbed Diabolika and it was said that she was 'certainly the most disastrous libretto on which the master could devote his energies'.

Lili soon escaped the solitude of Schönau, the country estate where Strauss composed, and was seen in Vienna in the company of handsome young army officers. When she returned home, there were rows. He accused her of being unfaithful. She riposted that Strauss was 'old'. Then she left for good and moved in with Frank Steiner, the son of one of Strauss's friends. But pretty soon Steiner grew tired of her and kicked her out. When Strauss refused to have her back, she played the wronged wife. No one believed her and she died unmourned in 1919.

Strauss's unfortunate fling with Lili had not put him off young women though – far from it. He immediately fell for Adele Deutsch, the widowed daughter-in-law of his banker, Albert Strauss. Despite being a widow, Adele was still an attractive young woman. Soon their engagement was announced. This caused another scandal because Strauss was a Catholic and so, theoretically, could not divorce. Lili was certainly in no mood to be abandoned. Also Adele was Jewish and anti-Semitism was rife in Vienna at that time.

Despite the opposition of his family and Lili's tenacious fight to hold on to him, Strauss would not be thwarted. He took Adele to Coburg, where he became a Protestant and was promptly granted a divorce. They married and returned to Austria.

Strauss was now fifty-eight and said his new marriage was 'the best of all'. Certainly his letters to his new young bride are full of a passion that would shame a man forty years his junior. When travelling, he would send letters to her written at midnight and she became so important to him that he dropped all his other mistresses. 'The poetry of love, be it Catholic, Protestant or Jewish consists of ardent, soulful living,' he wrote. 'Friendship? I cannot imagine it because I am not in that disconsolate state where I must bid farewell to earthly love. On this point, I will accept no reproach because I swear to you that to this very minute I have been faithful. I astound myself, but this is not a miracle because you are close to my heart.' He signsed off the letter: 'Millions of embraces from your Jean.'

Their affair was so ardent that friends referred to her as 'Cosima in three-quarter time'. In his new state of marital bliss, he produced some of his finest work. Even the authorities forgave him for abandoning the official Catholic faith and, temporarily, relinquishing his Austrian citizenship to become a resident in Coburg, so he was allowed to keep his new title of *Hofballmusikdirektor*.

The actress Sarah Bernhardt had wanted to be in Vienna for the celebration of his fifty years in music. He was seventy. 'Even if I run the risk of making Frau Strauss jealous,' she wrote, 'I would put my arms around the master and kiss and kiss him without end. This is the one way in which a woman can pay homage to him.'

Strauss certainly retained his extraordinary vitality in composition and performance until his death in 1899 at the age of seventy-three, and there is no reason to suppose that he lost it in bed.

17

OFFENBACH IN THE UNDERWORLD

In Paris Jacques Offenbach was seen as the King of the Boulevardiers. 'I have two-no, three-passions,' he once said. 'Cigars, women, and gambling as well.' But in true Parisian style, he had a long and successful marriage to a woman who had the good sense to turn a blind eye to his misdemeanours. His grandson wrote: 'Precisely because of the love for his family; the life of Offenbach (if we ignore his regular and routine peccadilloes) passed without incident between his desk, his rehearsals and his travelling; one could not make a novel out of his adventures, and today I know of absolutely nothing confidential which I have to conceal, forget or censor.' But Arsène Houssaye at the Comédie-Française knew him better. 'What a gay companion he was when his eyes did not stray from his wife (what a respectable beauty she was!),' he recalled. 'But, alas, I have seen him torn apart by cruel passion.'

Jacques Offenbach was born Jakob Offenbach in Cologne in 1819. Offenbach was not his family name. His father, Isaac Juda Eberst, was a music teacher who had changed his name when he moved to Cologne from Offenbach-on-Main. The young Jakob was a prodigy and his father showed him off and his older brother Julius – later Jules – in taverns, dancehalls and beer gardens.

When Offenbach was fourteen, his father decided that he

177

and his brother should go to Paris to complete their musical education. Isaac took them to the Conservatoire, which was run by the director Luigi Cherubini with an iron grip. He insisted that male and female pupils use separate entrances to the Conservatoire, so 'any hint of scandalous dalliance could be avoided'. Berlioz once entered by the door reserved for women and a porter and Cherubini himself chased the licentious inter-loper around a library table, before catching him and throwing him out.

By the age of twenty-three, Offenbach was ready to give a concert of his own music. It took place at Salle Hertz, a new concert hall built by the pianist Henri Hertz. Hertz had just become a lover of the Junoesque Polish beauty Thérèse Lachmann, who was known as 'Madame Hertz'. Unfortunately, she was a woman of extravagant tastes, especially in men. After she had extracted Hertz's vast fortune from him, she left to build a huge mansion on the Champs-Elysées, which is now the Travellers' Club. She became a spy and an adventuress and, as the Marquise de Païva, became the most notorious courtesan of the Second Empire. Meanwhile, Hertz headed for California with the bizarre notion that he could regain his fortune playing to the miners and fruit-pickers there.

Offenbach established his reputation immediately and was soon in demand, especially with young ladies. Although he was matchstick thin with bony fingers, a beaky nose and straggling hair, he had a ready wit and could make them laugh. He already had a reputation for his conquests among the chorus girls and bit-part actresses he knew.

At twenty-four, he was invited to a party given in honour of a hero of the latest uprising in Spain. Offenbach played the piano and sang, and made a deep impression on sixteen-year-old Herminie, step-daughter of the host John Mitchell, who ran the St James's Theatre in London. Six months later, Offenbach asked for permission to marry Herminie. The Mitchells were taken aback. Offenbach had no money, though it was clear that he had already embarked on a successful career. To show his good faith, Offenbach dedicated the ballad *A Toi* to Herminie.

The Mitchells were impressed. They gave their permission for the couple to marry on two conditions. Offenbach must make a successful tour of England and he must renounce his Jewish faith and become a Catholic. He did both and the young couple were married in Paris in 1844. The newspapers announced that he had bagged a pretty, young heiress. Herminie was certainly pretty and young, but she was no heiress.

They set up home in Montmartre and within a year their first child was born. Four more soon followed, but success was still ten years away. Herminie devotedly scrimped and saved, while he scoured the boulevards in search of pleasure and inspiration. Offenbach came into his own after Napoléon III seized power. In December 1852, Louis-Napoléon proclaimed the Second Empire, an era notorious for its debauchery, luxury and shameless immorality. Offenbach effortlessly caught the mood of the times.

He discovered the legendary beauty Hortense Schneider. One of his singers had taken her as mistress, and when Offenbach set eyes on her he was immediately captivated and decided to audition her there and then. He hired her for the unheard-of sum of 200 francs a month before she had finished her first song. Hortense quickly abandoned her singer. Later she spread herself widely among those even richer and more influential. When royalty crowded into Paris for the *Expositions Universelles*, another courtesan nicknamed her *Passage des Princes*, after the street of the same name.

The story is told of the licentious Duc de Morny – or, in other versions, the Khedive of Egypt – who asked his servant to bring him Schneider. He waited bathed and scented, only to be confronted by the rotund figure of Paul Schneider, the steel magnate. She was certainly a mistress of both Bertie, the Prince of Wales who became Edward VII, and Prince Jérôme Bonaparte. Hortense was a natural choice for Offenbach's *La Belle Hélène*.

As Offenbach grew more wealthy, he was a regular fixture in the restaurants and cafés of Paris. But every Friday night, he had dinner at home with his family. Friends from the theatre were invited over afterwards. But only male members of the cast would be invited. Actresses were something he dealt with discreetly out of the house. After dinner, Herminie and her daughters would retire early while the men told risqué stories. She also shielded her daughters from the theatre and the naughty operettas their father put on.

The greatest of these was *Orpheus in the Underworld*. Offenbach wanted Hortense for it but, by this time, she had priced herself out of the role by demanding 500 francs a month. Besides she was too busy squandering the fortune of the young Duc de Gramont-Caderousse, who boasted when they met that he had already blown a million francs on the gaming tables. He had tuberculosis and was determined to kill himself quickly with wild living, rather than become a slave to his illness. With the aid of Hortense and a string of other lovers, he succeeded, leaving her 50,000 francs and another million for the disabled son she had born him.

Orpheus was a huge success right across Europe. When Napoleon III's troops beat the Austrians at the Battle of Magenta, they marched home to the tunes of *Orpheus*. The following year, Offenbach was granted French citizenship.

Offenbach followed *Orpheus* with his only ballet; *Le Papillon*. It was to be his first production at the Opéra, a sought-after accolade. The butterfly of the title was danced by the young ballerina Emma Livry. While rehearsing for her next production, her wispy skirt fluttered dangerously near a gaslight and she went up in flames. Firemen threw a wet blanket over her, but her burns were so severe that she died in agony eight months later.

The success of *Orpheus* and *Le Papillon* allowed Offenbach to buy a holiday home, the Villa Orphée at Étretat on the Channel coast. Many of the actresses and singers Offenbach knew particularly well bought cottages in the vicinity. He would visit them if he needed to relieve the depression that began to dog him, or Herminie would summon them if he got too unbearable.

His relationships with other women were usually brief and

to the point. They never affected his marriage, though they certainly affected his wealth. The Viennese journalist Friedrich Uhl once wrote that Offenbach 'would have died rich ... if it hadn't been for the women and the damned card games'. To be fair, Offenbach was just as generous to his wife as his mistresses, often surprising her with jewellery instead of paying the bills.

However, there was one young woman who came close to rocking the boat. He was forty-four when he saw the twenty-year-old Zulma Bouffar on stage at Bad Homburg. Immediately he went to her dressing room to introduce himself. She had been born in the Midi to a theatrical family. At the age of twelve, she was hired by a German company and found herself singing risqué Parisian songs in one of the restaurants in Cologne where Offenbach had played as a child. He hired her as a singer and took her as his lover. They stayed together for twelve years or more, even though, during that time, other lovers would come and go. Herminie certainly suspected something and complained to friends.

When Offenbach went to Prague with Zulma, he went to the lengths of getting a friend to plant a story in the newspaper saying that Zulma and other members of Offenbach's company not involved in the Prague production would be performing in Nantes, knowing that Herminie would see the piece. He begged his friend and the newspaper's editor 'to be totally discreet'.

On stage, Offenbach became more daring. In *La Belle Hélène*, Hortense Schneider appeared on stage in a brief, gauze tunic, and was plainly naked underneath it. The fame the role brought her guaranteed a long and wealthy retirement.

Offenbach went even further with his 1865 production of Orpheus when he cast the notorious English courtesan Cora Pearl, born Emma Crouch in Plymouth, as Cupid. She was another of the *grandes horizontales* of Paris to have slept with the Prince of Wales. Napoléon III once paid £10,000 for a single night with her, and it was said that she 'possessed such a talent for voluptuous eccentricities that Prince Gortchakoff described her as the acme of sensual delight'. On one occasion, she had herself served up on a silver salver at a gentlemen's dinner party. When the lid was removed, she was revealed naked except for a string of pearls and a sprig of parsley.

At the time, Cora was entertaining Prince Napoleon, a dissolute cousin of the Emperor. This caused problems and because of her royal liaison she had to have a dressing room set apart from the others with a private entrance. On stage, she appeared draped head to foot in diamonds. When Hortense appeared in a similar dress, someone in the audience remarked that she must have discovered a diamond mine. 'A mine ... and miners,' said another wit.

Cora was paralyzed with stage fright. Her voice was thin and her English accent grating. A number of aristocrats in the audience – largely her clients – shouted bravo. But when militant students from the Left Bank protested noisily at this outrage to public morals, Cora left the theatre for good, once again deploying her talents solely for private performances.

In operas such as *Bluebeard*, *La Vie Parisienne* and *The Hundred Virgins*, Offenbach repeatedly returned to sex as his theme. However, he overstretched himself to the point of bankruptcy. But that did not stop him continuing with the same panache. In three weeks, he wrote three full-length operas and one one-acter. He drove everywhere in a carriage and was seen dining at the best restaurants. And as one visitor put it, it seemed that the whole of Paris was his mistress.

A quick tour of America restored his fortunes and the Offenbachs moved to a new apartment. Above them lived a doctor and his pretty young wife. Late one night, on his way back from the theatre, Offenbach burst into the couple's apartment and saw her undressing. He explained that he simply got out of the lift on the wrong floor. But knowing his reputation, the doctor pursued him with a revolver.

After writing *Tales of Hoffmann*, Offenbach died of a heart attack in 1880. When the comedian Léonce, who had played Pluto in *Orpheus*, turned up the next day, the concierge explained: 'Monsieur Offenbach is dead. He died very gently, without realizing it.' 'Oh,' said Léonce gravely. 'How annoyed he'll be when he finds out.'

Herminie had been with her husband for thirty-six years and found she could not live without him. Her grief never lifted and she died in 1887. Zulma felt much the same. Their affair had still been going strong in 1875, when they had a discreet holiday together in Aix-les-Bains. She continued to appear in his productions, but slowly her star began to wane. She moved into theatre management, but lost her money and ended her days in a home for retired thespians.

18

A BRUSH WITH THE BARBER

His uncle, a barber, suggested that the young Rossini join the ranks of castrati to preserve his delightful singing voice, but he was saved. 'My brave mother would not consent at any price,' he said. Throughout his life, many women offered him similar tender protection.

Gioacchino Rossini never forgot his brush with the barber. One of his early operas was *L'equivoco stravagante*. This translates directly as 'The ridiculous misunderstanding', but it also means 'The eccentric person of dubious sex'. It tells of Ermanno, a tutor, who falls in love with his pupil Ernestina. But Ernestina falls for the young aristocrat Buralicchio. To get rid of his rival, Ermanno tells Buralicchio that Ernestina is not only a boy, but a *castrato* and a deserter from the army.

The opera was a failure, but Rossini was a success with the prima donna Maria Marcolini, who helped advance his career. She was the mistress of Napoleon's brother Lucien Bonaparte. But few doubted she entertained Rossini sexually too. She certainly inspired him. According to Stendhal: 'It was at her side, on her piano and within the walls of her villa near Bologna that he wrote some of his finest compositions.' La Marcolini was, Stendhal tells us, 'a woman in the fullest flower of her youth and talent, who swept him away from the great ladies that were his first protectresses'.

185

Unfortunately, he was successful with these other women as well. Some of them were not so great and they certainly did not offer him protection. It was around this time that he contracted gonorrhoea. A medial report in his later life mentioned that he had 'abused Venus from his earliest youth'.

After his opera *L'italiana in Algeri* (The Italian Girl in Algiers), about a slave girl of Suleiman the Magnificent, Rossini returned home to Bologna to celebrate. There 'his relaxation mostly took the form of sexual activity'. At this time, before he had gone prematurely bald and fat, Rossini was famous for 'his good looks and sexual conquests'.

The next diva to give him a leg up was Isabella Colbran, a thirty-year-old Spaniard who became his mistress, then his first wife. He first saw her singing with Giovanni Battista Velluti, one of the last great *castrati*. He was much impressed with Velluti's voice and wrote him a part, as it were. Rossini was even more impressed with Isabella though. 'Hers was the beauty of the most queenly kind: noble features which, on stage, radiated majesty; an eye like that of a Circassian maiden, darting with fire; and to crown it all a deep instinct for tragedy,' he said. But, sadly, that was not the whole story. 'Off stage, she had about as much dignity as the average milliner's assistant.'

When they met again in Naples, she was the mistress of Domenico Barbaia, who ran the San Carlo opera house. She was married, too, to the unfortunate Giovanni Colbran. Barbaia was a favourite of the king's and kept a tight reign on the purse-strings. But Isabella loved to make a fool of him and began spending her days making love to the twenty-three-year-old Rossini. He wrote *Elisabetta, regina d'Inghilterra* for her, in which Elizabeth I of England secretly marries her lover, the Earl of Leicester. Soon Rossini was famous all over Italy and, in 1816, immortalized the razor-wielding barber who had so nearly cut short his career with *The Barber of Seville*.

The first night in Rome was a disaster. On the second night Rossini pretended to be ill and stayed in bed. He awoke to hear a noise in the streets. Fearing that it was a mob coming to burn his house down, Rossini hid in the stable. The lead tenor found him there, told him that the opera had been a great success and the crowd was demanding to see the composer. Rossini said: 'Sod them, their cheers and everything else. I am not coming out of here.'

While Rossini was away, the San Carlo burned down. Barbaia had to supervise the rebuilding, but Isabella Colbran went to Paris with Rossini to perform in *The Marriage of Thetis and Peleus*. Next Rossini produced a scandal on stage. In his opera *Cinderella*, the women had to raise their skirts to try on the glass slipper and so revealed their ankles! Even more scandalous was that in the audience at the premiére of *The Thieving Magpie* at Pesaro, was Caroline of Brunswick, the estranged wife of the Prince Regent, the future George IV of England, with her Italian lover Bartolomeo Pergami. Although no whited sepulchre himself, Rossini refused all invitations to the Princess of Wales's receptions. Rossini was later attacked by a gang of thugs who worked for the Princess of Wales, only to be rescued by fans.

In 1820, Isabella's father died, leaving her a considerable fortune. The following year, when Rossini was thirty, he sent home for his baptismal certificate and proof that he was a bachelor. If he only had to think of himself, he said, he would have stayed single. As it was, he was going to marry Isabella, largely to please his mother, who had heard persistent rumours of their affair.

However, the best years of their relationship were behind them. Isabella's voice was failing and she retired from the stage in 1824. Meanwhile Rossini's career was flourishing and he travelled constantly. She chose not to accompany him. They stayed together, on and off, for eight years all told. After that, she lived alone, or with Rossini's father, in Bologna and developed a passion for gambling.

Rossini preferred to stay in Paris, which was full of young Italian sopranos. His name was linked particularly with the prima donna Giuditta Pasta, though Stendhal noted that he did not write any great composition for her, as he had for Maria Marcolini and Isabella Colbran. Then he got involved with

Olympe Pélissier.

Illegitimate by birth, Olympe began her career as a fashionable courtesan. When Rossini first met her she was the model and mistress of the painter Horace Vernet. Rossini was with Isabella at that time, but when he returned to Paris in 1832 alone, she invited him to dinner. Soon after he wrote the cantata *Joan of Arc* for her. The novelist Balzac, another former lover of Olympe's, described her as physically well endowed, sexually chilly, snobbish and insecure. Rossini's male friends dubbed her 'Mrs Killjoy the Second', as she kept him away from other sport.

Rossini valued her also as a nurse. He was suffering from haemorrhoids and chronic urethritis, a result of his gonorrhoea, and had to use a catheter every day to prevent the urethral canal from becoming blocked. The catheter took pride of place in his music rack. He called it 'the best of instruments'. But the condition was so painful that he may well have wished that his uncle the barber had had his way all those years before.

Rossini and Olympe stayed together for the next twenty years, with Olympe acting more as a second mother than a wife. When Rossini and Isabella formally separated, Olympe travelled to Bologna with him. Isabella graciously received her there, but made it clear that Olympe would never be his wife while she lived. 'God gave me strength, a long time ago, to see Rossini simply as a friend,' she wrote to a friend. However, there was jealousy all round when Liszt made a pass at her.

When Isabella fell ill, Rossini and Olympe visited her. Rossini cried. A few days later, Isabella died with his name on her lips. Nine months later, Rossini and Olympe were married. She nursed him through a nasty bout of rectal cancer. She was the only one who he would let change the dressings after the doctors operated, but he died in 1868.

19

I NEED AN AIDA

The operas of Giuseppe Verdi are known for their grand scale. In his private life Verdi was reserved to the point of being secretive. But he was a man of grand passions who eventually did find his Aida.

Verdi had a precocious talent and at sixteen he had already outdistanced one music teacher in his home town of Busseto. He moved in with another, Antonio Barezzi, and promptly fell in love with his daughter Margherita. But Verdi was so reserved that it was a year before anyone knew of his feelings towards her. But when it was realized 'the freedom the two young people had previously enjoyed was taken away from them'.

Verdi was sent away to Milan to finish his studies. When he returned to his beloved Margherita, he brought with him Dorina Seletti, the daughter of his music professor who denounced him as a 'rogue'. Despite the slight to his daughter, Barezzi stood by his young pupil. In gratitude, Verdi dropped Dorina and Margherita, who everyone now considered to be Verdi's fiancée, forgave him.

However, the feud between Seletti and Verdi tore the city of Busseto in two. At the height of the strife one of Verdi's friends circulated two sonnets, alleging that the local priest, a Seletti-sympathizer, Don Pettorelli, was sleeping with his serving maid. There was such an outcry that Don Pettorelli had to get rid of the maid 'in whom he shows a great deal of interest'. Nevertheless, when Verdi was appointed *maestro di musica* by the Duke of Palma, Don Pettorelli was forced to marry Verdi and Margherita. The ceremony effectively put an end to the feud. Verdi and his new bride were even invited to stay in Seletti's house in Milan on their honeymoon. Dorina's father said: 'The bed will be fine for the newly weds.' The couple quickly had two children, but they both died in infancy. Margherita also succumbed, she was just twenty-seven. 'A third coffin goes out of my house,' said Verdi. 'I was alone.'

But he wasn't. He had already met the soprano Giuseppina Strepponi. Unmarried, she had three children by various men who had helped her build her career at La Scala. Although she was living with one man and engaged to another, Verdi was to take her as his mistress.

He was also seeing Donna Emilia Zeltner Morosini. She was nine years older than him and married to a man old enough to be her father, who had just moved out of their *palazzo*. Verdi was so reserved that his missives to her can hardly be described as love letters. Fifteen of them survive, but only in one did he write of his feelings. 'I am always loving, passionate, on fire, half dead over you,' he wrote. 'There are so many things I would like to say to you.' He did not say them, but he remained friends with her and her daughters until the end of his life.

Giuseppina was starring in Verdi's opera *Nabucco* when they became lovers. Verdi moved on to Venice where he became involved with a woman he described in a letter to a friend as 'the Angel that you know' and 'the woman I like'. She may have been a singer, possibly Cadiz-born Antoinetta Del Carmen or Gertrude Bortolotti, whom he liked a great deal and often mentioned in his letters. In other letters, he refers to a 'gentlewoman' of Venice. 'Lacara Vamarana', daughter of the Duke Valier, is also mentioned, although 'the Angel' could have been the offspring of any of the old Venetian families. He was to go on seeing her for ten years.

On his way back from London in 1846, Verdi stopped in Paris, where a production of his *Jerusalem* was being staged.

I NEED AN AIDA

Giuseppina Strepponi was there. They wrote some of the dialogue together. It appears in the manuscript in their two distinctive handwritings.

> Strepponi: Alas! Hope is banished. My glory has faded. Family, fatherland, all I have lost.
> Verdi: No, I am still left for you. And it will be for life.
> Strepponi: Angel from heaven. May I die in the arms of a husband.
> Verdi: Let me die with you. My death will be ...
> Strepponi ... sweet.

During the summer of 1848, they lived quite openly together in Paris. Giuseppina had planned to settle there and open a singing school for young gentlewomen. But Verdi gave her a letter pledging his love for her. The letter was sealed. She kept it unopened for the rest of her life, her most treasured possession. She intended to be buried with it. Unfortunately, when she died, it could not be found. Later it was found among her things, her wishes were respected. The letter remains sealed to this day.

With that letter in her hand, Giuseppina returned to Italy to set up home with Verdi at the Villa Sant'Agata near Busseto and Verdi terminated his relationship with 'the Angel' in Venice. He also terminated his relationship with a serving girl, who may have been the mother of his child. Local tradition has it that a child called Giuseppe, abandoned at the Ospidale Maggiore in Cremona in May 1850, was Verdi's illegitimate offspring.

In April 1851, another baby, identified as 'Santa Streppini', was abandoned at the Cremona hospital. Giuseppina Strepponi had abandoned her previous children at a foundling hospital this way. All died as charity cases. Santa Streppini, under the name Santa Stropellini, was fostered out to a family with a farm adjoining Verdi's land. At that time, Verdi was not prepared to marry Giuseppina because of her scandalously promiscuous past. Marriage would have made him legally responsible for all her children. Besides, he liked his freedom. If they had been married, she would have been able to travel with him openly, enjoying the trappings of fame. As his mistress, she had to stay at home.

They did not marry until 1859, after they had been living together for twelve years. Even then, they did it secretly in Savoy, just outside Geneva. It is unclear why they married. It may have been because of the uncertainty caused by the Italian war of unification. Verdi was seen as a patriotic figure and the cause of unification might have been weakened if he was seen to be living in sin. Or it may have been because Streppino's youngest son had reached twenty-one and, consequently, was no longer a threat to the Verdi purse.

The marriage was happy enough until after the première of *Aida* in Naples in 1873. Giuseppina heard a rumour that Verdi was having an affair with the soprano Teresa Stolz. She had been engaged to the conductor Angelo Mariani, but had broken the engagement off when she started rehearsing the role of *Aida* for its Italian première in Milan. Giuseppina became suspicious of the frequency of correspondence from Stolz. She addressed Verdi as 'my dear naughty Maestro' and would often come and stay at Sant'Agata for weeks on end. The rumour that Stolz was his mistress was widespread. Few who saw them together doubted they were in love. It was said that Verdi went to Cremona every Saturday to make love to Teresa.

Despite the fact that the liaison was making his wife unhappy, Verdi refused to break it off. Giuseppina even had to put up with Teresa dropping by the house. She did everything she could to find Teresa a new fiancé, but Teresa stoutly refused. In 1875, the affair surfaced in the newspapers. By this time, Verdi and Giuseppina had been together for nearly thirty years. She could not risk losing him now. Resigning herself to the situation, she suggested that Teresa buy a villa near their own. That way they could at least carry on their affair discreetly. But when Verdi went to supervise the numerous new productions of his operas, he went with Teresa rather than his wife.

Giuseppina's reluctant compromise did nothing to help the situation. Verdi only responded with 'hard, violent and heart-rending words'. But still Giuseppina kept it together. She wrote to Teresa after a spat: 'I know – or rather, we know – that you love us very much, we believe that, we are happy to believe it

... If you are happy in believing we love you, you may be sure that we will never change as long as we live. So, my dear Teresa, put aside your fear of being unwelcome because you detected a hint of unhappiness in me. You will never be unwelcome in our house so long as you and we remain those honest, straightforward souls that we now are. With this and a kiss, I end my letter.'

Giuseppina was terrified that Verdi would abandon her for the younger woman. She hid her true feelings away in her diary in an essay entitled: 'A Philospher's Notes on a Woman's Heart, for the Guidance of Men.' It reads:

1. Between twenty and thirty years of age, a woman takes courtship and everything else as a joke – there is no danger, or almost none.

2. Between thirty and forty, it is more serious. At that crucial age, a woman is subject to dangerous moods. She dreams of sin and is concerned with remorse. When she shows you some kindness, she is showing off her remorse. She says that she is afraid of sin, but she is very much inclined to commit it. Really, she needs a bit of scandal so that people will pay attention to her. Let the man stay far, far away.

3. The woman of forty to fifty is left. Oh! Oh! With her, one has to act with the greatest discretion imaginable. Beautiful or ugly, her heart is like an Aeolian lyre that throbs and sighs in every breeze. If he lets her see even the slightest amorous intention, the man is lost. With women of that age, he has to limit himself to talking of love in general terms – not risk either a glance or a sigh.'

Teresa was in her thirties when Verdi first fell for her. She was in her forties by the time Giuseppina wrote this.

Giuseppina made the mistake of going to see Verdi's triumph with *Aida* in Paris. After the première, Verdi went back to Teresa's suite with her. Giuseppina was outraged. 'It did not seem to me to be a proper day to visit a Signora who is neither your wife, nor your daughter, nor your sister,' she complained. Later she apologized, saying the remake had just 'slipped out'.

'I knew at once you were unhappy with it,' she wrote. But she still denied what she saw plainly. If Teresa was really his mistress, Giuseppina told Verdi, 'let's end this once and for all.' 'I think sometimes I, your wife, am living *à trois*,' she wrote. 'I have the right at least to your respect, if not your caresses.'

Aida is, of course, the story of a *ménage à trois*. The Pharoah's daughter discovers that her lover, a captain in the Egyptian army is in love with her slave girl Aida, who turns out to be the daughter of the King of Ethiopia.

Despite Giuseppina's complaints, the Verdi *ménage à trois* remained intact. The three of them lived together in the Hôtel de Bade in Paris for three months. Verdi closed his ears to the gossip. Teresa planned to retire from the stage and Giuseppina longed for death to free her of this pain.

Things grew worse when they returned *à trois* to Sant'Agata. Giuseppina ordered Verdi to send Teresa away. Verdi threatened to kill himself if Teresa left. So Giuseppina herself left the villa until Teresa went back to Milan. 'Fate has decreed that everything that has made up bliss in this life is irredeemably lost,' Giuseppina confided. Teresa decided not to retire and took an engagement in St Petersburg for a fee of 140,000 gold francs. She also wanted to get away from the situation with Verdi and his wife. A flurry of letters were exchanged between the three parties, but Giuseppina eventually saw her young rival off.

However, twenty years later, after Giuseppina had died, Teresa became Verdi's constant companion until his death in 1901. However, she was not, like the fictional Aida, buried with her love. Verdi was buried next to Giuseppina in the municipal cemetery in Milan. A month later they were moved in a great state ceremony and reinterred at the Rest Home for Musicians, where they still lie.

20

MONSIEUR BUTTERFLY

Most of Giacomo Puccini's operas concern troubled women – *La Bohème, Tosca, Turandot* and, most of all, *Madame Butterfly*. Off stage, too, Puccini did his best to trouble women. But that is because they troubled him.

Puccini was brought up in a house full of women. He had six older sisters and his father had died when he was five. He earned a few lire playing the organ in local churches around his home town of Lucca in Tuscany. He played at beach resorts and weddings, and was engaged to play at dances at the local casino. But the young girls there troubled him. He had to turn his piano around so that he faced the wall – seeing the beautiful creatures in the arms of their partners was far too distracting.

Puccini's mother was worried by him playing at these parties. She thought that seeing too much of the world at such a young age might corrupt her darling son. Little did she know that he was also playing piano in the brothel on Via della Dogana. One of the girls there, Lola, took pity on the young Puccini and in his mid-teens he lost his virginity.

He practised what he had learnt from the skilful Lola with a black-haired girl from the local cigarette factory. Then he came under the tutelage of a friend called Zizz, who lodged with a widow named Maddalena. Zizz thoughtfully passed on what Maddalena taught him at night. The two of them set about seducing as many of the local girls as possible and they would raid neighbouring villages where they would delight in stripping young gypsy girls naked.

Puccini was poor and his friend and former school mate Narciso Gemignani would invite him for dinner. Gemignani was now a prosperous merchant and married to a handsome woman, then in her early twenties, called Elvira. They had one child and another on the way. Elvira was blonde with soft eyes, full lips and a classic hour-glass figure. Puccini noticed that her nipples hardened whenever he kissed her hand. She found her marriage dull and loveless. The young composer positively throbbed with life and she was ready for romance.

Puccini was working on *Le Villi* (The Witches) when Elvira realized that a successful opera would mean that he would leave Lucca, and she became concerned. Often she would burst into tears, but his mother urged him to go. His scandalous affair with Elvira was holding him back. When Puccini left to go to Milan, he was seen off by Zizz and the widow Maddalena, who stood brazenly arm-in-arm on the platform.

In Milan, Puccini immersed himself in the Bohemian life. He put on impromptu musical entertainments for friends, once even donning a bustle and blonde wig to play Juliet. After a month, Elvira turned up, saying that she could not live without him. She brought, her two-year-old daughter Fosca, her new-born son had been left at home with her husband. Puccini installed Elvira and Fosca in a shabby two-room apartment, while he headed for Turin where *Le Villi* was going into rehearsal.

The opera was not a success, but Puccini was fêted when he visited Lucca. He was honoured with a banquet and toasted by Zizz. Few Lucchesi took the drunken threats of disgruntled Narciso Gemignani seriously.

In Milan, Puccini, Elvira and Fosca moved every few weeks to escape landlords, eventually moving out to Monza, ten miles away, where the rents were lower. Puccini revelled in his poverty. In home-made shoes and faded blouses, he said Elvira looked even more attractive. Soon they had a son,

Antonio, who was registered 'father unknown'.

The Lucchesi, who had looked kindly on the young lovers, were now outraged. When Puccini's opera *Edgar* opened in Lucca in 1891, it was clear that Elvira could not return there with him. She went to stay with her sister in Florence. Drinking with his buddies back in Lucca, Puccini boasted of his philandering. These remarks were reported back to Elvira by her family. She wrote chastizing him, but, like all men who have been found out, Puccini claimed that he had been slandered by women who simply wanted him for themselves.

'These pure women are capable of anything,' he wrote to Elvira. 'You know I am your love and you are my only, true, holy love.' There was nothing to worry about, of course. He was still hot for her. 'You will see what orgies we will have...', he said. 'I miss you ... the evenings are worst, in bed without my little mouse.'

This set the pattern for their relationship. She grew suspicious of his every move. There would be jealous outbursts and rows. They would split up, then, within days, they would be begging each other for a reconciliation. They moved to Torre del Lago, near Viareggio, where Puccini and his friends established the Club La Bohème. The members drank wine, played cards and swapped ribald stories. Puccini also used the clubhouse to entertain young ladies from Viareggio. Because of his then undiagnosed diabetes, Puccini needed to piss frequently while out on hunting trips. Club members joked that he just wanted to show off his penis, of which he was inordinately proud.

Despite the occasional jealous outbursts, Elvira turned a blind eye to most of his goings on. Her growing daughter Fosca was more blunt. 'If I were in Mama's place,' she told Puccini, 'I would pay you back in the same way.' Puccini laughed and kissed her. He needed sex like other writers and artists needed alcohol, he explained. 'You can write a march after a pail of wine,' he said, 'but for a love duet you need a clear head and a warm heart.'

Puccini did not neglect his conjugal duties with Elvira and

promised to marry her when her husband died. His other lovers were nothing to him he said. 'You imagine immense affairs,' he told her. 'In reality, they are nothing but a sport which most men dedicate a fleeting thought to without giving up what is serious and sacred – the family.'

However, she suspected that the tradesmen and village people sniggered behind her back and begged him to show more consideration. But he just could not stop himself. A friend referred to him as 'a male siren who sips each flower and changes every hour'. 'On the day when I am no longer in love,' he said, 'you can hold my funeral.'

His publisher Giulio Ricordi became worried. 'I am afraid the Puccini tragedy is becoming more serious,' he wrote. 'It is impossible for a man who is preparing his own physical and moral downfall with his own hands to compose. I write this with the greatest pain and sorrow. But in Puccini's present state I don't believe he can possess that vitality of thought that is needed to give birth to a creation.'

Puccini had just started work on *Madame Butterfly*. Unlike other composers, his taste did not usually run to sopranos – too fat – or amorous aristocrats. He preferred chorus girls, waitresses and fans. He liked sex brief, immediate and uncomplicated, and Elvira kept a constant eye on him.

They went to New York, where Lina Cavalieri – dubbed 'the most beautiful woman in the world' – was starring in *Manon*. One night Elvira went through his pockets to find a note from Lina, confirming a tryst the next day. She was plainly an exception to his 'no sopranos' rule. Another exception was Maria Jertiza, the last rose of Richard Strauss. She shocked Puccini by singing his dying arias lying flat on the stage, rather than propped on one arm. This earned her the nickname *la dive prostrata* (the horizontal prima donna), although some thought there might have been other reasons for the sobriquet.

Puccini toured Italy supervising productions of his operas. One night when he was on his way from Lucca to Genoa he was spotted by a friend of one of his sisters changing trains at Pisa. He was waiting for the night express on which he had booked a double sleeper, and with him was an attractive young woman. When his sister wrote chiding him, Elvira opened the letter. She accused him of infidelity, which he admitted, but he said that it was, in part, her fault. She had not been very understanding recently. He bought her some diamond earrings. Then they indulged in a passionate bout of lovemaking and soon everything was patched up.

Puccini rewarded himself with a new car, a powerful Clement, which he would roar around the streets of Torre del Lago in. Elvira naturally suspected that he had bought the car to give him more mobility in his infidelity. She was right. He had recently begun an affair with a pretty school teacher from Turin and had persuaded her to spend a couple of weekends in a hunting lodge nearby.

Puccini would tell Elvira that he was going out in his boat to hunt waterfowl. Instead he would leap in his car and drive to Viareggio, where he would grab a bike and cycle to his tryst. The bicycle was his one concession to discretion.

Puccini was now a well-known figure. His photograph appeared in the papers regularly, and everyone knew his car. News of the affair quickly reached Elvira's ears. She decided to catch him at it. So after he left one morning, she headed off to the love nest. But Puccini had been delayed and the school teacher received several blows from Elvira's umbrella before she made her escape. Puccini himself suffered bad scratching around the face before fleeing to Milan. He wrote begging Elvira to be 'less nervous and less of a policeman'. When that did no good, he complained that he had malaria and had no one to nurse him. She took him back.

In England, he was lionized by Sybil Seligman, the beautiful wife of the merchant banker David Seligman. Like many Edwardian gentlemen, Seligman enjoyed food, drink and baccarat, but women were his principal pastime. He maintained a string of mistresses without disturbing his domestic arrangements. Sybil was thirty at the time, a little older than most of Puccini's amorettes, but he responded as an amorous Italian should.

'It began as a passionate love affair and only with the years developed into one of the few genuine friendships Puccini was able to form,' said Sybil's sister Mrs Violet Schiff. 'It lasted to his death.'

Back in Italy, the Clement skidded off the road into a ditch and Puccini was badly injured, though his publisher suspected that his long convalescence was caused by the venereal disease given to him by a lady from Piedmont. Ricordi wrote again, criticizing him for his sexual excesses. The lady concerned was a young law student called Corinna. Her surname has not become known because Puccini dismissed their three-year relationship as 'the Turin affair'. She tried to arrange a meeting with Elvira to sort the situation out but Elvira refused.

By now Elvira was forty-two. She was worried about being unmarried and terrified of being abandoned. She knew that she could not compete with the young women her husband so vigorously pursued. She took to wearing black and seldom left the confines of their villa. Nevertheless, Puccini was as good as his word. When her husband died, he married her. But that did not end his quest to find the perfect mistress.

Puccini was still unwell and walking with the aid of sticks. So the newly married Elvira hired a nurse for him, the sixteen-year-old Doria Manfredi, daughter of a local peasant family. Elvira and Puccini were involved in something of a second – though actually first – honeymoon at the time. He barely noticed Doria even though she picked fresh flowers for his room every day.

When Puccini was fully recovered, Doria was kept on as cook and housemaid. Then one night, Elvira came downstairs to find Puccini and Doria together. They maintained that they were involved in an innocent conversation. Elvira said she had caught them in *flagrante delicto*. Doria fled home, where Elvira followed her the next morning, threatening to drown 'the whore … as sure as there is a Christ and a Madonna'. Although the villagers had never liked Elvira, they knew of Puccini's reputation and believed her accusations. Puccini sent a note to Doria's family assuring them of her innocence. He also took the extraordinary risk of meeting her to comfort her. It did no good. Three weeks later, Doria swallowed rat poison and, after five days of agony, died.

The villagers then rounded on the Puccinis for hounding the poor girl to death. The press whipped the scandal up to fever pitch. Puccini, a national hero, was quickly vindicated and was soon seen as another victim of his wife's insane jealousy. Doria's family sued Elvira, who mounted a stout defence. Puccini wanted nothing to do with the case and fled to Paris, where he went to the Ballets Russes production of *Cléopâtre* every night to admire Ida Rubenstein's body.

Elvira was found guilty and sentenced to five months imprisonment and a 700 lire fine. Puccini settled the matter on appeal by giving Doria's family 12,000 lire, which they used to buy themselves a house and erected a monument to Doria. Every year on the anniversary of her death, Puccini laid a wreath on her grave, marked 'to my poor little butterfly'. He made a more lasting tribute in *Turandot*. Doria was the model for Liù, the slave girl who stabs herself to death.

But Puccini had not learnt his lesson. Soon he was having a discreet affair with Blanka Lendvai, the sister of his friend the Hungarian musician Ervin Lendvai. For three years they carried on. Elvira grew suspicious and tore up her photograph and her letters, but Puccini simply re-routed their passionate correspondence through a friend in Viareggio.

The affair with Blanka was still going on when he met Josephine von Stängel, a twenty-six-year-old German baroness who was separated from her husband and spent a great deal of time in Italy. They travelled to Bayreuth together where she divorced with the intention of marrying Puccini. But he remained loyal to Elvira, who became so suspicious that Puccini and Josephine had to abandon the 'three delicious days' they planned to spend together at Lugano in 1915. With Italy's belated entry into World War I, they had to meet in Switzerland. The affair ended when the Italian consul refused to issue Puccini a return visa because he was consorting with an enemy national.

After the war, he began an affair with another German, the singer Rose Ader. She was some thirty years his junior, but their letters bristle with passion. She was Jewish and settled in Brazil after the rise of the Nazis forced her from her homeland.

Enormous sexual vigour informed all of Puccini's music and his life. But in his mid-sixties he wrote to Sybil complaining of the loss of his sex drive and saying that he was intending to undergo monkey-gland treatment to restore his libido. In fact, at the time he was suffering from cancer and died shortly after, reminding Fosca on his deathbed what a remarkable woman her mother was. As he had said twenty years before: 'On the day when I am no longer in love, you can hold my funeral.'

21

ELGAR'S ENIGMA, AND
HIS VARIATIONS

The English have never had a reputation as passionate lovers and Sir Edward Elgar is the most English of composers. But he was a great lover of women. No less than five of his famous *Enigma* Variations are musical portraits of women. Maybe that was the enigma.

Elgar's father owned a music shop in Worcester. The young Elgar would practise the violin in the room upstairs. One day a young woman who worked in a nearby glove factory smiled up at him as she passed. He smiled back. The next day, the same thing happened. Next time he saw her, he called down to her and invited her up. And up she came. She was not interested in music, but showed some small interest in books. So, by way of a literary seduction, he started reading her a passage from Voltaire's *Candide*. 'You silly mutt,' she said and left. Then he fell for Helen Weaver, the pretty and musical daughter of the owner of the shoe shop directly across the High Street from his father's shop. Elgar called her Nelly and named some of his early compositions after her.

At Christmas in 1882, he headed off to Leipzig ostensibly to immerse himself in music there. In fact, it was to see Helen who was studying music in Germany. He arranged to stay at the same boarding house. When he arrived, Helen's companion, seventeen-year-old piano student Edith Groveham, fell for him.

The three of them went out together. Elgar read Longfellow's prose romance *Hyperion* to Helen. *Hyperion* itself contains a scene of literary seduction, and this time it may have worked. In his letters, Elgar refers to Helen as 'my *braut*', which is German for bride.

However, he did not forget about Edith. He sent her a copy of *The First Violin*, which is about a seventeen-year-old English woman who is seduced by a brilliant violinist. And he kept up a correspondence with her for some time.

In the summer, and back in Worcester, Elgar and Helen got engaged. This caused problems with Helen's family, as they were Unitarian chapel goers and wanted someone of the same persuasion for their daughter. The Elgars were a Catholic family. By the end of the summer, her family's opposition began to take its toll. Besides, Helen decided that she really deserved some one with better prospects than this provincial dreamer. She broke off the engagement. Soon after, Elgar's first composition was performed in London. But it was too late. Helen had already made plans to emigrate to New Zealand. She may have ended up on the other side of the world but musicologists have found traces of his lost love throughout all his most English of music.

To mend his broken heart, Elgar took a holiday in Scotland where he met a girl recorded in his diary only as E. E. He pursued her around the Grampians, meeting her in Oban, at Inverness at the Omnibus Station Hotel and in Edinburgh. He dedicated his *Idylle* to her and their romantic interlude.

When questioned about its dedication to 'E. E., Inverness', he said: 'Miss E. E. at Inverness is nobody – that is to say I shall never see her again. I wrote down the little air when I was there and dedicated it to her "with estimation the most profound" as a Frenchman would say, that's all.'

In 1886, Elgar was inspired by a meeting with the seventy-five-year-old Abbé Liszt, took a room in Malvern and started taking in pupils. One of them was a beauty in her late thirties with China-blue eyes called Caroline Alice Roberts. The coachman who took Alice to Malvern remarked that he thought 'there was more to it than music lessons'. Indeed there was. Elgar began taking an interest in Wagnerian love duets and finished the sketch of a song with words translated from a French romantic poem:

> Is she not passing fair,
>> She whom I love so well?
> On earth, in sea, or air,
>> Where may her equal dwell?
> Oh! tell me, ye who dare
>> To brave her beauty's spell.
> Is she not passing fair,
>> She whom I love so well?

Alice was a writer and a poet. She had published a long poem and a novel long before she met Elgar. Her work concerned people less well off than herself and what could be done to help them. Indeed, they were about love between the classes. In Elgar, who was nearly ten years her junior, she found a lower-class lad who was plainly a genius. The fact that he was dark, good-looking, young and romantic helped too, of course. He was a figure right out of her fiction. She abandoned her career to forward his.

When they announced their engagement, her family were horrified. The Robertses did not consort with tradesmen. Elgar was a mere violinist, the son of a shopkeeper, a Catholic and a decade younger than Alice. He had to be a fortune hunter. One of Alice's aunts, who was planning to leave her a substantial sum, wrote her out of her will. In the family's eyes, the fact that this young man had grandiose notions of composing music, as Alice seemed to think, also counted against him. It meant that his temperament was unstable and his income uncertain. It would be hard to think of a more unsuitable match.

But Alice was determined. Like the heroines in her books, she would propel her lover to heights he had never dreamed of. She agreed to a Catholic marriage, which took place in Brompton Oratory in London, where they knew almost no one. The honeymoon was on the Isle of Wight. The marriage might have seemed bohemian bliss to Alice, but they did not really have to rough it. She brought her maid Sarah with her.

In 1890, at the age of forty-four Alice gave birth to a daughter, Carice. They returned to Malvern, where Elgar got a job teaching at the local girls' school, called of all things, The Mount. He enjoyed working there, giving lessons to a succession of young girls, even though they were always chaperoned by an elderly dragon to make sure he kept his hands on the piano.

The headmistress, Miss Rosa Burley, was just twenty-five and rather attractive. He unburdened himself to her, complaining that he was lonely, unhappy and disappointed in love. She began taking violin lessons with him herself. And when the Elgars went to Bavaria to pay homage at Bayreuth, Rosa and one of her older pupils, Alice Davey, came along. 'No one had told me,' observed Rosa, 'what, at first sight, was the most striking thing about Alice Elgar – namely that she was considerably older than her husband. Indeed, he was an unusually youthful thirty-six and she was a rather mature forty-five, she seemed almost to belong to a different generation.'

At Bayreuth, Rosa was overwhelmed. 'Tristan was a shattering experience,' she wrote. 'Mrs Elgar, always deeply affected by romantic music, was the most touched ... but on all of us the heavily erotic melodies worked such a spell as to make sleep impossible for the whole night.' Rosa noted that Alice fussed over Elgar like a doting mother, which irritated him. But her devotion to her husband made her an unshakeable foe.

'She married him in defiance of the opinion of her friends,' Rosa said, 'and it was clear that she would stand by him whatever misfortune might befall. Hers was truly a great love.' However, after Alice died, Rosa confessed to Carice that her relationship with Elgar had gone further than mere friendship.

Soon after, he attracted another fan, Dora Penny, the twenty-one-year-old stepdaughter of one of Alice's friends. She would regularly cycle the forty miles from Wolverhampton to stay with the Elgars. They would take long walks in the woods alone together and he immortalized her in Variation X of the *Enigma*, as Dorabella – beautiful Dora – the girl with the tinkling laugh. In return, she called him His Excellency and they talked of a mysterious thing called 'it' that was hidden in his music.

There were always other young women around the house – Florence and Winifred Norbury, Lady Mary Lygon and Isabel Fitton, who took viola lessons from him. They were also accorded Variations. They would go cycling with him, climb hills, fly kites; and there was not a hint of jealousy on Alice's part. 'Mrs Elgar was a wonderful woman,' recalled a niece of the Norbury sisters. 'His work and his well-being were everything to her and I believe she made these friendships with other women – all young and attractive – who could do the parts she could not manage. She was almost too sweet with him ... Their part was to get him ready for work.'

Nor were these relationships Platonic. With his aquiline features and dark insecurities, Elgar was attractive to women. Several of his youthful companions were eager for their romantic feelings to be requited and laid claim to him. There was talk of an illegitimate daughter.

But Alice knew she was in no danger, even though she was growing old and had lost her looks. Without her, Elgar could not make music. He was ambitious, but lazy. He would do nothing without her encouragement. She knew it. He knew it. And the young women who craved his attention knew it. They were there to stimulate him. Sex, Alice realized, was less important to a man who had a creative outlet than to one whose only outlet was sex. If these women wanted to stimulate him, she let them get on with it. His sexual passion for them informed his work. But as long as he wanted to make music, he was stuck with Alice, for life. The only female who posed a threat was Carice, who was promptly packed off to Rosa. Even though The Mount was near enough for her to be a day-girl, she was boarded so that she would not disturb the great composer's concentration.

In 1902, Elgar began a daring affair with Alice Stuart-Wortley, the daughter of the Pre-Raphaelite painter John Millais and wife of the MP for Sheffield. The Elgars often met the

Stuart-Wortleys socially. Privately, Elgar called Alice Stuart-Wortley 'Windflower' and a secret correspondence grew up between them. Windflower's letters have been preserved, but Elgar's letters to her have been destroyed, probably by her daughter Clare in an effort to conceal any evidence of their affair.

How much Elgar's wife or Windflower's husband knew of the affair it is impossible to say. But it continued for years. Elgar's London flat was right round the corner from the Stuart-Wortley's house and Windflower would pop around to the flat when Alice was out. The two of them would sometimes spend time alone together in the country. Nothing was said. Windflower again was immortalized in music.

In 1920, well into her seventies, Alice Elgar died. Although most of the women who he had been interested in romantically were still alive and unattached, musically he fell silent. Alice had been right. Without her, he could not compose. Soon, even his passion for Windflower grew cold. But he had one last stab at it. Before Alice's death he had already been captivated by the twenty-five-year-old violinist Jelly d'Arányi, when he heard her playing his *Violin Sonata*. Soon after Alice died, Elgar, who was sixty-three, invited Jelly home and soon developed a 'violent affection' for her. He plied her with compliments and called her 'my darling tenth muse' – plainly there had been nine beforehand.

They frequently lunched at his club in Pall Mall. One afternoon he suggested taking her, by cab, to Richmond Park. 'Surely that isn't the place to go in midwinter, not for an old man and me,' Jelly thought. Fearing he fancied *coito al fresco*, she insisted on going to the British Museum to look at the mummies instead. Afterwards, he wanted to take her home for tea. She refused. He made a lunge at her. She left in a cab 'cursing old men'. It was the composer Vaughan Williams she really fancied.

Elgar died in 1934. His Dorabella married and lived until 1964. Rosa Burley and Isabel Fitton never married and lived until 1951 and 1936 respectively. What became of Helen Weaver no one knows. She remains an enigma.

22

GRAINGER WAS STRANGER

The Australian Percy Grainger was a very strange man indeed, and it is hardly surprising, given his family background. His father, John Grainger, was an Englishman who had adopted hard-drinking Australian ways after he emigrated in 1877. Two years later, he was introduced to Rose Aldridge, daughter of another hard-drinking English immigrant in Adelaide who thought nothing of taking his horse-fearing wife and children out on a Sunday to watch him subdue a troublesome horse. And to bring the children into line, the harshest and most brutal corporal punishment was used.

When the blonde, blue-eyed Rose met John, he seemed so very different from her father. He spent hours reading poetry to the Aldridge girls. He was a talented painter and singer, and started a string quartet. Rose was aware of John's shortcomings. He had a flirtatious character and, at one time, she thought he was going to marry her sister Clara. But when he switched his affections to Rose, she jumped at the chance to have him.

Her mother warned against it. John was dark. The whole of the Aldridge family had a Nordic look and she did not trust dark-eyed people. All the troubles in life come from dark-eyed folk she used to say. 'Do you really think you will be happy with Jack in the long run?' she asked her enamoured daughter. 'If I am happy with him for six months, that's all I care about,' Rose replied. She'd be lucky.

Before their marriage, in Rose's eyes they were the perfect couple. They never exchanged a cross word. She loved and was loved. But the moment they got back from their honeymoon in Sydney, things began to go terribly wrong. A letter awaited Rose on her return. It was from England and informed her that John had a fiancée there, who had borne him a child. It blamed Rose for keeping John in Australia. When he had not returned to marry the mother of his child, the girl had killed herself.

Rose herself was soon expecting. Once the pregnancy was confirmed, she refused to have anything more to do with her husband. He was removed to a separate bedroom and replaced by a statue of a Greek god which faced the bed. Rose believed that by contemplating its naked beauty her unborn child would imbibe some of its godlike qualities.

When Rose gave birth, John boasted to the doctor that this was not the first child he had sired. He boasted of his sexual stamina to anyone who would listen. One night during the Franco-Prussian war, he said, he had had fourteen prostitutes in Paris. Denied love at home, John went back to his drunken whoring ways. Rose took her personal problems to the doctor. She complained of John's drinking and unfaithfulness. The doctor, who was between wives at the time, suggested that they run off together.

Inevitably, John had contracted syphilis. Rose was terrified that the baby might have inherited it. She lived in morbid fear of what was then an incurable disease. Throughout her life she was terrified of the insanity the last stages of the disease brought. Frightened that the child might catch it, she would not touch the infant. She hired a nanny, to whom Percy became fiercely attached. When he was five, Rose got over her fear and sacked the nanny, to Percy's great distress.

Rose called her baby boy Bubbles, because of his beautiful blond curls. When they grew darker with age, she bleached them. They grew close, very close. Rose and Percy slept together until he was thirty-six. She did everything in her power to alienate him from his father. Percy was told never to touch him for fear of catching the dreadful disease. But his father was a kindly man who never scolded or beat his son. His mother thrashed him severely if he tried to skip his piano lessons, and he loved her all the more for it. She also turned the whip on his father when he was drunk, who did not.

As a child, every aspect of Percy Grainger's life was controlled by his mother. He was not allowed to use baby talk or play with children of his own age. His mother kept him out of school and taught him herself. In his youth, he showed more of an aptitude for art than for music. He loved to draw the Greek statues that were found around the house. But when Rose caught him making copies of his father's collection of nude paintings, she put a stop to it.

Rose could not control what was going on in his head though. Like other boys, he loved stories of the Vikings and the blood-thirsty battles of the ancient world. But unlike other boys, he never grew out of it. 'Many children are cruel to animals and many little boys are harsh to girls,' he wrote, 'but this fierceness wanes as they grow up. But I never grew up in this respect and fierceness is the keynote of my music ... The object of my music is not to entertain, but to agonize – to make mankind think of the agony of young men forced to kill each other against their will and all the other thwartments and torturings of the young ... Is it because our era (with its myriads of young men doomed to face death in the sky and wholesale drownings as sea) needs to have its injustices to the young brought home by art?'

As in art, so in life. Throughout his life, Grainger was deeply into S&M. Adopting his mother's veneration for all things blonde, blue-eyed and Nordic, he became a proto-Nazi. But when he had a chance to put his lust for pain to some good use during the World Wars he ran away to America.

In 1895, when Percy was only twelve, he was good enough to play the piano in public. A packed house in Melbourne Town Hall gave mother and son enough money to set sail for Europe, leaving papa to fend for himself. John Grainger died alone in Melbourne of tertiary syphilis in 1917.

The thirteen-year-old Grainger was enrolled at the

Conservatorium of Dr Hoch in Frankfurt. It was there that he met Mimi Kwast, the daughter of his piano teacher. She was in love with the composer Hans Pfitzner, another proto-Nazi and the cuckolder of Mahler.

Her father did not approve of Pfitzner and Rose, still controlling every aspect of her son's life, decided that Grainger, then sixteen, should have his first experience of love. She sent him out for a walk with Mimi and insisted that he hold her hand. The whole thing was too much for the youthful Grainger, who was soon pouring out his undying love to Mimi. Although Mimi was in love with another, she responded. Soon she was insisting that her sixteen-year-old suitor marry her. When Grainger balked, she teased him saying his mother was the only woman he would ever love.

When Rose heard that Percy and Mimi had been seen walking around town hand in hand, she suddenly grew jealous. She went to see Mimi's father, with an eye to putting a stop to the relationship. But he heartily approved of the match. The affair only came to an end when Pfitzner sent a telegram from Berlin, telling Mimi that he would kill himself if she did join him there at once. She flew to his arms. They married in England the following year.

Later, Grainger cruelly described Mimi as a 'lump' who became a 'mountain' before she died. It was not true, of course. When Grainger was praised for heroically giving Mimi up after it became clear that Pfitzner, who as we have seen was not entirely faithful to her, was her true love, he denied it. 'I never dreamt she would not come back to me,' he said. It was all too much for his dear mother, though, and she promptly had a nervous breakdown.

In Frankfurt, Grainger began to become aware of his abnormal sexual desires. 'By sixteen or seventeen, I was sex crazed,' he wrote. Flagellation was his bag and he had already begun auto-erotic experiments in sado-maschocism. Stories of people whipping and being whipped particularly turned him on. 'These passions were quite unconscious and I had no idea what caused me to shake at such descriptions. Each person must have some subject that fires him to madness, whatever it is. To put up with less seems crazy.'

Other people would have to put up with it too. Among other things, Grainger was an exhibitionist. He would present himself stark naked, spread-eagled on the lid of a grand piano at an open window, no matter how cold the weather. Or in deepest winter, he would strip off out of doors and pose naked as a statue. He was happy to pose nude for photographs and encouraged his girlfriends to do likewise. He liked to sketch himself naked, too, and hung out with homosexuals.

In Frankfurt, he met the cellist Herman Sanby, who raved over 'the Adonis from the Southern Hemisphere', his 'Iceberg from Australia'. In return, Grainger positively salivated over Sanby's finely cut features, his mane of dark brown hair, his beautiful hands and his 'fire'. 'I have sat, eaten up by it time and again,' he drooled. 'There can be in his tone a quietly ruthless slowly pushful and sending force that if I were a woman would lay me out wholly submissive, I wish I had the chance – I should be splendacious towards his possiblities.'

At his mother's request, Grainger wore his peroxide blond hair long. Many people mistook him for a homosexual. He was outraged. For him, homosexuality was far too run of the mill. 'There are those that say a man gets more perfect happiness with a man friend than with a woman sweethcart,' he said. 'George Moore [a friend] says that there are few women a man would wish to meet in Paradise. I know nought of such sex differentiation. With me it is race, not sex that matters. If the race is right, and the land is right, I am in heaven.'

For Grainger, a lover had to be a Nordic blonde. Of course, the perfect example of Nordic womanhood was readily to hand – his own mother. She had retained her good looks and they were often mistaken for brother and sister, and they slept together. Grainger described the relationship with his mother as 'the only truly passionate love affair of my life'. But he was also attracted to young girls and studied the female nude in the many museums and art galleries of the city.

'So the body, the naked body as well as the clothed, became

for me a vehicle of expression, a tally for life, a symbol of nature's world just as music, poetry and prose,' he wrote. 'In art I saw the pure, the unspoilt, the natural, the unblemished exalted and deified, and in talk of my parents and of art-loving friends I heard the artificial and pretentious, such as artificial flowers, modern clothes, the use of scent, powder and rouge. So as I grew up to be fourteen or sixteen or twenty years old I looked upon grown women with horror as being dirty with their beauty grease, foul in their powder and rouge, disgusting in their indolent grossness, repellent in their lovelessness and worldliness. Mid-teenage girls were half-spoilt goods, but I looked upon girls of thirteen and twelve down to six and five as being the only representatives of womankind that answered the requirements of an art-wonted mind and eye. I was not anti-woman, I was only anti-filth, anti-decay. I was not pro-infantile, I was merely pro-pure, pro-clean, pro-fit, pro-natural, pro-sweet, pro-nice. I was not so lacking in manly feelings as to love the nasty for the nice, as to tolerate females looking and behaving as revoltingly as men.'

He wanted children of his own, but for his own special purposes. He wrote to a girlfriend: 'I wish to procreate children ... I propose this: Never whip them till they are old enough to grasp the meanings of lots of things, then say to them: Look here! I want to ask a favour from you kids. I want to whip you, because it gives me extraordinary pleasure. I don't know why, but it does. It gladdens me more than eating even. I know it's rotten for you, but then: I am particularly kind to you kids. I've worked hard to make you free in life, so that your childhood not only may be jollier now than ordinary children's, but may last ever so long, if you're pure minded like I am, and don't grow worldly out of pure cussedness, or inherited "throw-back". I don't deserve any reward for this, or for all the freedom I allow and encourage, for that is every grown-up's duty to the young, but I say this to you: I'm kind and a good old thing, and polite and obliging. Now why not do me a great favour, as one equal to another, let me whip you; because, only, it gives me such unexplainable delight. Don't you think the children'd let me? I have hopes. Then encourage them to whip each other as a form of athletic fight. (They have a game like that in Japan, I've just lately read.) I believe one could easily get decent, plucky, blue-eyed children to do it ... You know that I long to flog children. It must be wonderful to hurt this soft unspoilt skin ... and when my girls begin to awaken sexually I would gradually like to have carnal knowledge with them ... I would love to explain things to them and open their eyes in this area the whole way of the world without shame or shyness or cowardice ... Why should a man not be sensual with his own children? All these mixed father – and lover – instincts I have had since I was four-teen or fifteen. I have always dreamed about having children and whipping them, and to have a sensual life with my own daughters.'

Fortunately, he did not get the opportunity to indulge these desires. In fact, he advised his girlfriends not to get pregnant. 'Do you know that woman's breasts, after she has had children, always hang down and she can never get them nice and firm again,' he warns one girlfriend. 'Think about it.' None of his loves ever bore him children, which was probably just as well because he knew he was depraved.

'I cringe and quail because of my awareness of my evils,' he wrote, 'the evil deeds I have done and the far more evil thoughts I feel within my bosom.' But he forgave himself, pro-vided he was appropriately chastized. 'The core of me, my inner self, my senses have stayed like those of a child,' he said, 'a child that knows he is naughty and looks to be punished for it.'

Grainger knew no shame. He was positively proud of his immoral urges. He scrupulously recorded them in his letters and photographed himself in acts of depravity, meticulously noting the film speed, exposure, camera aperture, date, time, location, number of lashes and type of whip employed. These details were written on a board which he proudly held up to the cam-era.

All his girlfriends, with the possible exception of Mimi Kwast, were involved. There is ample photographic evidence of

215

that. His frantic desires, he explained, were simply his 'mad side'. They were also the well-spring of his art. 'The only real thing to me is the love of pleasure,' he said. 'That is why I say I hate love, that love is the cruellest thing in human affairs. I like only those things that leave men and women perfectly free. The only kind of love I like is Platonic love. But there was heaps of that between Mother and me. The reason why I say I worship lust but hate love is because lust, like Platonic love, leaves people perfectly free.'

Whatever hang-ups Grainger had about his depraved desires were removed by a trip to Amsterdam in 1900. There he saw every possible perversion played out before his eyes. He began a collection of pornography about German whipping clubs and Improving Institutes for Girls with titles like *Käthe's First Chastisement*. And with this amoral awakening, he put aside Christianity and its moral dogmas. 'It is no use living merely not to die,' he said. 'One should live really to live.' And when it came to living, Grainger meant only one thing. 'I live for my lusts and I don't care if they kill me or others,' he told a friend. 'No sadist can call life poor or disappointing who can realize his cruellest, wildest dreams. When we successfully follow and realize our lusts we are lords indeed. I would not exchange with the angels.' Evil became his god.

'The fact is that I really worship evil and find everything else un-worthwhile,' he wrote. 'But it may (nay, must) be said that all my worship of cruelty cruises only around sex-instincts.' So he was not so wicked after all. 'Apart from sex I am not such a bad fellow. But as I am really not interested in anything but sex it just boils down to this: that I hardly think of anything but sex and that all my sex thoughts are full of evil and cruelty. And one of the greatest and most continual worries is that I may die without the full evilness of my sex feelings being known to the world or recorded.'

No worries there then. That's what I am here for. 'If I knew of a country where I could publish an unabridged account of my sex-life and sex-feelings I would be a happy man indeed,' he wrote in 1956. That country is now.

In Frankfurt, some of his sexual sadism was transmogrified into anti-Semitism, though he got on with Jews individually, particularly those he admired. But he was a racist who craved global apartheid that would separate his beloved Nordics from Latin peoples, Jews, Blacks and anyone else who did not have blue eyes and blonde hair. He even thought homosexuals and heterosexuals should be segregated, but which side of the fence he would have placed himself no one is sure.

In an effort to bring his dystopia about, he sought to drop any word of Latin and Greek derivation from the language he used. And he spent much of his life compiling a 'blue-eyed' English dictionary, containing only words that date back to before the Norman conquest. His parents began to feel that he was becoming too 'Germanized'. So his father sent him a book called *Deeds That Won The Empire*. Walt Whitman was a better antidote. After reading *Leaves of Grass*, he began to become obsessed with America and democracy. He started work on *Marching Song of Democracy* which was dedicated to 'My darling mother, united with her in the loving adoration of Walt Whitman.' He had other plans for the world.

'If only one could get the whole world to unite in making the earth a temple of sexual intensity,' he wrote. 'Men and women both eager for the fleshy bliss of it all. If only young girls could be trained from the very start to be selfish, as dirty-minded, as unnatural, as health-reckless as boys – both sexes could go to hell in joy and oblivion.'

Grainger loved to read books about young girls and girls' schools. He longed to travel all over the world, trying out women from every land. 'Woman's flesh is for me like being in a temple of some tremendous worship,' he wrote. The world, he thought, should unite 'in praise and adoration of woman's body, dwelling ever, and ever brutally but lovingly on the very titles of her sexual parts; giving remembered sexual deeds out of their hoarse whiskered throats. It thrills and lifts me up; this fiery devotion of men to sex in women.'

In 1901, in a new effort to 'un-Germanize' him, his mother took him to London. Momentarily leaving aside his predilection for everything Nordic, he fell for the half-Irish, half-Polish Mrs Frank Lowery, an elegant lady in her forties who lived in Cheyne Walk. She invited him around to play for her. He performed an impromptu piano transcription of *Love Verses from 'The Song of Solomon'*. So passionate was his rendering that, on the last noted, she fainted. He had to revive her by loosening her clothing. After that, he was a regular visitor to Cheyne Walk.

Mr Lowry allowed his wife complete sexual freedom. And with Mrs Lowry, Grainger recorded, he had his first orgasm. He thought he was going to die. He was afraid that the affair might lead to a scandal, but he was pleased that his 'sexual equipment' worked after all. Still, no matter how earth-shattering an experience orgasm was, Grainger concluded that it was not nearly as good as a sound flogging.

Mrs Lowry introduced Grainger to the composer Ferruccio Busoni, who offered to teach Grainger for free provided he went to Berlin. Busoni lived there in a house he filled with cripples and paupers who acted as his willing slaves. In Berlin, Grainger lodged at a boarding house run by Mimi Kwast's mother, who tried to interest him in her second daughter Evchen. Then Mrs Lowry turned up. Soon she was evicted from her hotel because the management objected to Grainger's night-time visits. She moved into the boarding house too, scuppering the romance with Evchen.

Meanwhile Busoni's pretty wife took a fancy to him, but he was more interested in their two boys, Raffaello and Benvenuto, who were 'fine featured, bright eyed, soft limbed … as fair to see as children could be'.

Grainger went on a concert tour of Australia, New Zealand and South Africa. He travelled out there on a RMS *Omrah*. He loved to travel by ship and would persuade the captain to let him shovel coal in the boiler room stripped naked for an hour each day. While the rest of the party travelled around by train, Grainger would don his running shorts and jog to the next engagement. In South Africa, he walked from Pietermaritzburg to Durban, a distance of six to five miles, in less than a day, just making his cue at an evening performance.

GRAINGER WAS STRANGER

On a tour of Denmark, Grainger found himself greatly attracted to Herman Sanby's fiancée Alfhild de Luce. One night he kissed his friend and paid her the highest compliment in his pantheon. 'Mother must have looked something like you when she was young,' he said. Sanby had his own line in compliments. He told Alfhild: 'You look a lot like Percy. Your eyes are a different blue, your hair a different gold, but somehow you are the Percy I love in the shape of a woman.'

They began a bizarre *ménage à trois* with Sanby taking a back seat, but getting a voyeuristic pleasure out of seeing the other two get it on. He was not at all put out by Grainger openly declaring his great love for Alfhild in front of him. Both were amused when the Scandinavian newspapers reported that Grainger and Sanby were lovers. The only thing that dented the affair was when Grainger showed Alfhild a picture of his mother and Alfhild thoughtlessly remarked that she 'looked like the devil'. This led to some bad blood between them. Years later, Grainger wrote testily: 'I did not force my sex-will unduly, did I?'

In pique, Grainger looked around for a Nordic beauty of his own. He found one in the shape of Karen Holten, who he took back to London with him. Rose liked her instantly and she stayed with the Graingers. At night, he crept up to Karen's room, naked, for a spot of whipping and sex. He was getting to like sex.

'When one, without a condom, feels one's erection embraced by the vagina for the first time after a period of postponement then it is the purest uncorrupted voice of nature that sings to me,' he wrote. 'I want to throw all separators [condoms] to hell and glide gently with my thick strong phallus into your inner fjords, your oily greasy slimy inner roads, that fog-up and bewitch away all mental consciousness, my phallus smelling sharp and animal-like of rotten fish, your sex passages smelling sharp and animal-like of something bitter and sour, and feel the thick rich cream stride forth from my body's interior dark earth and grow fruitfully forward against your womanliness's warmth and intoxicating sun, and stride up and forward with maddening thudding pumping pulse, enormous and threatening, till all personality is intoxicated away ...' And so on for a another couple of pages or so.

When he was away, Grainger lovingly detailed everything he was getting up to on his own for her delectation. In 1911, he wrote to her: 'After the concert I read the whipping books and was naughty two splendid times ... My room was so overheated that one sweated and was pink all over the body and I had two lovely whips (from Utrecht) with me. Some weeks ago in Bussum I began to brand a K [Karen] in my flesh right in the middle of my primeval forest, after first having shaved the trees away. But last night I was mad-sensual and burnt deeper in so that one heard the flesh melt. I still only have the I (the < is still lacking) and after that I whipped myself and was naughty the first time, then I read on for a long time, and then bit my breasts with my tie-clip and was blissfully naughty again. I really believe that I feel relieved and healthier after such a night.'

He told her that it 'hurts amusingly' when he stuck needles into his chest. Then he tied bigger and bigger knots in the cotton and drew it through the flesh until the cotton finally broke. There are gruesome descriptions of his whipping and his wounds. He even longs to whip himself with a whip of wire, as nothing else is sharp enough. Sometimes he admits to being naughty four or five times in as many days and boasts of giving himself up to a 1000 lashes.

He wrote from Port Said, telling her of his experiences in a brothel with four 'not unattractive' women. He was disappointed with the pictures of nude women the Arabs tried to sell him, but he enjoyed watching a beautiful golden-brown girl do the can-can naked. Her nipples he noticed were formed differently from Europeans and ended in a tiny slit. He paid five shillings to watch an Arab boy screw a Greek girl and was impressed with how bored she looked. Afterwards he was upset that, although he had examined them closely, he could not remember what her breasts looked like. He also liked the Arab boys who dived naked for pennies. And in Australia he liked swimming with naked men. One chap particularly impressed him. 'His sexual parts were so astoundingly Grecian; graceful and round without being clumsy and floppy. It is to my mind the very rarest thing to see men or boys with prettily formed appetizing sexual parts.'

In his letters, he addressed her as 'Sweetest most delicate cream-fleshed treasure', 'Oasis in the Desert', 'My heart's plum' and 'My meat-mate'. He happily relates picking up two sisters in Norway, describes fooling around with other women, compares their naked bodies to hers and begs her to send a nude photograph of herself. She was, after all, his 'playmate'.

'Sometimes, when I call to mind how long I still must wait until your flesh and my flesh meet,' he wrote, 'and that it is quite impossible for us to be united in half-an-hour's time, a madness overflows over me and boundless anger ... Then I must pull, hit, cut, whip, tear and burn some pain in myself. Afterwards I feel much less unsatisfied.'

But it is not just himself he wants to whip. He wants to whip her and have her whip him. She should be tied up. 'You shouldn't have a single stitch of clothing on your body,' he told her. 'But I "as man", must be allowed to wear a shield for the tediously easily destroyed parts of a man's body. I think it must be furiously painful for you to be whipped on your breasts, don't you think? (Couldn't you try on yourself sometimes?) If it hurts terribly, you can count more strokes on me. But I can't give up wanting to whip you there; it is one of the greatest longings of my little life.' And just to get her in the mood, he tells her stories of the whipping of penitents in Sweden. If she would let him give her a hundred lashes, she could give him two hundred, with a pause for breath between each group of fifty. He liked it particularly if the whip left 'leopard patterns'. And it did not end there.

'After the whipping, if you were "madly angry" with me, couldn't I try and rape you?' he asked. 'Or is that disgusting? Perhaps it is disgusting. Or would being tied up and raped be amusing and good? Tell me your little opinion.' He had a yen to rape Danish girls, too, he told her. She should not be afraid that the whipping would injure her. 'It hurts so much more than it harms.' The danger, he explains is separating the nipple from the flesh. But she should not worry. Her nipples are much stronger than his and the flesh around them more soft and giving. He felt a strong urge to experience all the sexual things he had ever planned with her because, as one person, she could be a thousand times more understanding than if he tried to do them with ten different people. Though he suppressed the urge to tell her of his teenage dream of attaching fish hooks to a woman's breasts and raising her on a pulley. And afterwards he is going to kiss her and cuddle her and treat her like a princess.

He wanted to get as good as he gave though. 'I would like to be whipped until I fell asleep from it,' he told her, 'and you should tear pieces out of me with your small teeth.' He likes it best when she bites his breast. And he had other longings. 'My swollen sex-organ (so ugly, animal, low, ignoble) seeks, mad with longing, your trembling forgiving misused mouth,' he told her. 'I long for you to see me in all my beastly lowness.' And he wants her to pull his hair out. He wanted to pull out her pubic hair. Perhaps they could pull out each other's pubic hair simultaneously?

'I long to kiss your pudenda when your pubic hair has been plucked out. I will be able to like you all round there and it will be smooth as butter, and soft. Why can't my tongue reach your little penis there? If I could kiss your little penis how blissful it would be. To think he has never been kissed and is so straight and willing. When will I be allowed to pull out your pubic hair?'

Her sexual organs are of immense importance to him. 'I long to lie in bed on my back, while you kneel over me, with you mouth to my mouth, while my hand glides into your vulva. I long for the smell of sweat and the smell of sex. I wish that you could get hold of your climax's moisture and smear it on my mouth and face and eyes. I wish for me to bite pieces out of your vulva and eat them.'

He wanted his testicles eaten like two boiled eggs. But would she like to be licked by a dog – or by another woman? 'Where is that woman who wanted to see you without clothes?

If she is ugly shut your eyes and let her lick you. But for God's sake don't waste time in fidelity.'

And sometimes he can be almost tender. 'I wish you were here with me. I would undress you and carry you to the bed and bite you and lie so heavily on you and kiss you everywhere (I remember places I have not kissed yet) and be quite careless and sleep right inside you and wake up late and do it all over again.'

'There shouldn't be so many lonely places on your body. Everything should be visited and hotly greeted.'

But he had one regret: 'I wish I could hunger after you twenty times hotter than I do.'

They were made for one another. 'I have no one to tell my wickedness to except you.' The relationship lasted eight years, but ended because Rose would not let them marry and her jealous outbursts became unbearable. Rose sensed that Alfhild was more of a threat and took against her from the start.

Back in London, Grainger was fêted. The great actress Mrs Patrick Campbell threw herself at his feet and begged him to play. He performed privately for H.G. Wells and Lady Elcho, long-standing mistress of the former prime minister Arthur Balfour. He also met the French composer Gabriel Fauré, who had once been engaged to Marianne, third daughter of Pauline Viardot. Fauré had left his wife behind in France while he womanized his way across England. Among those he bugged were Mrs Patrick Campbell, the contralto Mrs George Campbell Swinton and the composer Adela Maddison, who was the wife of the director of the music publishers Metzler & Co.

Adela left her husband and followed Fauré back to France. But not only did he return to his wife, but to his long-term mistress Marguerite Hasselmans, wife of a violinist at the Paris Conservatoire Opera. And he was having an affair with his pupil Marguerite Long. His multiple mistresses caused a little tension in the Fauré household. He would not speak to his long-suffering wife Marie and would only communicate with her in writing. 'He crucified me with his silence,' she said. But she stayed with her faithless husband for forty-one years and bore him two sons.

Even though Rose had seen off Karen Holten and Alfhild de Luce, who then married Sanby, she was determined that Percy should get married. Of course, the wife would have to look after her mother-in-law as well as her husband. The only way Grainger could disabuse his mother of this fantasy was to list his sexual deviations for her. The principal obstacle to matrimony was his craving for young girls. 'What troubled my mother was either my enjoyment of flagellation or my declaration that if I had daughters I would probably establish a lustful relationship with them – either through flagellation or by incest with them,' Grainger said.

His mother compared him to the girl in Kipling's poem who taunts a suitor by rejecting his gift of red and white roses and saying she will only love him if he brings her blue ones. 'If only you did not prefer blue roses, I should be happy,' she said. 'I fret very much about your strange fancies … Forget the wrong-coloured roses, sometimes I think it is all a horrible nightmare and that I shall wake and find reality again as I used to know it. If you only had the power of loving me, as I do you, you could never indulge in your fancies … although I love you quite as much as I used to, I am no longer proud of you … I feel so ashamed of having a child with such fancies as you have. If you were as I once thought you to be, you would be a grand man and outgrow them … unless you overcome them, they will overcome you, as years go on, you will have stranger fancies, and God knows how you will end.'

But Grainger could not give up his strange fancies. Nor could he even pretend to his mother that he had because his body was covered with welts. His doctor wrote of the whiplash marks that covered his body, and also of his inner conflicts. 'It might be crucial for complete fulfilment of the love-action that his love-partner met the "approval" of his mother,' he said. 'He knew well that his love-action was never to be approved by his mother. Neither her love nor her sorrows, however, could disengage Percy from his compulsive sexual acts.' Grainger simply could not deny himself his vicious pleasure.

'A man cannot be a full artist unless he is manly, and a man cannot be manly unless his sex-life is selfish, brutal, wilful and unbridled,' he wrote to Alfhild Sanby by way of explanation. However, in 1911 Grainger delighted his mother by announcing his engagement to Margot Harrison, one of his pupils. But Rose did not get on with Margot's mother and Percy was forced to write to his fiancée breaking off the engagement. Whereupon Margot and her mother came to the Graingers' house and tried to cut a deal.

Rose, an early advocate of free love, said that she was delighted if Percy and Margot remain lovers. Margot should move into the Graingers' establishment and go on tour with Percy later that year as part of a trial marriage. Margot was keen. Her mother gave her approval. But her father was outraged and stepped in.

With the outbreak of World War I, Grainger scuttled off to America. The reasoning behind this move was unassailable. He had set his heart on becoming Australia's first great composer, and he could not do that if he was dead. However, when America joined the war, he joined up as a bandsman. He remained an avowed pacifist – or coward as he sometimes put it – but realized that staying a civilian would invite criticism that would harm his career. Nor was his pacifism in conflict with his love of violence, as he explained to the editor of the *American Vegetarian* in 1946: 'Since war has ceased to be hand-to-hand fighting, its appeal to the savage side of our nature doesn't amount to much. It isn't sporting.' War just wasn't warlike enough for Percy. Perhaps he should have started a Campaign for Real War.

After the war, he renewed his practice of seducing his pupils. One of them, known simply as E–, moved into the Graingers' house in White Plains. Rose grew so jealous that she began feigning death and threatening suicide to test Percy's love for her. Things came to a head when Grainger went on tour, leaving Rose and E– alone in the house together. Rumours began to spread that the love between Rose and Percy was not just excessive, but actually incestuous. Rose was outraged and wrote notes to his lady friends who she thought were spreading the gossip. This only fanned the flames.

'The unmentionable has been laid at my door,' Rose telegraphed Percy. She burnt his letters and begged him to do likewise to hers. But he continued writing to her, filling his correspondence with phrases like 'I long to be in your arms again' which could be easily misconstrued. One of his letters fell into E–'s hands. This was too much for Rose. She went to New York and jumped out of the window of a skyscraper. She was found on the roof of an adjoining building, fourteen floors below. She was still alive and conscious. But the fractured skull and a multiple internal injuries caused by the fall killed her before she could be moved.

'I returned to New York,' Grainger wrote to a friend, 'and heard the truth about E– from friends who told me that she had slandered me and my Mother in this disgusting way. Mother had been ill; her nerves were worn out; she hadn't long to live; the shock was too much for her; I firmly believe her mind gave way. She wanted peace; she took it ... I faced E– and told her she was a despicable liar; I told her that I had never loved her and could never love her; and that I never wanted to see her. What people believe I do not know; but in case I die before you, and hear anyone accusing me and my Mother of having lived in incest, I want you to come forward and tell them what I tell you now. This is the sacred truth and I want you to know it'.

The cause of Rose's illness, it is suggested, was syphilis, contracted from her husband before Percy's birth. He mentions in a letter that she had been 'fighting for thirty years a cruel disease (not of her Aldridge blood)'.

But even with Rose dead, the umbilical cord was not severed. He added her name, Aldridge, to his own. In a drawer in their home in White Plains, he found the pieces of her last unsent letter to him. Scrawled in pencil, she had torn it up. Percy pieced the letter together and found it detailed her futile, self-defeating efforts to scotch the rumour that they had had an incestuous affair. It accused him plainly. 'Your mad side has ruined us,' it said.

For the rest of his life, he carried the letter rolled up in a tiny locket on a chain around his neck. He refused to see Alfhild Sanby because, twenty years earlier, she had said that his mother 'looked like the devil'. But he did write her a series of vitriolic letters.

Grainger went to Australia to bury his mother's ashes. On the way back, he shared a cabin with gay surgeon and hernia pioneer Robert Hamilton Russell. They spent most of their time in heated debates over the relative merits of their respective deviances. With mother gone, Grainger's sex life took on a new vigour. He scrupulously recorded the details of each act in his diaries, in code, in Danish. Although one thing he wrote in plain English was 'women are mad'.

On the way home after another trip to America, Grainger fell for another Nordic beauty, thirty-seven-year-old blonde-haired, blue-eyed Ella Viola Ström. He was rehearsing for a recital in Honolulu in the ship's bandroom when she came in. Mistaking him for a band leader, she asked him for a lesson on the ban-julele, which is a cross between a banjo and a ukulele. For Grainger, it was love at first sight and he gave his radiant, fair-skinned pupil the lesson of a lifetime. Next day, she discovered that her teacher had been a world-famous conductor. She approached him gingerly to apologize. He told her that she reminded him of his mother.

Recording their meeting he said: 'Every romantic thought of my life seemed to rise out of dim memories and rush towards her for fulfilment ... It maybe she said to me "Hello little boy" or some other playful greeting, her bright eyes sparkling ... Likewise it was the girl in her – the playmate, the sister, the skittish-one (not the woman) – that I loved and worshipped.' Born in Stockholm, Ella had been a model for Augustus John in London and the mistress of Prince Iyemasa Tokugawa in Japan.

When the ship docked in Vancouver, Grainger found her in the writing room in tears. She had just learnt of the death of her lover. She was on her way to England so the two of them travelled together across America by train. Grainger got off at Albany to catch his connection to White Plains. But he turned up on the dockside in New York before her ship set sail, bearing gifts: $5,000 in life assurance, a slim volume dedicated to his mother and a book on keep fit.

Ella invited him to stay in her house in Pevensey Bay the following year. The year after that, 1928, they were married in Los Angeles. Ella knew nothing of his strange sexual interests when she married him. It came as quite a shock. She left him when his demands became excessive, but always came back. 'It was hell to be with him and hell to be without him,' she said.

Gradually, she came to except his sado-masochism and joined in. In 1930 he wrote a letter and sealed it, with strict instructions on the envelope that it should only be opened in the event of their bodies being found dead, covered in whiplashes. The letter said that no blame should be attached to their deaths as, for him, flagellation was the greatest pleasure and the highest expression of his love.

They went on having a spanking good time together for another thirty years. Even though cancer meant he had to be castrated in 1957, it did not stop the fun. He once said that he had enjoyed sex for fifty-five years and would rather give up music than his kinky pleasures.

Pursuing his earnest wish that the world should know every detail of his kinky sex life, Grainger built a museum in Melbourne in a style referred to as 1930s lavatorial. Frequently, Melbourne graffiti artists have daubed 'Gentlemen' and 'Ladies' on it. A constant stream of letters, photographs and diaries giving a blow by blow account of his perversion along with sundry equipment were sent from Grainger's home in White Plains. This caused no end of trouble for the Australian Customs and Excise who regularly impounded them. Often he had to appeal right up to the prime minister of Australia's office to get his material released, so that future generations could truly appreciate the cultural depths of the new world down under.

23

LIE BACK AND THINK
OF BRITTEN

Benjanim Britten was a slow starter. The poet W.H. Auden and the writer Christopher Isherwood both tried to seduce him in his youth. Neither succeeded. But once he got down with the singer Peter Pears, he was set for life.

Most people who knew Britten said that he had been born a homosexual. Britten himself said that his sexual orientation was the result of being raped by a master at his school. Certainly something very traumatic happened to him when he was wrestling with his sexuality in his youth.

The headmaster at South Lodge in Norfolk was not above caressing a boy's bare bottom to comfort him after a beating. But it is generally conceded that he was too much of a God-fearing man to have sexually assaulted his pupils. But given the sort of school Britten's *alma mater* was in the 1920s, he could easily have been abused by other members of the teacher staff.

Throughout his teens and early twenties, Britten steered clear of sex, though he had a number of seemingly chaste 'romantic friendships' with younger boys. He was twenty-three and working in London when he was propositioned by Auden, who already had a fierce reputation as a homosexual. Auden fell in love with Britten and wrote poems about it, but never succeeded in getting him into bed.

In Barcelona, Britten went to a club with composer Lennox

Berkeley where couples, men and men dressed as women, danced. Britten found it very sordid with 'sexual temptations of every kind at each corner'. In his diary, he began to note that a large number of his friends were gay. He went to stay with Berkeley and enjoyed nude sunbathing together. Berkeley had had a number of homosexual affairs, but Britten was not ready to move on to that stage quite yet.

In Paris, he made an effort to investigate the straight world and headed for the Folies Bergère. Arriving early, the commissionaire directed them to 'another little show'. In a nearby house, Britten was presented with 'about twenty nude females, fat, hairy, unprepossessing; smelling of vile cheap scent'. Plainly this did nothing for him.

'It is revolting,' he wrote, 'that such a noble thing as sex should be so degraded.' He was not impressed by the Folies either – 'Josephine Baker is as old as the hills, and can neither dance, sing nor act'.

Back in London in 1937, he had lunch with an old school friend who was homosexual and who told him that he really should get his sex life sorted out. But Britten, then twenty-four, still lacked the courage. All that changed when, soon after, he met the singer Peter Pears.

Pears was three years older than Britten and had the advantage of being educated in the sexually relaxed atmosphere of Lancing College in Sussex. He had had lots of crushes on boys and some assignations. He went up to Cambridge in the 1920s, when a flamboyantly homosexual manner was considered the thing.

'I am henceforth proceeding to plunge into the waters of life, alike homosexual and heterosexual, to indulge in all kinds of orgies, sadist and masochistic, and finally to end as a wreck, one of the very scum of the earth,' he wrote to a friend. Instead, he became a prep-school teacher and, though romantically attracted to the boys, kept himself to himself. He then won a scholarship to the Royal College of Music in London where he found himself at home in the homosexual underworld, though many women were attracted to him.

LIE BACK AND THINK OF BRITTEN

He met Britten though Peter Burra, a chum from Lancing, whom Britten was finding himself increasingly attracted to. Britten now considered himself, at least temporarily, a homosexual – though he had such a passion for sopranos that he thought it might lead him one day to becoming 'normal'.

Berkeley was pressing him, but Britten wanted to slow things down in order to 'arrange sexual matters at least to my satisfaction'. The problem was he was not so much attracted to young men as to pubescent and pre-pubescent boys. He regularly ditched amoretti when they reached puberty.

Pears took Britten for a spin on his motorbike. Christopher Isherwood took him to a Turkish bath on Jermyn Street, which was 'very pleasant – completely sensuous, but very healthy'. He still did not succumb but remarked: 'It is extraordinary to find one's resistance to anything gradually weakening.' All those around him considered that he was a queer and after a night in the baths he found himself more ready to be sexually active.

He took a young boy from the East End on holiday to Cornwall, with the consent of his family. At the suggestion of a friend, he adopted a young Basque boy. However, it is the name of Peter Pears that pops up most frequently in his diaries. He comes to dinner, stays the night. Soon he moved into Britten's flat at 67 Hallam Street, behind the BBC.

The situation was quite complicated because Britten was having sex with Berkeley, which was something 'Ben did not care for' and seemed happy to stop. But he did not give himself immediately to Pears. The consummation of their relationship occurred on a rather curious honeymoon in Grand Rapids, Michigan, where the couple were staying as the guests of the organist of the First Congregational Church.

'I shall never forget a certain night in Grand Rapids,' Pears wrote to Britten, six months later. Pears was a steadying influence on Britten, though Britten was the more masculine of the two, except in bed. There Britten liked to be the passive partner. He dedicated his setting of one of Rimbaud's more orgiastic pieces to Pears. Pears wrote to his 'little white-thighed beauty' saying 'I'm terribly in love with you' promising to 'kiss you all over'. Britten hoped that his commitment to Pears would stop his craving for young boys. It didn't.

His operas were packed with them. He slept with thirteen-year-old David Spense, who played Harry in the original production of *Albert Herring*. But according to Spense, Britten did not 'go too far' with him. Britten was hurt when parents kept young boys out of his company because of his reputation as a homosexual. On the other hand, some mothers positively threw their sons at him.

He would like to watch them naked in the bath, often sauntering into the bathroom nude himself. He would kiss them and would occasionally make advances. But he would not be upset if they refused him.

Pears did not exhibit any jealousy. In fact, Britten's attentions to the young boys who cavorted naked on the beach near his home probably helped keep their relationship stable. At least he was not out having sex with other men. Britten said he hoped that Pears would marry one day, as Lennox Berkeley had in middle age. The singer Kathleen Ferrier, he thought, would be a suitable match. If Pears married, Britten decided, he would simply have to 'lump it'. But he did not see why marriage should interfere with their relationship.

Britten and Pears had their odd tiffs that sometimes affected their professional relationship. But largely their careers were built hand in hand. Britten realized that he would have been Court composer if it were not for his 'pacifism and homosexuality'. In 1954, Benjamin Britten was interviewed by the police about his homosexuality, but no action was taken.

Until 1967 homosexuality was still against the law in Britain. But Pears and Britten lived together openly. Some visitors were shocked to see them sharing the same double bed like a married couple. When the *Ladies' Journal* published a feature on their home, they omitted to publish a picture of the master bedroom. Instead they printed a picture of a spare room, captioned 'Peter Pears' bedroom', with a single bed in it.

Pears and Britten slid into a celibate middle age. Britten

made the odd avuncular advance to pretty young boys, but most of his proclivity went into his work. He declared himself openly in his opera *Death in Venice*.

Britten's health declined and Pears began to have other sexual affairs. But their love never died. In 1974, Pears wrote to his 'dearest darling': 'It is you who have given me everything, right from the beginning, from yourself in Grand Rapids ... I can never be thankful enough to you and to Fate for all the heavenly joy we have had together.' Benjanim Britten died in Peter Pears' arms two years later.

24

THREE LITTLE MAIDS

Gilbert and Sullivan subtitled their comic opera *Ruddigore* 'Robin and Richard; Two Pretty Men'. No tittering. W.S. Gilbert was a respectable married man. And although the bewhiskered and moustachioed eminent Victorian Arthur Seymour Sullivan was a 'confirmed bachelor', it was only because he did not want to settle for one, two, or even three little maids when he could have as many as he fancied.

In 1866, when Sullivan was twenty-two and already a performed composer, he was staying in Ireland, when he began to receive love letters from a 'very young girl' who signed herself 'Aramis'. Her name was Annie Tennent and she was the daughter of the family he was staying with. She asked him to destroy her letters because, one day when he was famous, they would be published. He could not bring himself to do that, even though he did not usually keep letters. She was right, they have been published, so Annie's little secret is out. She was to be the first of many.

Sullivan's first serious love affair was with Rachel Scott Russell. Known in the family as 'Chenny', she was the second of John Scott Russell's three daughters. Seeing which way the relationship was going, Chenny's mother wrote to him, telling him that, under no circumstances, would they be permitted to marry. He did not have any money, and his wooing was to cease. But this ban only intensified the young lovers' passion.

'Fond Dove' or 'Passion Flower', as she signed her notes, managed to give her parents the slip for secret trysts, sometimes in the office of George Grove, of *Grove's Dictionary* fame. What they were doing on his desk is plain from her letters: 'Ah me! when I think of those days when cooing and purring was enough for us, till we tried the utmost – and that is why I fancy marriage spoils love. When you can drink brandy, water tastes sickly afterwards.'

Chenny entrusted these intimate love notes to her older sister Louise, who acted as go-between. But she wanted a little of the action too. In her letters to Sullivan, Louise chastizes him: 'You have taken as your right the only thing I have to give.' Naughty boy.

Chenny sometimes used to sign her letter 'Little Woman'. Later, his diaries were full of an 'L.W.' But this Little Woman was not Rachel Scott Russell or, for that matter, Louise. It was Fanny Ronalds, who also appears in his diaries as 'Mrs R.' This is because they were having a double relationship. In society, they would mix openly as companions and close friends. But behind closed doors they were lovers. In his diaries he records how many times he did it with L.W. in a simple code, which would be highly compromising if someone stumbled across it. He denoted sexual intercourse with the French word *accès*, which means access but also a bout. *Accès de joie* means a burst of joy. This would be followed by the number (1) or (2), occasionally (3) but seldom more. Later he turned to German to record his pleasures.

There was also a D.H. who visited him late at night and sometimes breakfasts with him. Often they breakfast very late, presumably following a long lie in. D.H. – Dear Heart, perhaps – may also have been Mrs Ronalds.

Fanny Ronalds was an American who was separated from her husband, but he would not divorce her. However, even when he died, Sullivan refused to marry her. They met in Paris but, during the Franco-Prussian War, when the Germans invaded, Fanny fled to England. Of course, she was not the only woman in his life. One morning, over a late breakfast, L.W. spotted a telegram from another lover. There was a 'painful scene', followed by 'another painful interview' at her house. But she forgave him, and he was soon seen out again with 'Mrs R'.

One day, at a house party, they bumped into Chenny Scott Russell, who had since married. Sullivan talked with her for over three hours, noting 'she is as handsome as ever'.

In Paris with D.H. in 1882, he could not resist visiting a brothel at number 4, rue M.T. His diary entry reads: 'Arr. at 6 a.m. Descended at Grand Hotel – rooms 197-199. Adèle came at 9. Breakfasted at Voisin's at 11. At 12 went to keep an appointment at no. 4, rue M.T. Stayed till 5.30 (2). Dined with Dicey and D.H. at Restaurant Poissonnière. Took Dicey home, then D.H. (1). Then home myself, very tired.'

This certainly was not the only time Sullivan visited a brothel. Like most Victorian gentlemen, he used them regularly and he always noted how long he stayed there. More interesting is 'Adèle'. Adèle was his former serving maid with whom he had arranged a romantic tryst in Paris and who later returned to his service.

He used a series of maids – Adèle, Louisa, Sarah, Ruth, Jane, Janette, Harriet, Delphine – when other outlets were not available. One, Clotilde, became quite possessive. They had 'squalls', but he usually found some way to patch them up. 'Oh, the bother of servants,' he wrote. 'It is enough to make one marry – but the cure would be worse than the disease. I can get rid of servants but not a wife – especially if she is my wife.' Nevertheless he left Clotilde £1,000 in his will, which was an enormous sum in those days.

Despite having D.H. and Adèle in town, he could not resist the lure of number 4. The following day, after dining with D.H. at Véfours, a celebrated restaurant, he 'went to no.4 till midnight (2)'. Two days later, he 'spent a couple of hours at no.4 (1)', then 'dined at Véfours with Mrs R.' and her daughter Fan. The following day he went to number 4 for an hour and a half (1), before calling on the Duke of Edinburgh, then spending the evening with Mrs R. The next day he spent an hour there (2). Then an hour and a half the next day (with no recorded score).

But the following day he gets a (1) for 'a couple of hours at no.4'.

All this was happening on his way back from Egypt, where he had a romantic interlude with Miss Charlotte C. in the Shepherds' Hotel in Cairo. L.W. caught scent of her younger rival and kicked up. But he smoothed things over when he got back to London: 'L.W. dined here (1). Left much better than when she came.'

While Sullivan was working on *The Mikado*, L.W. got pregnant and underwent the highly hazardous procedure of a Victorian abortion. His diaries show that he was very concerned about her safety. They also show that his sexual passion for her waned afterwards, but he remained close to her – thereafter she was referred to in his diaries as 'Auntie'.

In 1891, he headed off to Monte Carlo with Bertie, the Prince of Wales. He clocked up a considerable number of casual sexual encounters, if the ticks in his diary are to be believed. And he began a correspondence with a mysterious 'O'. Before he has left France there are love letters to a 'P.C.'

Sybil Seligman, who went on to become Puccini's lover, introduced him to Violet Beddington. He offered to marry her, secretly, telling her that he had only two years to live and that she would inherit the considerable fortune he had amassed. She was twenty; he was fifty-four. She married the novelist Stephen Hudson, who used the situation as the basis for his novel *Myrtle*.

In 1966, Arthur Sullivan's diaries came up for sale. The twenty morocco-bound volumes had a lock which had to be forced. Inside he recorded numerous more *himmlische nacht* – heavenly nights.

Gilbert and Sullivan's comic operas may have been a pillar of Victorian society, but any close examination of them reveals that they are positively heaving with sex. When it comes to having a rollicking good sex life, you can't beat those uptight Victorians.

238

BIBLIOGRAPHY
OF SOURCES

The All-Round Man: Selected Letters of Percy Grainger 1914-61, edited by Malcolm Gillies and David Pear, Clarendon Press, Oxford, 1994

Amadeus: A Mozart Mosaic by Herbert Kupferberg, Robson Books, London, 1987

Arthur Sullivan: A Victorian Musician by Arthur Jacobs, Oxford University Press, Oxford, 1986

Beethoven by Maynard Solomon, Granada, London, 1980

Benjamin Britten: A Biography by Humphrey Carpenter, Faber & Faber, London, 1992

Berlioz by D. Kern Holoman, Faber & Faber, London, 1989

Berlioz by Hugh Macdonald, J.M. Dent & Sons, London. 1982

Berlioz: His Life and Times by Robert Clarson-Leach, Hippocrene Books, New York, 1983

Berlioz: The Making of an Artist by David Cairns, Andre Deutsch, London, 1989

Bizet by Winton Dean, J.M. Dent & Sons, London, 1948

Bizet by D.C. Parker, Routledge & Kegan Paul Ltd, London, 1951

Brahms: His Life and Times by Paul Holmes, The Baton Press, Southborough, Kent, 1984

Chopin by George R. Marek and Maria Gordon-Smith, Weidenfeld & Nicolson, London, 1978

Chopin: His Life by William Murdoch, John Murray, London, 1934

Clara Schumann: A Dedicated Spirit by Joan Chissell, Hamish Hamilton, London, 1983

Clara Schumann: The Artist and the Woman by Nancy B. Reich, Victor Gollancz, London, 1985

SEX LIVES OF THE GREAT COMPOSERS

Claude Debussy: An Essential Guide to His Life and Works by Jonathan Brown, Pavilion Books, London, 1996

Claude Debussy: His Life and Work by Léon Vallas, Oxford University Press, London, 1933

Composers in Love and Marriage by J. Cuthbert Hadden, John Long Ltd, London, 1913

The Composers in Love, edited by Cyril Clarke, Peter Nevill Ltd, London, 1951

Daughter of Paris: The Life Story of Céleste Mogador, Comtesse Lionel de Moreton de Chabrillan by Charlotte Haldane, Hutchinson, London, 1961

Debussy by Victor Seroff, John Cader, London, 1957

Debussy by Edward Lockspeiser, J.M. Dent & Sons, London, 1963

Debussy: His Life and Mind by Edward Lockspeiser, Cambridge University Press, Cambridge, 1962

Debussy: Man and Artist by Oscar Thompson, Dodd, Mead & Company, New York, 1937

Debussy Remembered by Roger Nichols, Faber and Faber, London, 1992

Edgar Elgar: A Creative Life by Jerrold Northrop Moore, Oxford University Press, Oxford, 1984

Edward Elgar: The Windflower Letters by Jerrold Northrop Moore, Clarendon Press, Oxford, 1989

Elgar As I Knew Him by W.H. Reed, Oxford University Press, Oxford, 1989

Fair Ophelia: A Life of Harriet Smithson Berlioz by Peter Raby, Cambridge University Press, Cambridge, 1982

F*anny del Rio: An Unrequited Love* by Ludwig Nohl, Richard Bentley & Son, London, 1876

The Farthest North of Humaness: Letters of Percy Grainger 1901-14, edited by Key Drefus, Macmillan, London, 1985

Franz Liszt: A Chronicle of His Life, translated by Stewart Spencer, Princton University Press, Princeton, New Jersey, 1989

Franz Liszt by Alan Walker, Faber & Faber, London, 1983

Franz Liszt: The Man and The Music by Ronald Taylor, Grafton Books, London, 1986

Franz Schubert: A Biography by Elizabeth Norman McKay, Clarendon Press, Oxford, 1996

The Galley Slave of Love: The story of Marie d'Agoult and Franz Liszt by Charlotte Haldane, Harvill Press, London, 1957

Gioacchino Rossini: The Reluctant Hero by Alan Kendall, Victor Gollancz, London, 1992

Gustav Mahler: Memories and Letters by Alma Mahler, Cardinal, London, 1990

BIBLIOGRAPHY OF SOURCES

Haydn: Chronicle and Works by H.C. Robbins Landon, Thames & Hudson, London, 1976

Haydn: A Documentary Study by H.C. Robbins Landon, Thames & Hudson, 1981

Haydn: His Life and Music by H.C. Robbins Landon and David Wyn Jones, Thames & Hudson, London 1988

Hector Berlioz: Rational Romantic by John Crabee, Kahn & Averill, London, 1980

Jacques Offenbach by Alexander Faris, Faber & Faber, London, 1980

Jacques Offenbach: A Biography by James Harding, John Calder, London, 1980

Johann Sebastian Bach by Russell H. Miles, Prentice-Hall Inc, Englewood Cliffs, New Jersey, 1962

Johann Strauss: The End of an Era by Egon Gartenberg, The Pennsylvania State University Press, London, 1974

Johann Strauss: Father and Son and their Era by Hans Fantel, David and Charles, Newton Abbot, 1971

J.S. Bach by Albert Schweiter, Dover Publications Inc, New York, 1966

The Life of Beethoven by Alexander Wheelock Thayer, Princeton University Press, Princeton, New Jersey, 1967

A Life of Love and Music: The Memoirs of Hector Berlioz, translated by David Cairns, The Folio Society, London, 1987

The Life of Mahler by Peter Franklin, Cambridge University Press, Cambridge, 1997

Life of Rossini by Stendal, Calder & Boyars, London, 1970

The Life and Times of Johann Sebastian Bach by Hendrik Willem van Loon, George Harrap & Co, London, 1942

Liszt by Eleanor Perényi, Weidenfeld and Nicolson, London, 1974

Lives, Wives and Lovers of the Great Composers by Fritz Spiegl, Marion Boyars, London, 1997

The Marriage Diaries of Robert and Clara Schumann, edited by Gerd Nauhaus, translated by Peter Ostwald, Robson Books, London, 1987

Monsieur Butterfly: The Story of Puccini by Stanley Jackson, W.H. Allen, London, 1974

Mozart by Haynard Solomon, Hutchinson, London, 1995

Mozart: A Documentary Biography by Otto Erich Deutsch, Simon & Schuster, London, 1990

Mozart and Constanze by Francis Carr, John Murray, London 1983

A Mozart Diary, complied by Peter Dimond, Greenwood Press, Westport, Connecticut, 1997

Mozart in Vienna 1781-1791 by Volkmar Braunebehrens, Andre Deutsch, 1990

My Life by Richard Wagner, Constable, London, 1994

SEX LIVES OF THE GREAT COMPOSERS

Nocturne: A Life of Chopin by Ruth Jordan, Constable, London, 1978

Percy Grainger by John Bird, Paul Elek, London, 1976

Portrait of Liszt by Adrian Williams, Clarendon Press, Oxford, 1990

Puccini Among Friends by Vincent Seligman, Macmillan, London, 1938

Puccini: A Biography by Howard Greenfield, Robert Hale, London, 1980

Puccini: A Critical Biography by Mosco Carner, Duckworth, London, 1992

The Real Mahler by Jonathan Carr, Constable, London, 1997

The Real Wagner by Rudoph Sabor, Cardinal, London, 1987

Richard Strauss by Michael Kennedy, Oxford University Press, Oxford, 1995

Richard Strauss: A Chronicle of the Early Years by Willi Schuh, Cambridge University Press, Cambridge, 1982

Richard Strauss: A Critical Commentary on his Life and Worlds by Norman Del Mar, Barrie & Jenkins, London, 1972

Richard Wagner: A Biography by Derek Watson, J.M. Dent & Sons, London, 1979

Richard Wagner: His Life, His Work, His Century by Martin Gregor-Dellin, Collins, London, 1983

Rossini by Richard Osborne, J.M. Dent & Sons, London, 1986

Rossini: His Life and Times by Nicholas Till, Midas Books, Tunbridge Wells, 1983

Saint-Saëns and the Organ by Rollin Smith, Pendragon Press, Stuyvesant, New York, 1992

Schubert by Peter Gammond, Methuen, London, 1982

Schubert by George R. Marek, Viking Penguin, London, 1986

Schubert: His Life, His Work, His Time by Joseph Wechsberg, Weidenfeld & Nicholson, London, 1977

Schubert: The Music and the Man by Brian Newbould, University of California Press, Berkeley and Los Angeles, 1997

Schumann: Music and Madness by Peter Ostwald, Victor Gollancz, London, 1985

Sex and Sensibility: Ideal and Erotic Loved from Milton to Mozart by H. Hagstrum, The University of Chicago Press, Chicago, 1980

The Sisters d'Aranyi by Joseph MacLeod, George Allen & Unwin, London, 1969

Spirit of England: Edward Elgar in his World by Jerrold Northrop Moore, Heinemann, London, 1984

Tchaikovsky by Alexander Poznansky, Schirmer Books, New York, 1991

Tchaikovsky by Antony Holden, Bantam Books, London, 1995

Tchaikovsky: A Biographical and Critical Study by David Brown, Victor Gollancz, London, 1978

BIBLIOGRAPHY OF SOURCES

Tchaikovsky: A Self-Portrait by Vladimir Volkoff, Robert Hale & Company, 1975

The Unknown Brahms by Robert Haven Schauffer, Dodd, Mean and Company, New York, 1933

Verdi: A Biography by Mary Jane Phillips-Matz, Oxford University Press, Oxford, 1993

Verdi: A Life in the Theatre by Charles Osborne, Weidenfeld and Nicolson, London, 1987

Vivaldi by Alan Kendal, Granada Publishing, London, 1979

Vivaldi by John Booth, Omnibus Press, London, 1989

Vivaldi by Michael Talbot, J.M. Dent & Sons, London, 1993

Vivaldi: Voice of the Baroque by H.C. Robbins Landon, Thames and Hudson, London, 1993

Wagner: A Case History by Martin van Amerongen, J.M. Dent, London, 1983

Wagner and the Romantic Disaster by Burnett James, Hippocrene Books, New York, 1983

Young Liszt by Iwo and Pamela Zaluski, Peter Owen, London, 1997